The Collector's Book of Bells

The Indian princess bell. Said to portray Atala, daughter of an American Indian chief. Circa 1830.
PRIVATE COLLECTION

The Collector's Book of Bells

L. ELSINORE SPRINGER

*Drawings
by
Catherine Wightman Springer*

CROWN PUBLISHERS, INC., NEW YORK

Book Design: BETTY MacDONALD

Library of Congress Catalog Card Number: 76-168319

PRINTED IN THE UNITED STATES OF AMERICA

Published simultaneously in Canada by General Publishing Company Limited

Contents

Preface

EVERY BOOK SHOULD HAVE a valid reason for existing, and no lengthy search was needed to arrive at a raison d'être for the present volume. It materialized from a long-felt need for an informative publication devoted to bells as collectibles—a subject that has had relatively little attention in book form.

But with thousands of such bells known to exist, how does one begin to write of them? The whole subject being vast and complex, some plan seemed desirable, and in the end a three-way approach proved the most workable. Looking at the whole field historically, geographically, and also typologically has opened the way to showing as many classifications of bells as possible.

To make the selections was no small task. A basic list of generally accepted examples was only a beginning. It was soon apparent that a longer list should be probed if the book was to be at all comprehensive.

To this end a cross-section sampling of many collections was made. This served to focus attention on the fact that no single collection is really complete. No collector in the span of a lifetime could possibly have access to the existing multitude of collectible bells. By the same token, no one book can hope to embody all there is to know about bell collecting. Although certain omissions have been unavoidable, an honest attempt has been made to include not only the best known bells but many that are unique. Hopefully, the results are representative enough to satisfy the informational needs of those who are collectors—and perhaps even prove enjoyable to some who are not.

No attempt is made to delve deeply into the techniques of bell production. It is taken for granted the collector will study the technical aspects in other references.

Nor does the book claim to advance any startling number of new findings, though original research has resulted in a few heretofore unrecognized considerations that may help collectors reevaluate certain of their bells. From the start, the chief purpose has been only to survey in some organized fashion the best that is known in the field.

In two respects the material encompasses a rather wide scope, including gongs and rattles along with bells and modern examples along with the antique. Many bells not early in point of time, not even old enough to rank as antiques, are nevertheless collectible as examples of certain concepts in design and craftsmanship.

In one other respect, also, the material adopts a somewhat unorthodox viewpoint. Unlike some collectors' books that deliberately avoid references to museum holdings, this one ranges freely into the museum world— on the assumption that the serious collector's interest extends, at least now and then, to the unobtainable as well as the obtainable. From a historical standpoint, museums offer examples of bells that could never be viewed any other place.

Because it delves into a little-explored field where there was no precedent to follow, the writing has been hampered to some extent. It would have been hampered even more had it not been for the response of so many who gladly contributed of their knowledge to help piece together widely scattered facts. That so many did respond is evidence of the ever increasing interest in bells as a form of art to be collected, studied, and exhibited.

Fortunately for the publishers and the author, collectors and curators alike agree with them that illustrations are vital to interpreting a text. Many have had pictures taken especially for this book, some of them showing bells never before photographed.

It is impossible to acknowledge each piece of assistance from private and public collections. Many of course are acknowledged throughout the book. But a more personal note of appreciation goes to the following individuals who willingly took time from their heavy schedules to share their expertise: Mrs. Vivian Bose, for documenting a number of Indian brasses; Mrs. John Bunker, for permitting use of her newly published research on ancient Chinese bronzes; Mr. Michael G. B. Coultas for his patience in authenticating bits of Australian history; Mr. Carl U. Fauster, for verifying certain facts about American glass; Dr. Adalbert Kretzmann, for appraising several bells in the realm of Christian art; and Mr. Vinne Starr for his perspective on bellmaking in East Hampton, Connecticut. Through their respective researches both Mrs. Berenice Du Bois and Mrs. Lois Herring graciously added new dimensions to existing data on smoke bells and on Danish plates carrying a bell motif.

Appreciative thanks go also to these persons who gladly offered to lend objects from their own collections for photographing and study: Miss Helen Baxter, Mrs. Robert W. Cole, Sr., and Mrs. Myrl Huene.

Finally, it is inevitable that errors creep into a survey of this kind. Justified corrections will be welcome. However, it is hoped that readers will feel they can echo a German curator's comment upon reading Ernest Morris's *Tintinnabula*. As he expressed it, "What is told in this book, the truth is more than the mistakes."

The Collector's Book of Bells

1

Oldest of Collectibles

To VISUALIZE A WORLD without bells is virtually impossible, and for a very good reason. Quite likely there never has been a time when bells in one form or another were utterly unknown. They are as old as recorded time but with the exact date of their origin indefinite and indeterminable, forever lost in antiquity. Like certain other primitive objects, bells may have developed gradually in scattered areas and, it is reasonable to assume, without any single inventor.

Perhaps in the childhood of the human race early man heard with delight the ringing tones of a clay pot hung to dry in the sun, or warned his people by rattling pebbles in a hollow shell. From these crude beginnings, so historians believe, early bell forms evolved as the use of metals spread.

Whether the earliest metal bells were crotals or open-mouthed types is best left for the antiquarians to debate. More interesting to students of recorded history, including collectors, are questions relating to the artistry of these ancient bells and to their varied uses.

LURISTAN BRONZE BELLS

Of all the more ancient types of bells known, those from the Luristan highlands of ancient Persia hold unique appeal for collectors—largely for their sophisticated designs, but also for the almost unbelievable story of their accidental dis-

1. *Luristan horse bell of the birdcage type. Sometimes identified as symbolizing a pomegranate and thereby denoting fertility.* HALPERIN COLLECTION

3. *Harness ornaments recovered from Siyalk, oldest human settlement on the Iranian Plateau, circa 800 B.C. The hammered silhouette figures of horses atop the bells indicate a strong dependency on that animal.* ALADDIN HOUSE, LTD., ARTIFACTS & ANTIQUITIES, 648 NINTH AVENUE, NEW YORK

2. *Luristan horse bells as they appeared when excavated. Note the heavy patination.* ARCHAEOLOGICAL SHOP, TEL AVIV HILTON, TEL AVIV, ISRAEL

covery and introduction on the antiques market not too long ago.

In 1927 a Lur peasant unexpectedly uncovered an ancient grave, the lonely resting place of one of his ancestral tribesmen. The shallow grave was unpretentious but its bronze contents attracted the peasant. Scattered among the bones of man and horse were curiously worked bells, amulets, harness ornaments, and long pins. Sometime later, this same Lur visited a grocer's shop in Harsin and offered, in exchange for sugar and tea, certain of the bronze objects he had found while working his land.

After a long discussion the grocer offered "half the weight of the old iron in sugar and a twentieth in tea." Presently a Jewish trader arrived in Harsin and, offering sugar for bronze, weight for weight, soon gathered what would prove a most profitable collection. Word quickly spread through the Luristan hills that these pieces were magic "antiquities" that could be exchanged for gold in the markets of Kermanshah.

The treasure hunt was on in this region of northwest Iran (Persia) and the graves were robbed with surprising speed. The Lurs rapidly discovered the best way to locate the tombs, sounding with an iron rod near springs of water, then ripping away scrub and prying off stone slabs to expose the bronze treasures. These they gathered by the thousands, then funneled them through Iranian merchants to dealers in London, Paris, and New York.

Within the last forty years almost every public and private collection of antiquities has acquired or has refused to acquire these plentiful objects. The very quantity of Luristan bronzes, bells included, has led some skeptics to question the authenticity of many pieces. Yet the possibility of being able to verify each of these "finds" is ever so slight. As Dr. Bernard Goldman points out in his extensive writings on Luristan bronzes, modern forgeries of these pieces are difficult and frequently totally impossible to detect. Since this is so, the only advice for prospective buyers is to put their trust in reputable dealers accustomed to giving a certificate of authenticity with each antiquity sold.

There are other problems surrounding the bronzes. Just who were the Lurs and precisely when did they create their metalwork? All through the second millennium B.C. until the end of the first millennium A.D. various tribal cultures succeeded one another in the vast regions around the Zagros Mountains. To which should the bronzes be attributed?

Without any written records as a frame of reference, scholars differ in their interpretation and dating of these Luristan objects. Some consider them the work of the Kassites coming from Babylon toward the end of the second millennium, or of the Hittite metallurgists who followed. Others attribute them to the later Scythians arriving from South Russia during the eighth century, or thereabouts. The dates different scholars assign the pieces vary as much as do their theories. All that can be said is that apparently they fall well within the first millennium before Christ.

Despite such problems, this much authorities agree upon so far as Luristan bells are concerned: the majority of them being harness ornaments, they were obviously intended for seminomadic warriors who prized their horses. As was their custom, the Lurs buried rider and horse together in the same grave, along with the animal's ornate bell-trimmed trappings. Sometimes the grave goods even included elaborate chariot fittings with bells.

An open-work type of horse bell, or bird-cage type, was popular with the itinerant tinkers who worked in metals. Frequently they topped these with stylized animal forms. Inside, iron pellets rolled around, but often these are now missing. Over the centuries the iron decomposed though the bronze bells remained beautifully preserved.

Of equal artistic interest are the smaller bells apparently used as ornaments on horse bridles. They, also, are frequently topped with stylized animal forms. This preoccupation with animalistic art was of course natural to a horse-breeding, pastoral people. Deer, mountain goats, cows, and horses were favorite subjects.

The rich patina of age on Luristan bells adds to their appeal, aesthetically and historically. Usually this is encrusted and of a malachite green. The color may vary, though, from a soft gray-green to a rich kingfisher blue. Generally speaking, it is a patina quite similar to that found on contemporary Chinese bronzes.

OTHER ANCIENT BELLS

Fascinating as Luristan bells can be, other ancient examples from neighboring cultures are also deserving of a collector's interest. That interest may of necessity be mostly academic, however, since examples outside Luristan types are not so easily acquired by the average private collector.

Throughout ancient times any number of horse-loving tribes roamed the Eurasian mainlands, and they all shared certain cultural affini-

4. *Iron terminal with pendent bells, from Stepants-minda. The stylized horns supporting a deity signify the existence of bull worship.*

ties. Their bells reveal this in style, subject, and technique. Heavily encrusted little bronze horse bells topped with animal forms have been recovered from the Siyalk settlement. An iron terminal with pendent bells from Stepantsminda shows stylized horns supporting a deity and signifying the existence of bull worship in some form.

Other cultures, further removed and somewhat different, produced bells of another kind. In ancient Egypt a superior sort of bell-rattle called a sistrum was dedicated to the mystical worship of Isis. This unique instrument consisted of an oval band of metal fastened to a handle, rather resembling the oval frame of a hand-mirror. Thick wires were threaded across the frame and loosely inserted in holes on each side of it. When shaken, the sistrum made a metallic rattle designed not only to summon

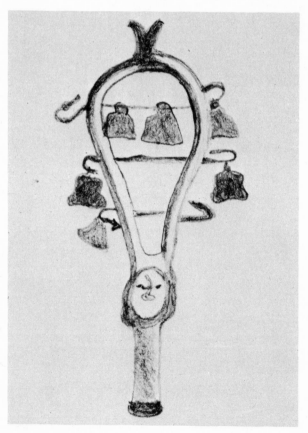

5. *Ancient Egyptian sistrum hung with small crude bells.*

worshipers but also to frighten off hostile spirits. To accentuate the bell-like quality, metal disks or rings or bars, even small bells, were hung on the wires.

Several variations of the sistrum have been unearthed in Egyptian tombs, along with other cherished objects lying buried with their owners. The tombs have also yielded necklaces laced with golden imitations of little bells.

The Assyrians made comparable use of little bells for personal adornment and sistrums for religious rituals. Sir Henry Layard aroused considerable interest in bells of the Assyrians while excavating in the ruins of Nineveh many years ago. He uncovered some eighty small cuplike shapes with iron clappers, all buried in a single caldron; stone reliefs were also uncovered to reveal spirited horses richly decorated with fancy harnesses having plumes and bells fixed on top of their headstalls. An Assyrian carving in the British Museum shows two horses drawing a carriage, each wearing around its neck six bells of various sizes.

ISRAEL'S USE OF BELLS

The rivalries between Egypt on the south and Assyria on the north constantly brought the little kingdom of Israel into the ebb and flow of cultural interplay, which in turn influenced the arts of the Israelites; so it is not surprising to find the early Hebrews supplied with bells and sistrums comparable to those of their neighbors.

Most collectors are familiar with the biblical references noting early Hebrew use of bells, but are perhaps less so with the poetic names ascribed to them by writers of the day. The *shalishim,* suggesting a shaking and rattling, were Egyptian-like sistrums and were sometimes translated as such among David's processional instruments that accompanied his bringing the Ark to Jerusalem. *Mezillot* were the bells used on the horses described by Zachariah. They warded off evil spirits by their jingling and were probably fastened on the headstalls, as they were in Assyria.

Of these two types little else is known, but more attention has been focused on the *pa-amonim*, the little bells attached to the lower seam of the high priest's robe. The Book of Exodus directs the making of this handsome garment with "a golden bell and a pomegranate, a golden bell and a pomegrante upon the skirts of the robe round about." The golden bells were said to symbolize thunder, and the pomegranates, lightning. The tinkle of these symbolic bells served to announce the whereabouts of the high priest and give him a twofold protection.

Hebrew religious law emphatically forbade looking upon God in His holy sanctum. Whoever did so must die. Yet in carrying out his duties, the priest might inadvertently come upon Him. Thus the priestly bells served to forewarn of a mortal's presence. Also according to Hebrew religion, God's protection was considered the best safeguard against evil spirits. Israelites nevertheless persisted in believing that demons could best be routed by the noise of a bell, which they could not endure. Again, then, the *pa-amonim* served by giving the priest added protection from such demons, who by tradition liked to inhabit sanctuaries.

Neither gold nor silver was mined in Israel, nor the tin needed for an alloy like bronze. Still it is a mistake to assume that early Israel imported its bells and other small metal objects. Metalworkers were held in high esteem and, coupled with musicians, come second in the three classes into which the Book of Genesis divides mankind. Tomb paintings show portrayals of traveling tinkers with portable goatskin bellows; and there is evidence that they knew how to cast small objects in gold, silver, brass, and bronze.

Only one inability is noted—how to prepare a proper bronze alloy for their temple cymbals. Written accounts state that when a bronze cymbal "from the days of Moses" became damaged, craftsmen from Alexandria had to be called in to mend it.

Although but distantly related to bells, early cymbals deserve some mention in passing. Collectors who encompass the whole range of bells, gongs, and rattles find these early examples of interest because certain of them, unlike modern cymbals, resemble bells in design and even in tonal quality. These musical instruments were common to the Egyptians and the Assyrians, as well as the Israelites, and their use in pairs supposedly originated from ancient man's belief in the power of symmetry.

The Israelites called theirs *meziltayim* or *zelzelim*, taking their names from the cymbals' shimmering sound. These were the only percussion instruments admitted into sacred Hebrew services. Two kinds are mentioned in the Psalms: the "loud cymbals" and the "high-sounding cymbals." Paul later refers to the "tinkling cymbals." These all presumably differed in size, design, and possibly in material. Quite likely the "loud cymbals" were the bell-like bronze sort known to the Assyrians. These were either bulging or elongated in shape, with noticeable handles. They were played not in the usual sideways fashion, but in an upright manner with the inverted cymbal striking the lower one.

GREEK AND ROMAN TYPES

Bells were widely used in ancient Greece and Rome. The classical writers allude to their various uses both in domestic and in religious life, and also in warfare.

Euripides, the Greek dramatist, tells how the Greeks decorated their horses with bells intended to spur them on and at the same time terrify the enemy. He also tells how Greek warriors had small bells concealed within the hollow of their shields. When the captains made their nightly rounds, each soldier was required to rattle his bell in order to show that he was guarding his post.

For much the same purpose Roman sentries wore a set of bells on their breastplates. Plutarch relates another curious instance of bells being used for Roman military defenses. Fearing his foes might escape at night by swimming across

6. Tentatively identified as a Roman lebetes-type bell. Handle and clapper remove easily so that when inverted the bell serves as a shallow bowl. PRIVATE COLLECTION

which were worn on a chain fastened over one shoulder and under the other. A statue of a Roman child wearing his *crepundia* may be seen in the Vatican's Museo Pio-Clementino.

Collectors often find it difficult to identify their ancient Roman bells as to original use, but with the help of classical writers they can at least catalogue them as examples of a specific type. True, some writers of the period rely on using "tintinnabula," the generic term for all small bells. Many, however, use precise and descriptive words suited to the various shapes of the bells.

There is, for example, the *lebetes* already mentioned. Homer uses this same word in describing the bowl-gongs given as prizes in athletic contests. Then there is the *petasus*, a shallow bell with flaring lip, so called because it resembles a wide-brimmed Roman traveler's hat of that same name. The *crotalum* implies a small closed sphere with rolling pellets inside. A *squilla* signifies a small shrill bell and is usually interpreted to mean some sort of a handbell.

PRE-COLUMBIAN TINTINNABULA

Absorbing stories are to be found in little bells belonging to the Indians of the Americas during the pre-Columbian period. They used them as costume decorations, as funerary offerings, sometimes as musical instruments, and occasionally as a medium of exchange. Produced by many cultures, the bells naturally assumed many forms —ranging from simple clay rattles and curious copper effigies to very ornate golden tintinnabula; but, whatever their form, all are significant and many reveal a degree of artistic cunning. Most of them date between 1000 B.C. and A.D. 1500.

Archaeologists from many lands have toiled for years to learn more about the Indians of the early Americas, but only in relatively recent times have scholars and collectors fully appreciated the varied artifacts from the world of the preconquest Americas. Tiny as most of them are,

the river where he held them, Brutus contrived a net with little bells on it. Dropped under the water, it gave notice of any who tried to swim away. It is not beyond the realm of possibility for collectors to feel that their tiny archaeological bells from Roman ruins might have been used for some such clever military defense as this.

Among the bells used in Roman religious practices, Herodotus mentions the bowl-like form used by the Spartans in funeral processions. This he calls a *lebetes*, the Latin word originally applied to copper caldrons.

With their population becoming more sedentary and urbanized, the Roman people found countless everyday uses for small bells: for opening the marketplace and the public baths; for decorating gates and doorways; or for protecting domestic animals and children from unseen evil. In the case of children, bells were usually among their *crepundia*, or playthings, all of

7. *Ancient finial from an Inca chieftain's staff. Dancing foxes decorate the tip. All but one of the original bells have corroded away.*

the bells found among the artifacts bring to life certain customs and beliefs of those ancient civilizations in a most interesting way.

They come from three major centers of preconquest civilization: the home of the vast Inca empires along the Pacific coast of South America, principally through Peru; the land of the Aztecs and the Mayas in Middle America, stretching from Mexico to Guatemala; and the smaller and less known region lying between the two, the countries of Central America, extending into parts of Colombia.

Uncounted quantities of small bells have been recovered from Inca burials in Peru. Scenes on ancient woven textiles and painted pottery show Inca warriors wearing bulbous crotals on their belts and smaller jinglets on their gaiters. Many ornate ceremonial pieces decorated with bells have also been uncovered. One splendid example

is an ornamental finial for a staff. On the tip, foxes are standing, dancing in a circle, supported by two tiers of bells. Along with painted masks and colorful plumes, bells were part and parcel of the Incas' ceremonial paraphernalia. And when it is estimated that these people celebrated one hundred fifty-eight festivals each year, the number of bells made for such use is easily imagined. Peruvian bells have never been available in any great numbers for the collector, however. This is largely blamed on the widespread looting of cemeteries during the period following Pizarro's conquest.

Several cultures emerged, flourished, and disappeared in the vast lands of ancient Middle America, each with its own way of life and each with a fondness for bells rivaling that of the Incas. So far as collectors are concerned, there were three major groups here whose arts are typically represented in their tintinnabula: the Mayas, the Mixtecs, and the Aztecs.

Archaeologists have been particularly involved with the Mayan culture in recent times during underwater explorations of their sacred *cenotes,* or wells of sacrifice. Even noncollectors cannot help being impressed with the quantities of little bells dredged up from such famous *cenotes* as the sacred well of sacrifice in the temple city of Chichén Itzá. In a single exploration, authorities estimate one thousand of these tiny artifacts were dredged up, most of them the size of a dime, many of gold, others of copper.

Among the most interesting always are the effigy bells demonstrating Mayan skill in figure portrayal. Some appear in the likeness of a deity or of a creature such as a bat or a monkey.

As archaeologists have reconstructed the life of the Mayas, it becomes clear that these bells were once used in ceremonial sacrifices at their sacred *cenotes.* Hundreds of them decorated the costumes of those luckless maidens and children thrown into such wells to appease the insatiable gods. Incredible quantities of them must also have been flung in with the human sacrifices, for many rare jewels and other treasures were customarily consigned to the gods in this way.

8. Effigy bells of the crotal type, dredged up from Mayan wells of sacrifice.

Even though of the crotal type with closed mouth, few of these tintinnabula are found with clappers. That is because they were "death bells," Mexican archaeologists explain. Before tossing them into the *cenote,* the Mayas usually silenced each little bell by opening it and ripping out its clapper. This tedious procedure was necessary, they believed, for they looked upon the clapper as the "soul" of the bell.

During their period of greatest artistic achievement, from A.D. 300 to 900, the ancient Mayas also sculptured small realistic clay figures from everyday life. These were hollow, and many became rattles with clay pellets enclosed. Occasionally one became a whistle as well as a rattle, with a mouthpiece embedded in the back. Traditionally women were among the favorite subjects, and they were depicted with dignity and style, indicating the high esteem women must have enjoyed among the Mayas.

Terra-cotta sculptures such as these were used as funerary pieces. Many are of course fragmentary when recovered from old graves; but the collector searching for a Mayan rattle of this type can almost surely find a perfect specimen from a dealer specializing in pre-Columbian art.

Of all the ancient American metalworkers, the Mixtecs attained the peak of perfection. Their gold bells and other ornaments were produced by technicians highly skilled in the art of goldsmithing. The people of this important cultural group inhabited the mountainous slopes of Monte Albán in western Oaxaca some time around A.D. 1000, and it is here that some of the most important finds in preconquest bells have been uncovered.

In the now-famous Monte Albán tomb no. 7, that of a fifteenth-century Mixtec chief, archaeologists found a glittering array of belled jewelry worked in gold, silver, jade, and turquoise. Probably the most superbly crafted of all the Mixtec costume bells are those with movable parts. One, for example, is a little pendant in the shape of a skull with an articulated lower jaw from which hang tassels and bells.

Although private collectors can scarcely hope to acquire originals of such priceless treasures, they can find very superior copies of them being painstakingly created by a few craftsmen in the Monte Albán region. One fact gives these copies a degree of intrinsic worth: they are made by the same centuries-old *cire perdue,* or lost-wax,

9. Five ancient bells brought up from the sacred well of sacrifice at Chichén Itzá. Four are effigy type and the fifth represents a perforated calabash. ROBERT STOLPER GALLERIES

10. *Hollow pottery figurines in the form of rattles, some with whistles, were made by the Mayan people between* A.D. *300 and 900 and used for burial with their dead. Of either warm red or sand-colored clay, they average in size from five to seven inches.* ALADDIN HOUSE, LTD., ARTIFACTS & AN-TIQUITIES, 648 NINTH AVENUE, NEW YORK

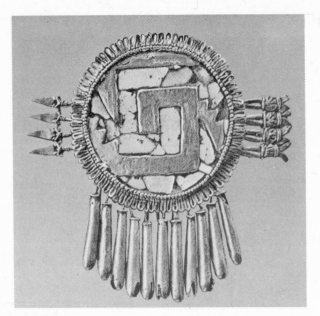

11. *Handsome Mixtec ornament of gold, inlaid with color and fringed with bells.*

method used by almost all pre-Columbian metalworkers. The process is an intricate and fascinating one that allows for great delicacy of design.

Over a clay core, wax is sculptured in the desired form; then an outer layer of clay is pressed on, completely covering the sculpture. The wax is melted out through vents in the clay while the mold is being fired, and molten metal can then be poured into the hollow mold. Finally, the clay casing is broken away to reveal the finished metal piece. It is a unique piece, since the mold for it has been destroyed.

As the last descendants of Mixtec culture, the Aztecs kept alive a high degree of skill in fashioning small bells of gold. Even their copper bells were distinctively ornamented with geometric designs. Many more of the gold tintinnabula might be seen in collections today, had not the Spanish conquerors swept them away, with hordes of other treasures bound for Spain, to be melted down for bullion. But at least the conquistadors left hundreds of copper ones behind, and these are the typical Aztec bells treasured by collectors. They are teardrop in shape and average from a fraction of an inch to three or more inches in length.

Fortunately, the conquistadors also left written records describing some of the bells they found. Diaz furnished one of the earliest ac-

counts, telling of a huge Mexican temple where "they kept vipers and venomous snakes, who had something at their tails which sounded like Morris bells . . ." Cortez wrote of two helmets he was sending home, one being covered with blue precious stones and "edged with twenty-five golden bells crested with a greene foule sitting on the top of the helmet, whose feet, bill and eyes were all of gold, and several golden knobbes sustained every bell." According to another chronicler of the conquest, Cortez himself carried back, among other magnificent treasures for his betrothed, an emerald in the form of a bell, with a fine pearl as its clapper.

The matchless bells of the Mixtecs are rivaled only by those found in another region lying along the narrow strip of Central America. Here the Indians of Costa Rica, Panama, and parts of Colombia belonged to a single culture. Little is known of them as a people; but exquisitely designed gold bells retrieved at such Panama sites as Coclé and Chiriquí are evidence of a highly developed artistic skill flourishing about A.D. 1300.

Large deep graves have yielded elegant little gold bells in the form of tiny three-dimensional animal figures, much of the work being filigree and repoussé. The jaguar was among the popular zoomorphic subjects for ornaments from this culture, for the cat-god was a popular deity. The detailed workmanship of these Lilliputian figures is equaled only by the inventiveness of their designs.

Several fine examples were found at Coclé in 1940 by Dr. Alden Mason while he was engaged in archaeological studies for the University of Pennsylvania Museum. All were added to the museum's extensive collection of more than one hundred pre-Columbian bells and rattles.

A few archaic pre-Columbian cultures once existed in Western Mexico and around Tlatilco on the outskirts of present-day Mexico City. They did not resemble the cultures of other areas, nor even each other's; yet they did possess one trait in common, a notable skill in free modeling of clay. Many unusual bell-rattles have

13. *Typical Aztec copper bell, teardrop in shape, with geometric patterns.* Cire perdue *casting.*

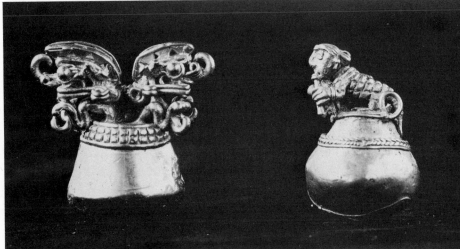

14. *Two aboriginal gold bells excavated in 1940 by Dr. Alden Mason from a burial in Coclé, Panama. Circa 1300.* MUSEUM COLLECTION, UNIVERSITY OF PENNSYLVANIA

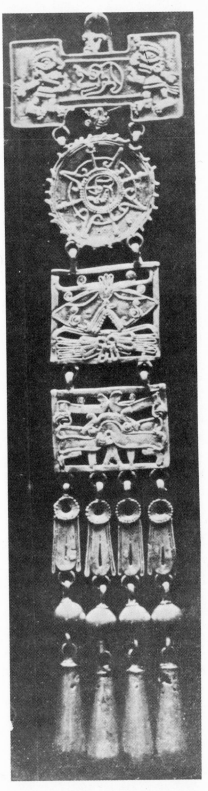

12. *Aztec bells on a costume ornament depicting, from the top, gods playing ball, a sun disk, a knife symbolizing the moon, and an earth monster. Cast by the* cire perdue *method.*

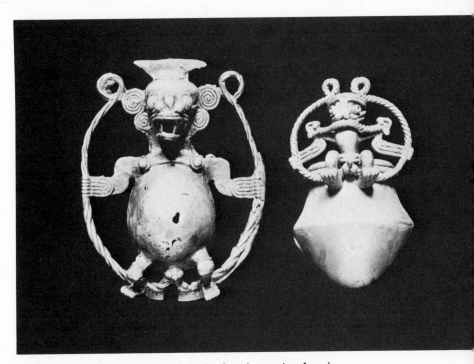

15. *Exquisitely detailed gold bells showing animals seizing coiled ropes. Both found in aboriginal graves—the larger in Costa Rica or Panama; the smaller, probably in Colombia.* MUSEUM COLLECTION, UNIVERSITY OF PENNSYLVANIA

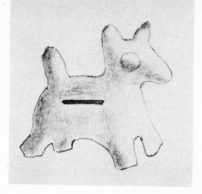

17. *Rattle from Western Mexico. The dog was a favorite subject for rattles like this to place in graves and thus ensure the birth of more animals.*

16. *A Middle American Indian modeled this naturalistic black clay rattle at Tlatilco in Mexico about one thousand years before Christ. It was found at the lowest stratification and under layers of lava.* ART ROBINSON COLLECTION

been unearthed around Tlatilco by workers digging for clay to make bricks. The ancient graves yielding them date between 1500 and 1000 B.C., making Tlatilco one of the oldest known village sites in Mexico.

The village farmers of Western Mexico created pottery figures typical of the everyday scene, and usually with the traditional clay pellet encased. Their modeling was comparatively simple in form, yet expressive. The Colima culture in particular has become famous among archaeologists for its figures of dogs in polished red or black clay. By popular misconception such figures are sometimes looked upon as ancient toys. Actually they were created as burial offerings to be placed in graves with the dead.

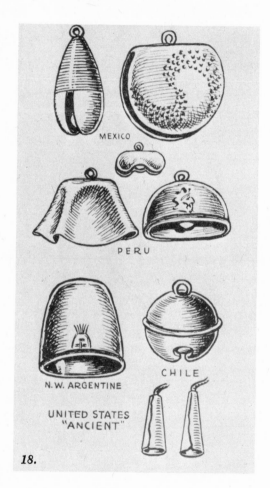

18.

One further observation is due *los cascabeles de los antiques*, the bells of the ancients, as they are called in present-day Mexico. Little has been said about them as musical instruments because very little is known of pre-Spanish music. Yet in the monumental study recently completed by a Mexico City musicologist, more than one hundred rhythmic devices have been found and identified. Bells and rattles are among them.

19. *Wheel-like chime of black clay made by the Mexican Indians of Oaxaca, copied from ancient instruments made by the Zapotecs between 300 B.C. and A.D. 300.* PRIVATE COLLECTION

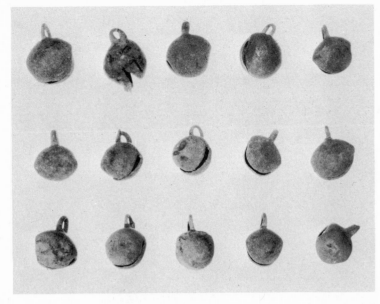

20. *These copper bells represent one of the largest yields found in Arizona, all fifteen being buried in a single cache with 100,000 beads contained in a jar.* ARIZONA STATE MUSEUM

An enterprising bell collector interested in instrumental artifacts might well find this a fertile field for further research. And for a start there is a bell known to most collectors that is actually descended from a rhythmic instrument used by the Zapotecs at Oaxaca between 300 B.C. and A.D. 300. This is the wheel-like chime of black clay made by the Indians in Oaxaca today. Grasped at the center, it can be twisted and turned to give a pronounced rhythmic tinkle; steadily revolving it on a slender branch slipped through a hole in the center core produces a softer sound.

UNITED STATES "ANCIENTS"

The region known as the United States of America was still an unmapped wilderness when Cortez left Mexico. It remained for Coronado's men to map this unknown North and they, like their fellow Spaniards in Mexico, left written accounts of what they saw—among other things, Indians wearing copper bells with faces carved on them.

Studies have proved that bells were, in fact, common to prehistoric cultures inhabiting this northern region from earliest times. Yet for years archaeologists have been puzzled about the little copper crotals being found in burials and ruins in certain parts of Arizona and New Mexico, but nowhere else in the United States. Microscopic tests indicate that these crotals were cast by skilled metalworkers using the *cire perdue* method. As no evidence has ever been found of such work being done by prehistoric people in the United States, there is little doubt that such bells were imported from Mexico. They are quite similar to those made there in pre-Spanish times.

Unprepossessing in appearance, these little crotals are still of interest to collectors as evidence of the early long-range connections between this area and Middle America. Obviously they were carried as a medium of exchange by isolated traders and missionaries who penetrated the unmapped wilderness north of Mexico. The dates assigned most of them range from around A.D. 1100 to 1400 and because of their relative scarcity, it is believed not many aboriginals of the Southwest had them as ornaments. No more than twenty-eight have ever been found in a single cache, and even smaller occurrences are extremely rare.

21. *Life-size photograph of a copper bell that was found among ruins in the San Pedro Valley near Mammoth, Arizona. The bell is believed to be as large as, or larger than, any known copper one unearthed in Mexico.* ARIZONA STATE MUSEUM

Occasionally an ancient burial site in the area yields a more exceptional find. Among the eighty-five small copper crotals in the Arizona State Museum is the largest one yet discovered in the Southwest. Archaeologists have acclaimed it as large as, or larger than, any found in Mexico.

Similarly, the Pueblo Grande Museum in Phoenix boasts a unique and very early example of aboriginal bells, discovered by Mr. and Mrs. Moulton B. Smith near an old pipestone quarry under some Pueblo ruins. Four copper crotals are combined with pipestone beads and tied into a bracelet with a bow of cotton weaving. Authorities estimate that the bracelet was worn sometime between A.D. 700 and 1100.

About this same time the Mogollon-Mimbres people in what is today New Mexico were acquiring by trade another kind of copper bell of teardrop shape. These resemble the ones commonly excavated in Aztec tombs. They are graduated in size and are often found in the same cache with turquoise jewelry, beads, and quite beautiful pottery.

Fragmentary clay bells found among artifacts belonging to the Mimbres people are among the most prized of the bells from the ancient Southwest, and are apparently the only ones indigenous to the region. Few have survived, and each one found has received considerable attention from archaeologists. The one known as the Luna County clay bell was detailed in a 1956 issue of *El Palacio,* the monthly review published by the Museum of New Mexico:

A fragmentary clay bell, consisting of a little over one-half of the original, is also of interest since pottery bells are comparatively rare in the Southwest . . . Since it is broken, one can get a fair idea of how it was made. It is formed from reddish-brown clay. The exterior is smoothed, unslipped, and unpolished. Inclusions of tempering material are visible on the exterior surface. Along the suspension hole are indications of wear . . . Smudging and carbonization visible on the interior, as well as cordage marks, support the earlier theory of how such bells were manufactured: "A sphere of clay for the clapper was placed within a ball of cotton textile or, perhaps, another substance covered with cloth and then wrapped with a few turns of string. Around this the bell was fashioned. Firing consumed the material within, leaving the clapper in place." (Allen, 1953, p. 16)

Outside of the Southwestern United States clay bells have been found in the Valley of Mexico and at Quirigua, Guatemala. "It is significant that pottery bells occur late in the protohistoric and historic times and have not been found at any site where copper bells have also been discovered. Apparently these clay bells were made in the localities where they have been found, and suggest a home-made substitute for metal bells. Whether this substitution was necessary because copper bells were not then being made, because metal bells had stopped being traded in, or simply because copper ones were rare, cannot be told at this time." (Withers, 1946, p. 53)

About 1945 several varieties of native aboriginal bells were offered directly to collectors by Colonel Fain White King, who was concluding a long span of digs throughout the Americas with excavations at Wickliffe, Kentucky. The buried city uncovered here belongs to the Mound Builders culture that once existed throughout the Ohio Valley and extended into Georgia. Among the artifacts commonly found in their mounds are conical copper tinklers. Although not bells in the true sense of the word, they gave a noticeable tinkle when used like a thick fringe on clothing. The later Indians eagerly adopted tinklers as a costume decoration for their rhythmic dances.

The most advanced of the Mound Builders were the Hopewellians, who were known to be active traders for the copper they were gifted at working. Among the pieces they hammered out were little effigy rattles. The Ohio Historical Society has examples of their small turtle-shaped crotals recovered from Mound City and dated between 400 B.C. and A.D. 500.

To a collector, any native aboriginal bells in effigy form are naturally the most desirable. Yet in any comprehensive collection even the more ordinary-looking "trade" bells constitute a desirable link between the prehistoric and the historic past.

And who can be sure? Some of these may have been among the little bells brought by Columbus, for in his diaries he makes frequent mention of the Indians he encountered and their delight in the bells he had brought over for trading. They willingly traded, he recounts, "bringing some pieces of gold, which these men wanted to exchange for a hawk's bell, for there was nothing they desired more than these bells."

22. *Bracelet of prehistoric copper bells strung with pipestone beads and tied with a bow of cotton weaving, shown as found by Mr. and Mrs. Moulton B. Smith in Pueblo ruins. Worn probably between A.D. 700 and 1100.* COURTESY OF MOULTON B. SMITH

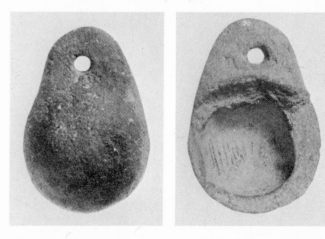

23. *Luna County clay bell from the Mimbres people of the ancient Southwest.* COLLECTIONS IN THE MUSEUM OF NEW MEXICO

2

Oriental Bells, Gongs, and Rattles

THE USE OF BELLS in the Orient has been well recorded for nearly five thousand years, and throughout those lengthy records this one fact is unchanging: their functions have been patterned primarily by the unique religious and musical dictates of the Far East, each bell having its own special use that in turn often influenced its design. As a result, in their Oriental bells collectors possess a heritage of facts too often lacking where Occidental bells are concerned.

The sound of stone was a favorite feature of early Chinese music. It is embodied in the *te ching*, or single sonorous stone, and also in that ancient instrument called the *pien ching*, a group of sixteen graduated stone chimes suspended in a large frame.

Usually in the shape of a carpenter's square, these stone chimes were often carved with representations of birds, beasts, and fish—real or imaginary. These were very special stones found in mountain streams and beautifully colored. Their sound, depending on the quality of the stone and on proper manipulation of the mallet, was "clear as a bell." It is said that when the great Confucius heard this instrument he was so affected by its music that he could not take food for three months afterward!

The Chinese name for a single clapperless metal bell is *chung,* and in its earliest form this bell was of bronze, square in shape, and used to mark the hours. Sixteen or more of these, when graduated in size and suspended in a

frame, became a *pien chung,* or chime of bells. According to ritual in Confucian temples, so Orientalists explain, the two sets of chimes were necessary to each other—the *pien chung* and the *pien ching.* The bell chimes sounded and the stone chimes answered, note for note.

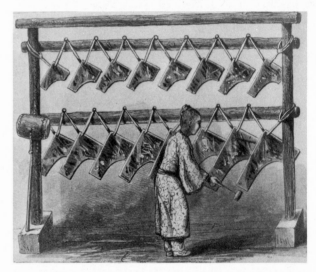

24. *A Chinese bell-ringer practicing on the* pien ching.

The *pien chung* has long since disappeared, but occasionally a collector finds a single and very early bell that once hung in such a chime set. This type can be distinguished from every other *chung* by a loop cast onto the front of the shank, or handle, thus permitting the bell to hang at the approved angle in the old *pien chung.* This loop feature was discontinued cen-

in proper tune or that they were struck to produce varying tones is unlikely. The boss, or striking point on a *chung,* is often clearly visible elsewhere on the surface.

That they were merely decorative or symbolic is more likely. On later examples they are coiled

25. *Unusually fine example of an elliptical* chung *that once hung obliquely in a frame as a part of a* pien chung. *The loop held it at just the correct angle. During the Sung dynasty, the loop was moved to the top so the bells would hang straight.* LA ROSE COLLECTION

turies ago; the more modern bells of similar type, still used for musical purposes, hang vertically.

One feature characterizing almost every *chung* has survived since ancient times, although it has often undergone modifications. That is the set of four panels containing, usually, nine protuberances each. These protuberances—knobs, studs, coils, spikes, or whatever their form—are always a matter of curiosity to the collector, and several theories have been advanced as to their purpose. That they were filed to keep the *chung*

26. *A* po chung *on a beautifully carved rosewood frame topped by the scaly dragon P'u Lao.* PRIVATE COLLECTION

27. *Addorsed dragons create an artistic stand, originally for some type of clapperless bell.*

to resemble snails, perhaps the sacred snails of Buddha, some say. On still other examples the knobs become spikes, said to represent fire-rays. All these ideas are only conjectural, however. To insist on a completely satisfactory explanation is asking the impossible, according to Director Won-Yong Kim of Korea's National Museum. "Nobody in the twentieth century," states Mr. Kim, "would know what those snail-like ju —studs—protuberances are meant for. No records about them have survived . . . and all guess and legends are purely groundless. One thing is clear, that they are all mere decorations whose real meaning is known only to those ancient Chinese . . . My guess is that they may represent nail-heads which had some functional significance in making up a drum made originally of wood before they invented a bronze bell."

Still one other type of single clapperless bell is deserving of the collector's attention. That is the *po chung*, of varying shape and traditionally stationed in a frame before a Confucian temple to serve as "a guardian, a proclamation, and a warning."

It is worth noting that the decorative frame supporting a *chung* and even the hammer used to strike it, are frequently symbolic in their carvings and also deserving of the collector's attention. Animal forms are a favorite motif, especially the dragon. The beneficent Chinese dragon should not be confused, however, with the ferocious dragon of heraldry and medieval mythology. Although now widely replaced by the lion as the guardian of Buddhist faith, the dragon was for centuries the symbol of China's glorious imperial power. By tradition in Chinese art, the dragon with five claws appears only on the imperial objects of the emperors; the four-clawed dragon, on objects for the lesser nobles; and the three-clawed is the one seen on most old bronze and teakwood carvings.

Dragons may be classed in nine families. Of these it is the P'u Lao that is depicted on top of bells in token of its habit of crying out loudly when attacked by its archenemy, the whale.

Along with the various *chung* types known to ancient China there was also the *to*, which is a handbell with free-swinging tongue. Apparently the tongue in the early *to* was of wood, for it is recorded that Confucius wished to be "a wooden-tongued bell of heaven."

28. *Though definitely associated with Shang bronzemanship, the* p'ang *remains a "mystery-bronze" as to function. Found buried always with chariots and their fittings.* LITTMANN COLLECTION

Any true appreciation of Chinese bells is linked with an understanding of the major dynasties in Chinese history, for each has its own identifiable bell forms. The earliest great era that produced bells in significant number was the Chou dynasty (ca. 1030–256 B.C.), which inherited a tradition of superb bronzemanship from the earlier Shang dynasty. A much admired bell piece known to collectors who specialize in ancient Orientalia comes from this period immediately predating the Chou dynasty and serves as an example of that earlier superb bronzemanship. This is the *p'ang*, a bow-shaped object with bells at the terminals. It is an extremely early piece and never shows up in any excavations of tombs dating later than 1027 B.C. According to the most recently published material on the *p'ang*, this much discussed object has long been considered a chariot fitting, since it is always found in tombs with chariots; but its exact usage has never been satisfactorily determined.

The period called Late Chou, or sometimes Warring States, was also the age of emerging Confucianism. As already implied, Confucius valued music as a moral force and bells as highly desirable musical instruments; so it is not surprising that bronzemakers of this period lavished their finest efforts on bells. In one Chou burial site alone dozens of magnificent bells from chime sets were unearthed, along with handbells and horse jinglets.

During the period of Warring States the *chung* became larger and more elaborate, decorated with mythical *t'ao-t'ieh* masks and arabesques symbolizing clouds and thunder. Handles of zoomorphic motif were often beautifully modeled in the form of back-to-back creatures, real or mythical. Dragons were a popular subject. Where there were projecting knobs, these were flattened into serpent coils and a panel of inscription added between sections of knobs.

The Han dynasty that followed (202 B.C.–A.D 220) produced an even greater quantity of bells. Never in Chinese history was so much attention devoted to the tomb and its contents as in the

29. *A chariot bell on a socket, the jingles being encased within the pocket formed by crossbars. Found always in tombs of the Western Chou period (1027–771 B.C.)* HALPERIN COLLECTION

Han dynasty, when it was seemingly important to supply the dead with all things necessary in the life beyond. Quantities of bells, many of them attached to horse fittings, are still being recovered from tombs of that period.

Although it is the rare private collector who is fortunate enough to possess a bell from the Chou dynasty, or an even earlier period, an authentic Han dynasty bell is not beyond acquiring by the serious collector. The various horse bells are favorites. In several respects, these particular pieces have much the same appeal found in Luristan bells and, in fact, are comparable in their simplicity of design and distinctive patina.

Han bronzes were made under a set formula handed down from the Chou dynasty. Analysis of their content reveals the special combination

30. *Motifs on this* chung *of the Warring States are typical of bronze workmanship from the period: the* t'ao-t'ieh *mask as a border, the zoomorphic handle, the flattened knobs.* MUSEUM VAN AZIATISCHE KUNST, AMSTERDAM

31. Cloud and thunder patterns, motifs found on many an old chung. *Such ornamentations were believed to influence the gods.*

of metals that combined with the soil where they lay to form their varicolored coatings. The oldest patina—according to Chinese belief—is cherry red. But among collectors in the Western world the bluish green is desirable and is the color common to Han horse bells. Often it is mottled with red or yellow and tinged with turquoise. The aesthetic value of this accidental patination was not lost on the early Chinese. Forgers went to great trouble in imitating it. One case is recorded of a family where each generation buried fake pieces in specially treated soil, to be dug up and sold by the next generation once removed!

During the four hundred years between the fall of the Han dynasty and the rise of T'ang (A.D. 618–906), China went through a period of great change marked by the introduction of Buddhism with its far-reaching effects on all the arts. Life was very cosmopolitan under the luxury-loving T'ang emperors. Musical entertainers were popular with all the noblemen, and many varieties of bells, gongs, and cymbals were used by the players.

This period is also notable in the history of Chinese ceramics, for it was during the seventh and eighth centuries that Chinese potters perfected true porcelain, a hard and translucent ware that rings when struck. The character *tz'u,* which in the Han dictionary still denoted stoneware, now came to mean true porcelain.

Bells of this ware closely resemble Chinese bronze bells in their decorations, and collectors often assume that they are copied from the bronze. There is no proof, however, that symbolic decorations originated in bronze, since the Chinese exhibited an unbroken tradition of skill in pottery making that continued from ancient times until the beginning of the present century. And archaeological finds show ancient stoneware bells and bronze bells similarly decorated.

32. The coiled protuberances and other styles of decoration on this chung *assign it to the much later Ch'ing dynasty. Note also the traditional cloud and thunder patterns. The hollow tube at the top, typical of some Chinese and of all Korean* chung, *is designed to regulate the tone and reverberation.*
PRIVATE COLLECTION

The celebrated pottery tomb figures of the T'ang period include horses and camels saddled and ready for the journey to life in the beyond. Many are decorated with sizable bells, well detailed. Too, there are figures depicting court musicians along with their instruments, including various bell forms.

Increasingly beautiful porcelains heralded the Sung dynasty (A.D. 960–1280). Of these the celadons are probably the best known to bell collectors. The name is believed to have come from that of Céladon, a shepherd dressed in silvery green who appeared in a pastoral play produced in Paris in 1610.

To the Chinese these beautiful wares are known as *ch'ing tz'u,* meaning a blue green porcelain. A number of kilns produced celadons. One, in fact, was the indirect heir of an old Han

33. *Modern copy of a T'ang dynasty pottery figure depicting a woman court musician playing cymbals. Pair of old brass cymbals at the right are of bell metal and are properly played with a sliding motion.*
PRIVATE COLLECTION

dynasty kiln firing fine-quality stoneware with a glaze of silvery green iridescence not unlike that on celadons.

Most of the early bells in this ware show a lacy raised design, but for the most part their beauty lies in their characteristic greenish white glaze. Sometimes this is crackled, originally an accidental result of the glaze shrinking more than the body in firing. Once its decorative effect was noticed, however, a crackled glaze was often purposely achieved.

Celadon ware formed a large part of China's early export trade under the foreign Mongol regime (A.D. 1279–1368). Junks carried it to Indochina and the Arab world, where it was much in demand among potentates because they believed it would crack or change color if it came into contact with poison. Much of it went to the Philippines, and even today a celadon bell is not an unlikely find in the better antique shops there.

Single-color celadon bells can be traced well into the Ming dynasty (A.D. 1368–1644), when the potting became heavier, the glaze greener and more glassy. But this was a period of immense progress in China's ceramic arts and there was considerable experimentation in decorating porcelains. Color decoration developed from the haphazard to the definitely artistic.

34. *Scrolls and mythical animals ornament this example of a celadon bell.*
HALPERIN COLLECTION

The Ming love of color emerged also in cloisonné enamel. Although early bells of this work exhibit a certain roughness due to imperfectly filled *cloisons,* later examples are technically perfect. Usually clapperless, they were made for ornamental use only. To strike them would mar the enamel. Genuine bells of this type, incidentally, are not to be confused with the smaller, brightly enameled bells of more modern manufacture that collectors sometimes mistakenly describe as cloisonné.

Aside from its preoccupation with color, the Ming period is distinguished by beautifully ornamented ritual objects in bronze and brass. Objects from the Hsüan-te reign (1426–1435) of this period are particularly excellent. The relief work is strong and crisply defined; the ornamentation, elaborate with tigers or dragons and other symbolic motifs. This combination of skills in the metal arts is exemplified in richly ornamented brass bells bearing the Hsüan-te reign mark or some calligraphic reference to dates. Such bells are all the more desirable if they hang in a Ming bronze frame formed by

35. *Two rare cloisonné bells, both with predominantly blue background somewhat darker than the* soufflé *blue of Oriental porcelains. Flowers and trailing vines are rust red, creamy white, and pale green. Bell with birds perched on top is the more pitted and apparently the older.* VIRGINIA BREWER COLLECTION

the lizardlike body of Ch'ih Lung, the three-clawed dragon of old bronzes.

Buddhist beliefs strongly influenced Chinese art, and this is especially apparent in the many sculptured images of Buddha or, next in the hierarchy, the eight Bodhisattvas, those all-but-perfect saints on the threshold of becoming Buddhas but who refrain in order to save others. Among these the most beloved in Chinese art is Kuan Yin, saint of mercy and protectress of children. Although Ming sculptors were not alone in this respect, it is no accident that they were particularly attracted to her as a subject of expression. The combination of symbolic accessories associated with her challenged their fondness for detailed portrayal.

Collectors intent on understanding more of Buddhist symbolism find many facets for study in the fully modeled figures of Kuan Yin sometimes found as handles on bells. Her image conveys those contradictory impressions that signal-

36. *Ming dynasty bell in a candle-fitted bronze frame formed of Ch'ih Lung dragons. Inscription on bell reads:* MADE IN THE YEAR OF HSUAN TE [A.D. 1426] OF MING DYNASTY. PRIVATE COLLECTION

ize the Bodhisattva figures in art: a calm repose in the stance and restless movement in the encircling robes; meditative detachment in the half-closed eyes and argumentative gestures in the hands.

Traditionally there are thirty-two symbols that mark the ideal Bodhisattva figure. Seldom, if ever, are all these shown in a single representation. The lotus flower, though, is invariably shown with Kuan Yin and is one of her special attributes—the flower that sprang forth wherever Buddha's feet touched the earth. Usually Kuan Yin is also characterized by the *ushnisha,* or topknot, symbolizing a source of superhuman intellectual powers.

The fall of the Ming dynasty in no way hindered the progress of China's artistic accomplishments, for it was followed by a period of great creativity under the early Manchus of the Ch'ing dynasty (1644–1912). Continued experimenta-

38. *Porcelain bell in* famille rose, *as admiring Europeans chose to name this ware. Attributed to the late Ch'ing dynasty. Modern rosewood frame.* PRIVATE COLLECTION

tions in color resulted in one of the most beautiful types of Oriental porcelain bells available to collectors. It is of a ware recognized by connoisseurs as famille rose. The manner of coloring that characterizes famille rose was developed and perfected early in this period and remained one of China's major and most popular palettes for overglaze enameling. The bell, cylindrical in shape, is softly glazed and decorated in shades of blue and bright salmon rose against a pale green background.

Jade has always been highly valued in China, and beautifully carved objects made of it date

37. *Dragons carved in heavy relief decorate the bronze bell on which Kuan Yin stands in calm repose, except for the argumentative gestures of her hands. Visible attributes characteristic of her figure are the lotus on which she stands and her topknot.* PRIVATE COLLECTION

39. *The jade pagoda commissioned in 1709 by the Emperor K'ang Hsi on the occasion of the birth of his grandson, the future Emperor Ch'ien Lung. Presented to the Museum of Art, University of Oregon, by an anonymous donor in 1956.* PERMANENT COLLECTION, MUSEUM OF ART, UNIVERSITY OF OREGON

back long before the days of Ch'ien Lung (1736–96), an emperor devoted to the arts. It was under his rule, however, that jade carvings reached an amazing peak of perfection. Perhaps this was more than mere happenstance, for Ch'ien Lung had been exposed to the beauty of jade since birth. On that occasion his grandfather, Emperor K'ang Hsi, had commissioned the making of a jade pagoda almost six feet tall, of "moss-in-the-snow" jade with a spinach green jade finial. The whole was hung with eighty gilt bronze bells. Truly an object of virtu, the pagoda was the largest and costliest of its kind ever made and undoubtedly it graced

40. *Jade gong from the Ch'ien Lung period. Three carved white-jade carp hang in an ebony trellis and are struck with a mallet. Symbolically the carp was both important and propitious to the ancient Chinese, denoting courage, patience, and success.* SPAULDING COLLECTION

Ch'ien Lung's palace when he became emperor. The furnishings throughout his palace represented the finest achievements of China's craftsmen.

Among bells of jade are some that are really flat gongs, carved from thin slabs seldom more than half an inch thick. Hanging one or more to a frame, these symbolic carvings were used as prayer gongs. Because of its unique qualities, jade has long been regarded by the Chinese with special reverence, and for this reason quite naturally became to them the voice of prayer. The great Han dictionary describes jade in these words:

> It is endowed with five virtues. Charity is typified by its lustre, bright yet warm; rectitude by its translucency, revealing the colour and markings within; wisdom by the purity and penetrating quality of its note when the stone is struck; courage, in that it may be broken, but cannot be bent; equity, in that it has sharp angles, which yet injure none.

By the year 1796, which marked the end of Ch'ien Lung's reign, the modern period of China's artistic endeavors was beginning. Increasing Occidental contacts and the demands for cheap wares were having their inevitable consequences—uninspired products, mere "trade goods," as connoisseurs express it. Nevertheless, there is something to be said in favor of collecting those bells that date no earlier than the

41. *Heavy Chinese bell of indeterminate age. A baby frog is the finial that is depressed to sound the bell.* AUMAN COLLECTION

42. *Canopy bells from the Twilight period of Old China.* PRIVATE COLLECTION

Twilight period of Old China (under the Manchus, 1839–1912). Derivative as most of the pieces are, the level of workmanship on them remains generally high.

The small brass bells made for export trade in no way compare with the earlier bronze specimens. Yet brass is a pleasing medium for copies of antique bells. With their details carefully executed and their chasings never traced but worked out by each individual artist, as of old, these bells serve to show how inseparable Chinese art and Chinese symbolism remain—even under the impact of modern trade demands. A brass tortoise-shaped bell carrying an ancestral tablet on its back illustrates the point, for the tortoise is sacred to China as symbolic of the universe, betokening strength and endurance and long life. The markings on its shell are be-

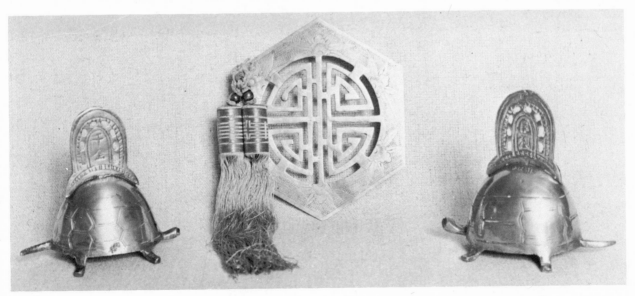

43. *Pair of brass bells often presented as christening gifts. Inscriptions on the ancestral tablets (one dedicated to a boy, the other to a girl) wish* HAPPINESS AND LONG LIFE. *Center gong shows the Chinese symbol for longevity.* PRIVATE COLLECTION

lieved to have suggested the characters in Chinese writing and to have constituted the basis for the Eight Trigrams of the *I-Ching,* an ancient mystical book of divination.

As the Twilight period of Old China drew to a close, a combination of circumstances was responsible for producing the little mandarin hat-button bells that became such a popular export. First, there was a brief renaissance in enameling; then, as the old officials gradually disappeared, they left behind their many badges of rank to be turned to other decorative uses. Among these were the jewel-like buttons from their hats, many of which became mounted handles on small enameled bells, thus preserving something of the Old China in modern objets d'art.

The Manchus, who founded the Ch'ing dynasty, considered hat badges as a primary indication of rank for all officials on ceremonial occasions. In their early form, these Manchu hat badges were long spikes protruding from a red fringe at the center of the crown. Each spike consisted of a high mount set with small stones and supporting an elongated jewel. This upright jewel was of ruby, sapphire, crystal, or gold, conforming to the traditional colors of the Manchu battle standards.

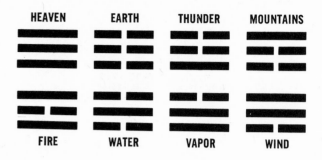

44. *The Eight Trigrams. Each is different but all use the same two lines representing the whole creative principle: − − for female Yin (darkness, earth) and — for male Yang (brightness, heaven).*

Being reserved for ceremonial occasions, these upright jeweled spikes were removed from the hats at other times. Before long, however, a court edict prescribed a second set of hat ornaments for semiformal wear so that the mandarins would never be without this badge of their official rank as magistrates. The newly prescribed jewels were round and firmly fastened to the apex of the hat with various filigree disks. These are the ones most commonly seen as handles on the hat-button bells. (*See* Color Plate I.)

About this same time, under a 1730 set of laws, the four traditional colors for both upright and spherical jewels were subdivided by

45. *Brass bells showing how inseparable Chinese art and Chinese symbolism remained even into the present century.* Left: *Stylized representation of a peach tree and its fruit, symbolizing the Tree of Life and longevity.* Center: *China's beneficent dragons support a jade gong.* Right: *Bell of a type commonly sold in American stores fifty years ago. Frame, a musical dragon.* PRIVATE COLLECTION

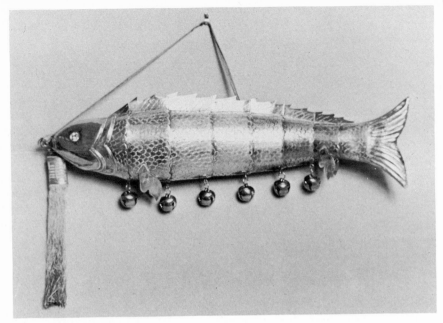

46. *Articulated thirteen-inch carp in the form of a wind chime. Modern.*
PRIVATE COLLECTION

introducing a distinction between clear and opaque. Under these laws the first eight ranks, starting with the nobles, were represented by ruby, coral, sapphire, opaque blue, crystal, moonstone, plain gold, and engraved gold; silver was used for the ninth. As before, small single stones of prescribed types decorated the mounts. This order remained unchanged throughout the Ch'ing dynasty except for occasional modifications. Court laws were introduced, for instance, permitting the use of glass as a substitute for the more precious substances. After that, pink porcelain was often used in place of coral, and opaque yellow in place of gold.

All in all, the collector has quite a range of types to seek in these colorful little bells whose handles once "ranked" the mandarins. The buttons themselves differ in mounting as well as in shape and substance; and there is always the challenge of trying to complete a set of handles showing the full range of colors appropriate to the nine mandarin ranks.

The enamel work on these bells is found in smooth solid colors, in shaded escalloped designs, and in various symbolic patterns all of one color or of mixed colors. Those with the symbolic patterns often show Taoist influence, as in the bat motif or the plum blossom. Both are emblems of long life—the plum, because Lao-Tse, founder of Taoism, was born under a plum tree.

47. *Old mandarin magistrate wearing headdress from which the official hat-button insignia rises at apex of the crown.*

48. *Detailed study of the Eight Immortals as they appear in miniature*

Although the influence of Buddhist beliefs is always emphasized in Chinese art, the Taoist system of religious thought has been responsible for a great deal of symbolism—including the Eight Trigrams—and has given to Chinese art some of its most romantic subjects. Chief among these are the themes connected with the Eight Immortals of Taoism. These figures and their characteristic attributes, which they always carry, are a favorite subject with Chinese craftsmen and are to be found as handles on another series of brightly enameled bells. In a group they may be shown in any order or, if preferred, in the order in which they achieved immortality. Each has an interesting story:

Li T'ieh-Kuai was a handsome man and the special friend of the founder of Taoism, whom he often visited in the celestial regions. On these visits he left his body behind, but on one occasion he returned to find it missing altogether. Spying the body of a dying beggar, he took possession and thereafter walked the earth as a cripple. His symbol is a crutch, with sometimes a pilgrim's gourd.

Chung-li Ch'uan, chief of the Eight Immortals, was a stout Han general who seems to have been responsible for forming the group. His emblem, a magic fan, he used to revive the dead.

Lan Ts'ai-ho, one of two women in the group, is usually represented wearing a blue gown and with one foot bare. She is the patron saint of gardeners, her symbol being a basket of flowers.

49. *Small enameled bells with handles depicting the six male figures among the Eight Immortals.* PRIVATE COLLECTION

orm on enameled bells (taken from a silk collage). **PRIVATE COLLECTION**

Chang Kuo-lao was a famous magician, always accompanied by a white mule that he rode backward. Whenever he stopped, he folded his mule like paper and put him in his cap-box. A musical instrument made of a bamboo tube is his symbol.

Ho Hsien-Ku, noted for her filial piety, walked the fields seeking bamboo sprouts for her sick mother, she herself living only on powdered mother-of-pearl. The kitchen ladle in her hands at the moment she was whisked into immortality became her emblem, later changing to the lotus.

With equally interesting stories, if they could all be told, Lu Tung-pin is symbolized by his two-edged sword used to overcome evil; Han Hsiang-tzu, patron saint of musicians, by his flute; and Ts'ao Kuo-chiu, patron saint of actors, by his castanets.

Along with these lesser and more modern Chinese bells, there are fine old temple gongs still being offered today's collector. As recently as the 1930s there were resident monks in one hundred thousand temples in China, exclusive of those living in several hundred large public monasteries. With only a minimum of oral communication permitted, all these monks were using bells, gongs, and rattles as freely then as in the past. In the larger monasteries life was still

50. *Chinese boy skipping rope on a tiny frog. The entire bell is heavily enameled in blue, pink, and green.* **MC KINNEY COLLECTION**

51. *Typical modern Chinese bells available to collectors. Bell at far right has a green jadeite handle in the form of a closed fist.* PRIVATE COLLECTION

52. A, B, C, *and* D. *Four old Chinese monastery gongs* (below and on opposite page):

52A. *Priest's hand gong, or* ta-ting, *used to introduce prayers in Buddhist ceremonies.* SMITHSONIAN INSTITUTION

52B. *Heavy brass gongs fashioned in the likeness of old Mongol headgear.* PRIVATE COLLECTION

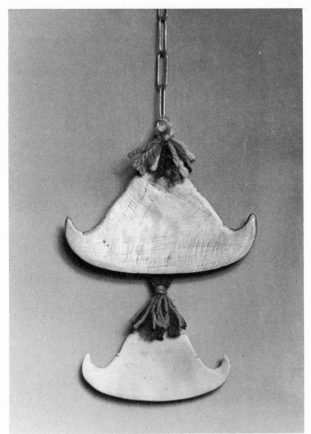

completely regulated by a complex schedule of signals on these instruments; and each liturgical orchestra demanded many such instruments. All of which adds up to the fact that collectors need not be satisfied simply with Chinese bells of modern make. From time to time old temple bells, gongs, and rattles do come on the sales market, as in these advertisements of the 1960s:

Chinese gong, very old, 18″, mallet, wonderful sound. Stand 4 feet, two parts. Extraordinary carved brown wood with elephants, etc. $250

Chinese temple bell, dragon handle, richly engraved, 10″ high. Frame stands 34″ high, blackwood carving, flowers, birds, dragons. Little damage on lower part. $125

Bowl gong, dark green bronze, with dragon in gold metal encircling bowl, 15″ diameter, 17″ deep. Padded stand in red lacquer and gold, ornated with metal pieces. $100

TIBETAN RITUAL OBJECTS

The mere mention of Tibet calls to mind prayer wheels and dorjes, in this land where for generations life revolved around the lamasery. Always considered rarities from that somewhat inaccessible country, such ritualistic objects are even more rare today, for there is reason to believe that everything of beauty left behind by the fleeing Tibetans was destroyed when the Chinese Communists seized full control in 1959.

On the other hand, escaping refugees were in many instances forced to sell their treasured

52C. *Large bowl gong signed by maker and inscribed* MADE FOR THE TEMPLE OF GREAT VIRTUE IN 1393. FREDERICK F. CROUSE

52D. *Gong harmonium called a* yun-lo—*actually a sistrum consisting of ten tuned gongs against a screen of red silk. Used in funeral processions.* SMITHSONIAN INSTITUTION

religious artifacts; and for a few unsettled months after their flight, some of their fine prayer wheels, bells, and dorjes passed into the hands of appreciative collectors.

Tibetan objects such as these are essentially related to their sacred functions, their ritualistic uses. They were made as a gesture of devotion, the artist all the while being governed by the rigid theological and liturgical canons of Lamaism, a special form of northern Buddhism. Working within these confines, though, the artist might occasionally exceed the merely liturgical dictates and create something a little more elegant.

The variations in the individual worshiper's prayer wheels illustrate the truth of this state-

53. Left: *Tibetan prayer wheel of silver repoussé and appliqué work in copper and brass, with a ring of human bone under the cylinder. The cluster of silver bells and weights facilitates turning.* Center: *Drilbu, or lamasery bell, showing face of Sherchin, the feminine divinity who represents all wisdom.* Right: *Lamasery watchman's rattle-drum beautifully appliquéd in silver, with silver crotals attached to hollow handle.* PRIVATE COLLECTION

54. *Temple-bound Tibetan women twirling their prayer wheels. The ritual is to walk around the temple a certain number of times, spinning the prayer wheel.*
COURTESY, COPLEY NEWS SERVICE

ment. All conform to the special pattern; but many are rather plain with a simple banding of silver, whereas others are elaborate with silver repoussé and appliqué work in copper and brass. The combining of several metals is typical of the best Tibetan metalwork. Also typical is the use of a piece of human bone in decorating sacred objects. On prayer wheels this is sometimes placed below the cylinder where the axis joins the handle.

The hollow cylinder of the prayer wheel contains inscribed prayers on thin sheets of paper. These are wound around the axis from right to left and covered with yellow silk. The wheel when set in motion must revolve in the opposite direction so that the writing passes before the worshiper in the way it reads, that is, from left to right. A weighted piece of metal on a chain is attached to one side of the cylinder to facilitate turning, and here is where small silver bells are sometimes included with the weight.

Each complete revolution counts as one reading of all the prayers contained on the scrolls. The usual invocation begins, when translated, "Hail, jewel in the lotus." This is addressed to Padmapani, who appeared out of a lotus for deliverance of mankind. He is revered by Tibetans, and according to their belief is incarnated in the Dalai Lama, the head of Tibetan Buddhism.

Larger architectural prayer wheels are placed in the entrances to temples and houses, to be turned by each person passing. On the gables of houses or over the hearth they are twirled by

55. *Tibetan ritual objects, with Japanese bell at far right included for comparison with lamasery bell at far left. Note the varying number of prongs on examples of the* dorje. *The Buddhist image hanging on tasseled clapper* (above) *holds incense. Brass cymbal* (below) *is struck with long wand during priestly rituals.*
PRIVATE COLLECTION

56. *Tibetan priest employs brass cymbal to aid his ritualistic performance. The rhythmic sound furnishes the cadence for his dance.*

57. *Obtained originally in the Mongolian city of Urga in 1819, this rainmaking bell was presented to W. F. Schilling by Dr. George W. Davis of Kansas. The idea of using bells to bring rain seems to have been introduced by Taoist priests of early Mongolia and Manchuria. Later it was adopted in neighboring regions.* THE SCHILLING MUSEUM, NORTHFIELD, MINNESOTA

58. *Ancient mirror-bell still showing traces of Sanskrit inscriptions and intricate cosmological symbols.* PRIVATE COLLECTION

the wind or the smoke. Sometimes a wheel is fixed in a stream and kept in motion by the current, thus praying night and day for all who prosper or languish within the eight-spoked Wheel of Existence described in Buddhist doctrine. And always, with each revolution, a little bell rings "yielding ten thousand warning chimes throughout the day."

Because Tibetan art rose out of a need to create objects for Lamaistic rituals, it is a unique art, peculiar to that country. This is well exemplified in the ornamentations on each bronze lamasery handbell, or *drilbu,* a type not found elsewhere. Eight mystic symbols circle the bell in delicate beaded relief. The neck of the handle shows one, two, or four faces of Sherchin, goddess of wisdom, topped by a lotus, then surmounted by a dorje; and the clawlike prongs of the dorje are likely to be gracefully carved. Upon close examination, additional decorative touches are often observed, invariably chosen from the Eight Buddhist Symbols: perhaps a wheel where the handle joins the bell; a fish for a clapper; or underneath, a conch shell etched where the clapper is attached.

The finest of these bells were cast in Derge, but some of the finest silver prayer wheels were made in Lhasa. Every region in Tibet had its specialty, much of the work being attributed to the skill of Nepalese artisans settling in Tibet. Once made, each bell and prayer wheel was sacredly cherished. It might become worn, but was always kept in neat repair and never found lying around discarded and broken.

Although Lamaism employs ritualistic symbols common to Buddhism elsewhere—and even to India's religious mythology—it has given these symbols unique treatment in its art, as already noted in the prayer wheels and lamasery bells. It has also adopted certain ones as peculiarly its own—as, for example, the dorje. This was originally the thunderbolt of Indra, the Hindu god of atmosphere, only with its clawlike points open. According to Nepalese beliefs, a contest occurred between Buddha and Indra in which Buddha wrested his opponent's instrument of power. Thus the *vajra,* as it is known in India, was appropriated by Buddhists as the favorite emblem of their faith. But Tibetans believe that, as a special favor, the original dorje fell from heaven and landed at a monastery in Lhasa, where it has been preserved ever since.

As the scepter of northern Buddhism, the dorje is used by lamas in conjunction with the ringing of the lamasery handbells. Abbots are pictured in their red robes and intricate helmets holding a dorje in their right hand and a bell in their left, the one signifying compassion and the other, wisdom. Used together, they represent imperishable spiritual perfection.

To be fully meaningful in a collection, a lamasery bell should be accompanied by a dorje. When Yale University's Tibetologist recently brought back two ritual handbells from a lamasery, he brought with them the companion scepters, each proportionately scaled to its bellmate. The larger of the two sets consists of a nine-inch handbell and a seven-inch scepter, this set being very possibly the largest of its kind in an American museum.

Although the typical lamasery bells and related paraphernalia are most desirable in a collection, they do not represent the sum total of bells available from Tibet. There are handsome rattle-drums used by the lamasery watchmen making their nightly rounds, some of them beautifully executed with silver appliqué and decorated with curious silver crotals. There are also peculiar rattles called Mongolian Rain Bells used by the weather-making monks in Tibetan villages. And each young monk designated as a State Oracle wears around his neck a discoid of fine bell metal, as a part of his regalia. While going into a trance on being questioned about important matters, he beats on this gong with a great thumb ring. From these few additional examples, it is evident that a variety of bells are to be found in a monastic culture like that once practiced in Tibet and now being continued at refugee sites like those in northern India.

RECURRING SYMBOLS ON JAPANESE BELLS

Too frequently when people speak in terms of Orientalia, they are assuming that the civilizations of China and Japan developed simultaneously. Civilization in China began several thousand years before that in Japan, and many facets

59. *A true "nine-toned bell" from the renowned Matsuodera Temple near Kyoto, Japan,* circa 1600. *Each of the bells on the five-foot cherrywood stand is rich in Buddhist symbolism.* RINGLAND COLLECTION

of Japanese culture were acquired from the Chinese. Bells were introduced with Chinese Buddhism about A.D. 552, according to some, although the Koreans claim to have first taught the art of bell-founding in Japan somewhat earlier.

In any event, Japanese artists soon learned to work under the same motivating forces that activated other Oriental artists: a reverence for nature, a strong religious bent, and a driving need to create truly functional objects expressing their beliefs. Much of the symbolism they employed showed Buddhist influence. Yet just as Buddhist art in China was tempered by Taoism, so in Japan it was tempered by Shintoism, stressing oneness with nature and the universe. Consequently, in many instances Japanese art developed distinctive characteristics stemming from the varied philosophical attitudes of the artists and from the somewhat paradisaical nature of their country's landscape.

60. *On all but one of the nine bells from the Matsu* *Temple dragons form the handle. On some, as in th* *tail, a pair of dragons supports and protects the sacre* *perial jewel represented by a bronze knob.* RINGLAND LECTION

61. Left: *A particularly significant example of a torii, its bell decorated with feather designs symbolic of the live cocks that once perched on such arches. Attendant with broom in hand purifies the ground for worshipers passing under the torii.* Right: *Shinto priestess's rattle representing the bamboo spray hung with bells and used by the goddess of mirth centuries ago. Red lacquered handle.* PRIVATE COLLECTION

62. *Small fox-god bells, also called* suzu, *the Japanese term for little bells. In groups of three, these are sold at Shinto shrines and used as votive offerings.* PRIVATE COLLECTION

63. *Heavy gilded elephant supports a large brass bell that is rung by means of the ornate finial, which twirls. This bell originally appeared as one of the cinema stage properties in a Japanese filming of* Yoki-Hi. PRIVATE COLLECTION

64. *Detailed and realistic modeling create an object of unusual interest and artistry. Crawling in the shadow of the bell is a large crab (to the Japanese, symbolic of good-natured aggressiveness). Watching overhead is a kiwi bird.* MYRL HUENE COLLECTION

To go into detail about all the symbolic designs used on Japanese bells would require a book-length study. Every decoration has a meaning. But even a brief survey of commonly met symbols will suggest possibilities for those who wish to delve further into the subject.

A good place to start is with some of the inanimate emblems associated again and again with Japanese bells. There is of course the thunderbolt (*vajra* in Sanskrit) surmounting the handle on typical Buddhist handbells—with the Japanese language assigning individual names to these, depending on the number of prongs converging at the tip. The three-pronged is called *san-ko;* the five-pronged, *go-ko.*

The *moncho* seen on numerous small bells make an interesting study in themselves. These are traditional family designs used on crests or coats of arms, the earliest dating from the eleventh century. Some are representations from the world of nature, but the majority are purely abstract. Certain groups, among them the samurai, were required to wear their personal *moncho* devices on formal dress. They appeared as well on flags, armor, and bells made for personal use. A *moncho* is sometimes found on a little *eki-rei,* or horse-station bell, which can easily be mistaken for a shrine bell. The *eki-rei* dates back to feudal days when the use of public horses was not permitted except to those who traveled on state business, mainly along the old Tokaido road between the two capitals of Tokyo and Kyoto. There were fifty-three stations along the Tokaido, and everyone who had a right to use the public horses was required to carry and show at each one his small horse-station bell as a token of his privilege. He might carry more than one bell, the number indicating how many horses he could rightfully use. Sometimes, in addition to the family crest, horse-station bells also carry their original owner's name.

Mirrors are closely associated with the mythological past of Japan, for the mirror is one of the three imperial treasures symbolizing the imperial throne. An early Japanese history of the eighth century relates the story of servants going to meet the emperor and presenting him with what were to become the three traditional imperial treasures: a Yasaka jewel, a white copper mirror, and a ten-span sword. Bells, too, were associated with royal prerogative, so it is not surprising to find them cast around the rims of ancient bronze mirrors.

These curious old mirror-bells were designed for religious use by the *miko*, the maidservants in Shinto shrines, in their dedication dances and rites. Because of their purely religious purpose, ancient mirror-bells are considered relics whose proper place is in a shrine. Priests sometimes specialize in collecting them.

Metal mirrors were rather widely used among early people, and their brightly polished surfaces served for magical as well as practical purposes. Those with bells cast solidly to the rim, however, are predominantly Japanese and unique to the Yomato people. Perhaps the artists who first conceived of these thought bells would add to a mirror's magical qualities in warding off evil.

Archaeologists date all ancient mirror-bells as well over eight hundred years old. Some have been recovered from tombs where they were placed to reflect the sun, and light the eternal darkness. Others have been found in damp woodland shrines. In either case, they come into a collection exhibiting a thickly encrusted verdigris that enhances their beauty; but the

65. *Wind-bell with pendent carp of hammered brass, formerly used in connection with boyhood celebrations on what is now known as Children's Day in Korea. The carp is the boys' national emblem there, the symbol for swimming against the stream of life courageously.* PRIVATE COLLECTION

bells are often so corroded that little tone is left even if the pellets are still within.

Art in Japan today, as in China and elsewhere in the Orient, is still marked by a love of antiquarianism, and mirror-bells are among the ancient types of bells being copied. The copies are true as to their shape, yet a collector who has ever seen even one piece of ancient metalwork with its original verdigris will not be fooled by them. Their patina is thin and in time disappears entirely. Too, the copies are heavy and lacking in the fine Sanskrit inscriptions and the intricate cosmological symbols found on the ancient mirror-bells.

The mystical number nine of Buddhism occurs frequently in Japanese metal arts decoration, though not with the same constancy as in Korean and Chinese art. The number nine represents the highest step attainable in life after traversing the eightfold path of Buddhism. To attain number ten, or nirvana, would mean the cessation of all striving, the cessation of all thought and feeling—in other words, extinction. Thus, number nine represents the ideal attainment, the highest perfection before extinction. Applying this concept to bells, the artist can arrange the embossings known as the "pitying snails of Buddha" in panels of nine each; or the priest at a Buddhist shrine can arrange devotional bells in groups of nine.

Among figures found ornamenting Japanese bells, there are both historical and legendary examples. The image of Daruma, probably the first teacher of Zen Buddhism, is recognizable in several guises. Dust has settled on some of the stories once surrounding this sixth-century sage, but the tale of his long and tortuous retreat remains and frequently gives rise to rather irreverent and humorous treatment of his image. Supposedly, he sat in meditation so many years that his legs shriveled away and he was legless the rest of his life. In the form of a chubby little crotal, his legless figure is shown with hands

66. Ancient carp that formerly hung in a Korean temple. The two rings on top keep it in a swimming, forward-moving position. PRIVATE COLLECTION

67. Called in China mu-yu *and, in Japan,* mo-ku-gyo, *literally wooden fish, this rounded bell with the staring eyes is used by Buddhist monks and priests.* SMITHSONIAN INSTITUTION

68. *Bells on either side of the* torii *illustrate the Japanese legend of tortoise and crane. Bell in the arch is of polished red stone intricately pierced.* PRIVATE COLLECTION

clasped overhead above a rather grotesque face. Such Daruma-shaped bells are sold in Japan as good-luck charms, especially for New Year's festivals when regular Daruma markets are set up and his roly-poly figure is offered in all sizes and materials.

The legendary figures of Tengu and of Buddhist angels float through Japanese art, but in contrasting roles. The origin of Tengu is not clear. In old folk tales he seems to have been a winged mountain spirit whose activities frightened little children because if they were bad Tengu whisked them away. Nowadays he is portrayed in more human form, with a long nose and a sharp chin. These unappealing features are effectively sculptured in double-faced

69. *Conventional phoenix birds and lotus blossoms decorate both sides of this flat, gilt bronze gong, also called a* kei, *which priests used to punctuate their prayers.* ERNEST MORRIS COLLECTION

clay bells, colorfully glazed. Effigy bells of this sort are a favorite Japanese medium for depicting the frightening features of various demonic characters from old folk tales. Possession of the effigies supposedly wards off whatever harm the evil spirits intend, and so they are called anti-demoniac bells.

The graceful figures of Buddhist angels add to the paradisaical quality of landscape scenes in Japanese art. With their fluent outlines, their scarves swirling upward, they are identified in the scenic engravings around numerous old handbells. Usually they are riding peacocks through the sky, symbols of beauty and dignity like the Buddhist angels themselves.

Because the Japanese people have always experienced a closeness to and a reverence for the beauties of nature, they place great value and importance on the art of portraying living things, even the tiniest insects. Nothing is too small or insignificant, for every living thing has its special meaning. One cycle of subjects is drawn from the Oriental zodiac and is comprised of the twelve creatures who rushed to Buddha's deathbed. The rat was first; among others were the mythical dragon, the monkey, and the cock.

The dragon ornaments many gongs and is much used on the *hin,* a bowl-shaped gong placed on a cushion atop an elaborate carved stand. The *hin* is sounded not by striking, but by rubbing a padded stick over the resonant edge until the vibration hums with a deep tone. The emblem of vigilance and power, as in China, the dragon is well suited to ornament

42

the *hin,* for gongs of this type have always been considered rather special and are usually associated with large monasteries and shrines, themselves symbols of vigilance and power.

Frolicking animals are favorite subjects and give Japanese art much of its vitality. The amusing see-no-hear-no-speak-no-evil trio of monkeys makes a fitting handle for several old bronze bells. Originally the monkey was a symbol of good luck, and was believed to possess the power of expelling evil and shielding people from misfortune. In earlier days little shrines sometimes kept small images of monkeys that visitors could borrow at will. If the image sat as a handle on a bell, it became doubly effective as an exorciser.

The cock in early times was considered a sacred bird and the creature responsible for the erection of Japan's picturesque torii. Since, according to Shinto belief, the sun goddess had established the early empire, many shrines were created to her; and since cocks were associated with the sunrise, live ones were placed on perches before her shrines. The perches were made of three wooden poles, one placed horizontally and the other two at either end as arch-

70. *Three old bronze shrine bells from Japan, each with some symbolic attribute.* Left: *Radiating fire-rays for life-giving energy.* Center: *Three feet for good fortune.* Right: *Sea plover's image denoting endurance.* PRIVATE COLLECTION

like supports. In time the perches, or torii, became symbols of the shrines. They were enlarged and more elaborately lacquered in red and gold. All Shintoists pass under a torii as a means of purification before entering the shrine itself.

71. Left: *Tortoise carries the weight of the world in the form of a bell beautifully engraved with pinecones and branches, symbols of vigorous old age. Inscriptions express a wish for happiness and long life.* Center: *Sixteen "snails" rather than nine fill each panel on this Buddhist bell.* Right: *Horse-station bell, or eki-rei, with ornate family crest called a* moncho. *The motif resembles a chrysanthemum.*
PRIVATE COLLECTION

72. *Japanese love of miniaturization can be seen even in the small* Kamidana, *or dollhouse-sized Shinto shrine, at which the family prays daily. Seemingly there is no conflict in the Japanese mind over worshiping before both Shinto and Buddhist symbols on the same god-shelf.* PRIVATE COLLECTION

No collection of Oriental bells seems quite complete without a small torii supporting a bell, just as some of the large ones do. An especially fine old example has a bell decorated with feather designs, symbolic of the vigilant and exultant cock. Beside the arch stands a Japanese attendant, broom in hand, to purify the ground before worshipers approach.

The *kitsune,* or fox, is not among the twelve zodiac creatures, yet he is significant in connection with those Shinto shrines dedicated to Inari, god of the rice, who is often shown riding a white fox. At his shrines the carving of a fox is seen at the entrance. At one time rural folk believed that Inari shrines were, in fact, erected for the fox because his image was always present; and a sort of fox-god cult developed, the deity and his mount blending into one. Crotals resembling the shape of a plump potato and used in varying sizes for Inari rituals or votive offerings came to be called fox-god bells.

Though the fox-god is only mythical, his figure remains as a Shinto symbol of good, sup-

posedly able to see everything, hear everything, and be aware of everything within a hundred miles. But there are other, more evil foxes in Japanese lore; and when they take demoniacal possession of a person, causing him to yelp and eat like a fox, then the *Yamabushi* must be sent for. He is the exorciser, and he uses clusters of fox-god bells to cast out this evil demon.

Another animal not included in the zodiac but highly honored in Japan is the elephant, and several attractive bell forms have been designed around gilded elephant images. Elephant worship is Buddhist in nature, largely due to the fact that one of Buddha's able disciples used an elephant as his trusted mount. The first historical account of this animal in Japan records its coming from China, the gift of the emperor. The elephant's symbolic role in China, as the sagacious and trusted bearer-of-the-jewel-of-the-law, was adopted in Japan; and after court rank was conferred on the first arrival, common people had to bow before all elephants.

Water birds and sea creatures parade endlessly through Japanese life and art. Geese,

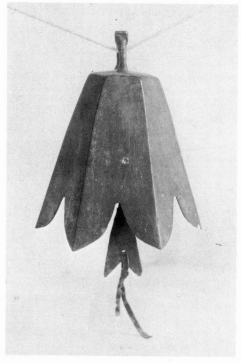

73. *Stylized lotus-shaped bell of iron.*

74. *The familiar and symbolic Buddhist pilgrim's bell.* PRIVATE COLLECTION

75. *Ancient Korean shrine bell known as a* shi-soku, *literally a four-legged bell. Here and there beaten gold shows through the encrusted patina. Considered to be one of the treasures rescued from "the hill of brass."* MICKEY COLLECTION

76. *Satsuma bell. The heavy gold decorations indicate a late period.* PRIVATE COLLECTION

cranes, tortoise, and fish, especially carp, have inspired designs for innumerable bells. The lobster and the crab crawl around in these designs less frequently but with interesting significance. The Japanese connect the lobster with longevity because his back is curved, as is that of an old person. The crab they connect with good-natured aggressiveness. Both these creatures are used as designs on bells and other objects to be given as gifts or prominently displayed in one's home.

Carp in particular, among fish, are venerated in Japan. They are looked upon as emblematic of strength and perseverance because of their ability to leap high waterfalls and overcome obstacles in the path of their migration. Children keep carp as pets; and on Children's Day in both Japan and Korea, large brass wind-bells with sizable carp pendants are hung from gables and trees.

Metal bells realistically shaped to resemble full-bodied carp have been made in Japan for

nearly a thousand years. It is perhaps a mark of their popularity with collectors that ancient carp-bodied bells, like ancient mirror-bells, are being reproduced. As already noted, however, these copies can be easily recognized. Their imitative patina bears little resemblance to that on genuinely old specimens.

A different symbolism is associated with the *mo-ku-gyo* (literally, a wooden fish). This is like the Chinese *mu-yu,* a great rounded bell resembling a stylized fish head with staring fish eyes carved on it. The shape is accounted for by the supposition that the fish is sleepless, keeping its eyes always open because of having no eyelids. It is therefore emblematic of watchfulness in the Buddhist striving for perfection. This is the bell mistakenly referred to sometimes as a "Buddha's ear." It is used by monks and priests in their prayers and in funeral chants.

The larger temple specimens are usually placed on their side and struck with a wooden mallet, producing a somber and hollow sound. Smaller specimens, ranging down to the size of a fifty-cent piece, are often used by beggars, sometimes to the point of annoyance, since their sound is more brittle and less sonorous. The beggars sit in front of a house and continue to tap, tap, tap their *mo-ku-gyo* until they are given the desired amount of money.

The origin of the curious *mo-ku-gyo* is given in the legend about Buddha's rude and stubborn disciple who was punished by being born a fish in the next life. Living in the sea, he was plagued by a heavy tree growing from his back. Every time there was a storm at sea, the tree tossed about and caused him great pain. As penance for his misconduct in the first life, the fish offered the tree to Buddha to use as he saw fit. He saw fit to have these oddly shaped bells fashioned from it.

Longevity has always been the boon most coveted by both Chinese and Japanese; thus, it is symbolized again and again. Of all the motifs

78. *A doll-shaped bell that is number one in the series of "Norigana's Seven Bells." In colorings of yellow and brown glaze.* MC LEAN COLLECTION

used to express the wish for a long life, the crane is the most constant throughout all of Japanese art. It stands almost as a sacred symbol of longevity and good fortune. Generals going into battle once carried their tame cranes with them; the gardens of feudal lords used cranes for adornment and also to bring good fortune to the owner. Later, when live cranes became less plentiful, carved figures were in demand. These were often used in pairs and were looked upon as being auspicious in still another way. Since they mate for life, a pair of cranes symbolizes marital fidelity.

The tortoise also bespeaks a long earthly life, since it can live as many as five thousand years; and it, too, is auspicious in other ways, for it

77. *Stone gong in fish and wave motif.*

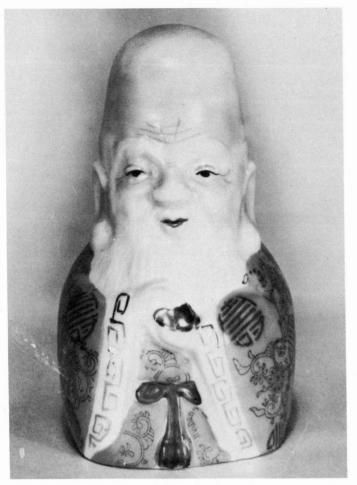

79. *Ceramic figure of Shou-lao, the Taoist god of long life. His robe is orange, and in his hand he holds the sacred peach of immortality.* WALTERS COLLECTION

symbolizes endurance and strength enough to carry the world on its back.

Japanese artists have taken these two compatible and versatile creatures, the tortoise and the crane, and united them in a decorative household bell that is a favorite with collectors. Here the enduring tortoise supports a crane who has wearied on his ocean flight. As the tale is told, the tortoise hears about the crane's important mission delivering the bell hanging from his beak, and so it takes pity on the bird's weariness and invites the creature to rest and ride on its shell.

On another and more intricately designed bell the tortoise is indeed carrying the weight of the

world on his back, in the form of a brass dome-shaped bell. The dome is prettily engraved with pine branches and cones, and two appropriate inscriptions. The tapping device atop the dome, to sound the bell, is the minute figure of a goose in flight. Miniaturization is a highly developed art in Japan, and the art is perfectly exemplified in the detailing of this tiny goose. He is, as in China, "The Bird of Heaven," symbol of love and truth.

Like the vast majority of other symbolic motifs used by the Japanese artist, emblematic designs from plant lore usually serve to express felicitous thoughts. The chrysanthemum, expressing purity, has long been Japan's national flower. It was chosen centuries ago by the imperial family for their *moncho* motif. Rising, as it does, unspotted by the mire in which it grows, the lotus also denotes purity and of course is a foremost Buddhist symbol. Designs of these and other flowers, such as the iris (for warding off evil) and the peony (betokening prosperity and wealth), are engraved on all sorts of bells. Even the little tinkling *furin* are often designed in the shape of favorite flowers. These wind-bells that grace every temple roof are in themselves symbolic, hung there originally to ward off evil spirits. In olden days they were often painstakingly chosen for their emblematic significance, that they might be doubly effective in exorcising evil.

Perhaps the most striking use of the lotus motif on bells is seen in the gilded eight-petaled bloom crowning the handle on the familiar Buddhist pilgrim's bell. Here from the center of the fully opened blossom rises a *vajra;* below the lotus, silvery cloud patterns are applied all up and down the tall eight-sided wooden handle. With other motifs around the bell proper and with even its tassel significantly knotted in a fourfold meander, this becomes a highly symbolic bell. For centuries, older Buddhists making long pilgrimages to distant shrines carried bells of this description. They rang them zealously as they chanted their prayers while passing through villages, hoping always for alms to help support their journey.

80. *Pair of colored clay bells sold as votive offerings to pilgrims at Kora Jinga, the chief shrine of the former province of Chikugo.* ERNEST MORRIS COLLECTION

Stylized lotus-shaped bells of iron have been found in ancient burials, as have little footed shrine bells in the shape of an eggplant or a gourd. The eggplant, *nasubi* in Japanese, is an omen of good fortune and is looked upon as one of three most auspicious subjects for one's dreams.

The pine is the emblem both of unflinching purpose and of vigorous old age, and its needles are credited with the power of driving demons away. The artist finds pine branches and cones a graceful and adaptable subject for the contours of small bells. Decorated with felicitous symbolism of this sort, they are popular with the Japanese as household gifts for relatives and friends.

Bamboo, denoting both durability and flexibility, is uniquely symbolized in a Shinto priestess's rattle that has several areas of appeal for the collector. The rattle consists of a lacquered handle mounted with a wire spiral on which are fastened a number of crotals. This is used by the priestess in her religious dance. The origin of her dance, and the bell she uses, are found in the legend of *Ame-no-uzume-no-mikoto,* goddess of mirth, who long ago sang and danced to lure the sun goddess from the cavern where she stayed, that she might again illuminate the world. Before starting her performance the goddess Uzume, as she was known for short, picked a spray of bamboo and with grasses tied small bells to it. This she used to make her performance more mirthful. The Shinto priestess's rattle, that strange spiraled instrument with its cluster of crotals, preserves the form of Uzume's bamboo-spray.

This résumé of recurring symbolism on Japanese bells has been purposely directed toward metalwork, since Oriental bells and gongs in this medium have always been more obtainable than those made of either porcelain or stone. Especially after the Second World War certain developments brought an unprecedented number of fine Oriental metal bells to this country and awakened a new interest in collecting and studying them.

Had the war continued, Japan's now famed "hill of brass" would have been melted away into armaments. Instead, at the war's end, for a period of three months, each American in the area was permitted three objects from this stockpile that had been requisitioned from homes and shrines and even palaces. As one professor later observed, probably more bronze treasures were contained in the "hill of brass" than in all of New York City's antique galleries combined. Many of the pieces retrieved were of course bells, some of them later identified as rare Korean treasures dating back nine hundred years or more and showing traces of beaten gold.

Meanwhile, Japanese porcelain bells and stone gongs had no part in this story and continued to grow increasingly scarce. Such examples as can be found are usually either Imari or Satsuma ware and were produced during the latter part of the nineteenth century. Although the Satsuma bells of this late period tend to be overdecorated and the figures poorly executed, they can serve to exemplify this old ware that was originally named for a Japanese warlord, Satsuma, who brought skilled ceramic workers to his country from Korea as early as 1600.

More easily available to the interested collector of porcelain are replicas from the Ban-Ko kiln, replicas of seven famous bronze bells now preserved as national treasures. The originals were used by a famous Japanese historian of the sixteenth century and are known as "Norigana's Seven Bells." The symbolic shapes of the originals and their colorations have been faithfully copied in porcelain. Although of recent manufacture, bells such as these can find a legitimate place in a collection, for they can convey a graphic understanding of Japanese symbolism that is difficult to assimilate from books alone.

3

Indian, Asian, and African Bells

INTRODUCTIONS TO THE HISTORY of Indian art carefully point out that it has always had an intelligible meaning and a definite purpose. "Art for art's sake"—even if comprehended—would have been regarded only as a monstrous human vanity. Each object was created as a means to a definite end, not as a work of art. Thus there is a kinship of spirit between Indian and Oriental art. This kinship is heightened by the fact that Buddhist influences, though most commonly associated with the Orient, are found too in India, where Buddhism originated.

Hinduism, however, has been the dominant influence, and it is exemplified most often on India's temple bells. Every deity—and there are many—has his image on countless bells used in the temples honoring his name. These handbells are called *ghanti* and are used, as in ancient temples the world over, not only to call the god's attention but to warn demons that it is time to depart. The Hindu temple is not necessarily a meeting place for worshipers. The cults are individual, and each worshiper rings the bell set up in the temple as he makes his offering of flowers, fruit, rice, et cetera.

The number of Hindu gods can be staggering to the Western mind and to the collector attempting to identify images of them on bells. To compound the confusion, these deities assume different earthly incarnations and may not always be depicted with their symbolic attributes. But there is a simplified approach to identifying god-handles on Hindu worship bells,

if collectors will first consider the triad of Hinduism's chief gods: Brahma the creator of life; Vishnu the preserver of all living things; and Siva the destroyer, who removes the old to make room for new life.

To symbolize the three aspects of the supreme spirit called Brahma, triple heads sometimes

81. *Krishna in his characteristic three-bend pose, playing a flute, ornaments an otherwise plain Hindu bell. Beside him is his consort Lakshmi.*

82. *Large and beautifully carved Hindu temple bell with standing figure of Hanuman, the monkey god. Behind him his tail winds upward to his shoulders.* PRIVATE COLLECTION

83. *"Evolution" bell showing* (left) *Anjana as the monkey side of the handle and* (right) *Vayu as the man side.* WALTERS COLLECTION

grace images of that deity. In popular worship, however, the Hindus seem to have forgotten Brahma the creator. His likeness appears less often in Hindu art than that of either Vishnu or Siva, whose cults are more closely related to the mainstreams of life.

As the preserver of life, Vishnu especially has many earthly forms he assumes whenever the world order of things is being disturbed. Two of his incarnations cherished by artists are those as Krishna and as Rama. Bell handles show Krishna standing in a graceful three-bend pose playing a flute. According to legend, the sweet tune of his flute once enchanted even the cows he raised. It is due to Krishna's fondness for cows that devout Hindus eat no beef.

Vishnu in the form of the legendary hero Rama is indirectly responsible for the popularity of another figure in Hindu art. This is Hanuman, the monkey god who is so often represented on metal objects to symbolize the bond of friendship. His image on bell handles can be found in a variety of poses, but almost always with his tail curling up his back and thus giving him unquestionable identity.

In the ancient Hindu epic Ramayana, an army of monkeys helped Rama rescue his wife when she was stolen away by Ravana, the king of Ceylon. Monkeys have been honored ever since and Hanuman, their faithful general, was rewarded with immortality. To this day traveling mendicants may be seen carrying small bells showing the figure of the friendly, helpful Hanuman—the better to fill their beggars' bowls.

Hanuman's parents, or at least one of them, appear on another type of bell that collectors term the "evolution" bell. It is a fairly common type, and yet two identical examples are seldom found, for each is individually carved and chased. On the handle two full-length Hindu figures stand back to back. On some the figures appear to be those of Vayu, the wind god, and the monkey nymph, Anjana, parents of Hanuman; on others, the two figures seem to be those of Anjana before and after she was turned into a monkey nymph.

84. *Large fourteenth-century bronze "Dancing Siva" with four arms, holding the flame of destruction in one hand and the bell of creation in another. The dwarf demon on whom he dances, Muyulaga-Kali by name, represents the illusion that Siva destroys evil. Similar details appear in miniature wherever Siva's figure is used as a handle on a Hindu bell.* COLLECTION OF THE WILLIAM ROCKHILL NELSON GALLERY OF ART

85. *Siva with his consort Parvati by his side. Her little figure is removable, as is the entire handle of the bell.*

The beautifully detailed chasing around the skirt of each "evolution" bell is unfailingly significant—a parade of elephants with a little mongoose dancing under each or perhaps a representation of Ganesha, the elephant-headed god of wisdom, circling through leafy branches. Another interesting feature is noted by B. A. Lascelles in his unpublished studies of bells. Throughout India he found pundits, or holy men, sometimes using this type of bell as an impromptu rice bowl. Upon closer observation, he discovered some of the better-made examples having handles that readily unscrew to release the clapper, so that the bell when inverted can serve as a handy bowl.

The power associated with each Hindu god is also personified as his consort. Vishnu's consort is Lakshmi, patroness of wealth and good fortune. Her image makes a fitting handle on bells used by street hawkers and other merchants.

The vehicle or mount of each god is likewise significant. Vishnu's is represented as a super-

natural being, half man, half bird, and his name is Garuda. He is usually shown as a man with the beak and the wings of a bird. As the mount on which Vishnu rides he becomes his servant also and is always present to attend him.

A most popular Hindu god and one of many qualities is Siva, who developed from the ancient storm god Rudra. Basically he is Siva the destroyer; but because death for Hindus is almost synonymous with rebirth, Siva is given a dual role as a destroyer and as a creator.

In his most characteristic position on bell handles Siva assumes this dual role and becomes Lord of the Dance. His performance symbolizes the eternal cycle of life from creation to destruction, and his four arms represent power. Two of the arms grasp emblems of his dual nature: the drum or bell of creation and the flame of destruction. His role in dispelling evil is emphasized by the demon dwarf he crushes under one foot as he dances.

A beautiful coppery-looking bell can be found showing Siva solely in the role of creator, seated with his wife Parvati by his side. As is sometimes true of Hindu bells, the entire piece is made in interlocking sections. Siva's image, seated, is separate and fits into a rimmed cup to hold it on top of the bell. The diminutive figure of Parvati is also separate and made with a pin designed to lock in a slot at Siva's side.

Here again, the powers associated with Siva are reflected in his consort Parvati. She is looked upon as the supreme mother goddess of India and, as such, she is beautiful and life-giving. She plays a dual role, however, and is known also as Kali, the goddess of death, horrible and destructive.

Nandi, the bull mount of Siva, is his principal attendant and the provider of music for his cosmic dance. He is also the guardian of all quadrupeds and his image is always conspicuous in the temples of Siva. His image also makes a handsome handle on bells, particularly if it is copied from the classic statue near Mysore, where Nandi reposes with one foot slightly raised, and wearing sculptured collars of heavy bells.

86. *Nandi, the bull mount of Siva, in a colossal stone carving at Mysore, where since 1659 the pious have kept the bull's likeness glistening with oil.*

Actually, it is the bull rather than the cow that is sacred in India, although the cow is venerated and, according to Hindu religion, not to be killed. But the most decorative bell collars are reserved for the sacred bulls, and the story of why they wear them is well known in Hindu mythology. As it is told, Lord Siva one day rode his sacred white bull Nandi through the lofty Himalayas. The journey was long and tedious, yet Nandi made his way with great skill in spite of many obstacles. Lord Siva, upon his return, wished to present Nandi with a worthy gift as a token of appreciation. He arranged for a most unusual necklace to be strung with rare and colorful beads combined with gold and silver bells. To this day in India it is quite customary to see sacred bulls wearing Nandi necklaces of bells as they plod through the streets.

Hindu gods other than the three comprising the Brahmic triad are to be found in one form or another on Hindu prayer bells. One is the

87. *Three Hindu temple bells of considerable age:* Left: *Sacred bulls rest on each corner of a miniature shrine sacred to Siva. Inside, a devout pilgrim sits in meditation.* Center: *Bronze temple bell sacred to Nandi, whose faithful image here, with its heavy collars of bells, is an example of Hindu metal sculpture at its best. Around the base an inscription in Telegu reads:* IN THE YEAR ANANDA ON THURSDA, THE FIFTH DAY OF THE BRIGHT FORTNIGHT OF THE MONTH KARTIKA, FOR CHADLUVADA RAMALINGA [*temple*] FOR THE MERIT OF YAMMALA PERA-REDI, THE YOUNGEST BROTHER OF KINDA SUB-HAMMA, THE BELL IS MADE AN OFFERING TO SIVA. *For 150 years the bell stood as a votive offering before Siva's image at the temple named in the inscription.* Right: *Vishnu assumes an attitude of prayer while the five-headed cobra shades his head. His figure is splashed with sacred vermilion.* PRIVATE COLLECTION

88. Hindu deities, all in attitudes of supplication. Left to right: *Garuda in human form but with a bird's beak and wings; Vishnu and his consort Lakshmi; Hanuman, the monkey god, resting his head against the curled tip of his tail.* PRIVATE COLLECTION

gentle elephant-headed Ganesha, the god of wisdom and good beginnings. Businessmen opening a new venture or travelers starting on a journey first invoke the blessings of this god. His mount and attendant is the rat, which is consequently sacred and therefore difficult to exterminate in parts of India.

Likewise, creatures other than sacred bulls are represented on Hindu prayer bells. The Nagas, really serpent demigods who inhabit deep waters in the underworld, are greatly revered—especially among the Sinhalese people of Ceylon. Their images not only rise as handles on bells,

89. Handsome temple bell from Bengal. The crescent marks it as sacred to Siva. Cast by the cire perdue *method.* PRIVATE COLLECTION

90. *Lengthily inscribed temple bell from Nepal, surmounted by a pair of dragons. The eighteen-inch carved frame is crowned by the removable figure of Kali, goddess of death. Ganesha, her son the elephant god, is depicted in richly detailed carvings at either end of the top and on all four corners of the base. Figures of the rat, Ganesha's mount and attendant, are conspicuous along the top of the frame.* RINGLAND COLLECTION

91. *A Naga rises as the handle on this bell, which is commonly found in solid brass, in contrast to the mixed metals of most Hindu bells.*

92. *The impressive hooded-cobra candlestick bell.* PRIVATE
COLLECTION

but as protective architectural symbols throughout southern India. Though sometimes renowned for trickery, they are widely worshiped as possessing the elixir of life and immortality, nourished as they are by the life-giving waters in which they live.

The finest of bells associated with this area of Hindu mythology is the hooded cobra candlestick bell. Its heavy and imposing outlines are familiar to most collectors, for it is frequently used as an illustration from the holdings of the Metropolitan Museum of Art. By any standards this piece is an excellent example of India's metal arts; and it serves to show how these arts reflect both Hindu and Buddhist beliefs in a single representation. The cobra's hood may be considered truly Hindu, yet it was one of the one hundred eight auspicious symbols associated with each foot of Buddha.

India offers many small collectibles in the way of old bells made from all sorts of mixed metals and distinguished for oddity of shape; the chief interest here need not be in the antiquity of the objects, some of which are obviously of great age. Rather, interest lies in the picture of life as it is evoked by these articles of religious and domestic purpose, a life permeated with strong artistic and spiritual impulses.

Among objects used in a temple or on a household altar there are little incense burners with crotals cast around the rim; miniature cymbals heavy with bells; occasionally finials and cultic standards hung with fancy bells, most of them made by the lost-wax method. The careful observer will notice that almost always the number of bells used on such articles is uneven. Some authorities go so far as to say that this numerical custom is all but imperative in the Hindu arts.

A certain special intimacy clings to a domestic bell that has been closely involved in the life of its owner, whether it is a utilitarian piece, a plaything, or a treasured personal adornment. Because Indian art is essentially religious, even common objects used in everyday life are often designed with a religious significance. This is true of some curious little punchwork rattles with animalistic handles. Correctly identified, these are scrubbers, forerunners of soap-and-rag. To the Western mind, anything as utilitarian as a scrubber might well have a mere ring for a handle. But the pious Hindu craftsman visualized something symbolic, perhaps a pair of peacocks proudly arching their necks or a pair of elephants at play. And of course it is such ornamentation that gives these their appeal.

93. *Small brass and ivory objects for the domestic altar are shown here on either side of a temple dancer's bell-laden cymbals. No ceremony or oblation is performed without the preliminary tinkling of a bell. Note,* from left to right, *the incense burner with fixed crotals cast on the rim, the curious ivory Naga in his basket, the peacock that symbolizes immortality.* PRIVATE COLLEC-TION

These scrubbers were once very common in India but are more rare today. They were used to scrub the body while bathing, and women coming in from the fields found them useful for scrubbing their mud-soaked feet. Some were used for generations until they became quite worn down. Originally they had little bumps or raised patterns on the bottom to provide better friction. As for the pellets encased in the base of each, says a New Delhi dealer in old brasses, "The sound, I suppose, was to cheer them when scrubbing."

To collectors who know of the blind earning their living as masseurs in India, these bells are also recognized as masseurs' bells. Among the street cries the call of a poor blind person can now and then be heard, begging to come and "rub your weary body," and always between calls comes the plaintive sound of the blind person's bell warning pedestrians and drivers he cannot see. The bell is sometimes of the scrubber type, serving as an aid to the stimulating body rub he begs to give.

Normally, the nineteenth-century brass, wheeled toys of south India are but slightly re-

94. *A cultic standard composed of braided cobra bodies and hung with chunky crotals cast by the lost-wax method.* PRIVATE COLLECTION

95. *Three examples of interesting little scrubbers. Typical of Hindu art are the stylized elephants* (center) *that do not look like their prototypes in nature.* PHOTO, COURTESY OF BERENICE DU BOIS

lated to bell collecting. The horses, elephants, and camels bearing their jaunty riders merely show embossed collars of bells in their casting. But the toy horse-on-wheels used as an illustration was found wearing a miniature collar of real bells, perhaps the whim of the *thathera,* the "beater of brass," who made the toy. More likely, adding the collar satisfied the whim of the child who wheeled the toy about and wanted to hear it jingle.

The heavy anklets and necklaces worn by women in India hold a never-failing charm for many collectors, since these pieces often incorporate bells in their design. The wealthy woman wears them of silver, and they are highly valued. She is, in a way, considered the family "banker" because she wears as jewelry whatever wealth the family has accumulated. Whenever times are hard, shops in the silver bazaars are well stocked with such personal adornments that have been sold for ready cash. Others less wealthy also wear heavy anklets and necklaces, but of mixed, or base, metals.

Of whatever metallic content, each adornment shows intricate construction and delicate detail. On some of the anklets, dozens of notched wedges are fitted together and strung on a firm hemp cord. The edge of each wedge is cast into a bell; and when tied around the ankle, this

semiflexible arrangement of radiating bell-tipped wedges is most ornamental.

A married woman in India often wears toe rings to indicate that fact. These too may be heavily decorated with bells, and the combined weight of the rings and anklets can be as much as two or three pounds. To this must be added the weight of necklaces, bracelets, pendants, and earrings—any or all of which may carry bells.

96. *Nineteenth-century brass wheeled toy with a collar of bells on the horse. This was probably added by the child who once owned the toy.* PRIVATE COLLECTION

97. *Exceptionally fine old brass anklets. Each, with its full quota of bells, weighs approximately one pound.*
PRIVATE COLLECTION

In her thickly illustrated book *Oriental Brasses,* Isabel Lockwood, discussing collecting costume bells in India, makes this comment: "There are other bells, some resembling so closely in shape and design the golden bells found in the sacred well at Chichén Itzá that they have provided a further theory as to the origin of this mysterious people and the Mayan civilization." Her observation is well made, for some of the most attractive Indian necklaces are laced with curious little bells that do bring to mind the Mayan effigy crotals.

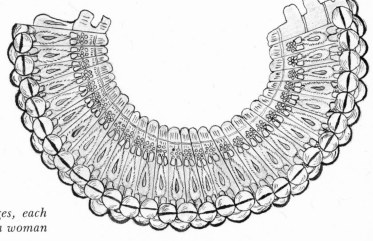

98. *Intricately contrived anklet of silver wedges, each with a bell cast onto its tip. Worn originally by a woman of high caste.* PRIVATE COLLECTION

99. *Weighty brass collar of bells, and a married woman's ring for the big toe.* PRIVATE COLLECTION

100. *This necklace illustrates the truth of Isabel Lockwood's observation that some little costume bells found in India resemble closely the tiny Mayan bells brought up from the sacred well at Chichén Itzá.* PRIVATE COLLECTION

Quantities of little bells are the symbol of a dancer's profession in India, binding her irrevocably to her art. "Tying on the bells" is a standard expression applying to someone who is taking a fateful step from which there is no turning back. The dancers use all manner of tinkling devices, the costume types just described and also odd bell clusters fitted to their fingertips. Although temple dancing has declined, it is still a highly acceptable form of worship.

101. *Dancer's bells strung with small perfume vials. The stopper in each vial is a miniature stiletto! Twentieth century.* PRIVATE COLLECTION

Young girls are dedicated at birth to become temple dancers, and they perform at all religious ceremonies. The dance in India has a divine origin, for the gods themselves are thought of as dancers. Siva, Nataraja, as Lord of the Dance, is only one example.

OTHER ASIAN BELLS

For the collector who travels, the search for costume bells is well rewarded throughout Asia. Indian women are not alone in their preference for adornments that tinkle and jingle. From Thailand on westward into Arabia there are still the native bazaars, despite changing times. Here a seller can be persuaded now and then to bring out a basket containing discards of objects from neighboring homes. In every lot there is always the possibility of finding a hollow coiled bracelet with a rolling pellet inside, a filigree necklace that tinkles, or a pair of early niello earrings whose soft silver patterns were hand polished before the days of whirring electric buffers.

Hereabouts in earlier days bells were often attached to common articles of clothing for both

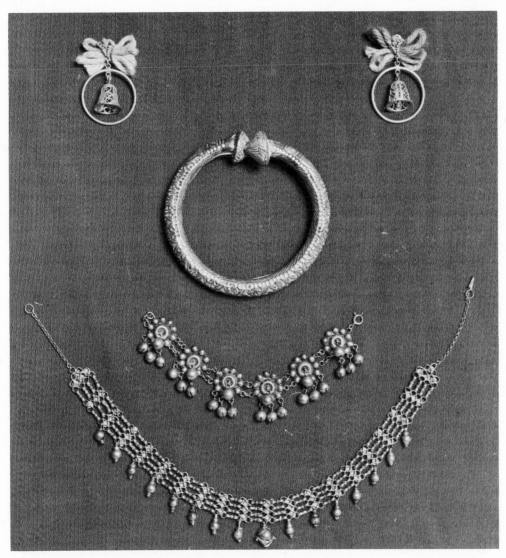

102. *Silver costume bells: Filigree earrings from Cambodia; coiled hollow serpent with bells enclosed, from Arabia; bracelet and necklace from the Fiji Islands.*
PRIVATE COLLECTION

women and men. For prestige, women wore stilt-like shoes called chopines, trimmed with fringes of bells, or platform shoes with bells concealed in a hollow heel. Occasionally an old pair of such footwear can still be found, somewhat the worse for wear. A most beautifully preserved pair of bell-fringed chopines is included in the showing of antique costume bells at the Traphagen School of Fashion in New York City. Many of the pieces in this unusual collection are of either Asian or African origin.

Obviously such beautifully crafted costume bells are worn for decorative effect. Yet in other instances they serve another purpose, acting as amulets to protect the wearer against harm. The Bagobo men of the Philippines are never dressed without a handsome curved knife hanging by their side. Its finely chased and beaded case, of solid bronze, is trimmed with a thick fringe of crotals made by the lost-wax method. The bells are as highly valued as the knife, for their rattle wards off malicious spirits.

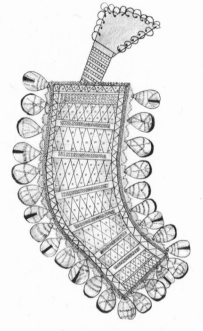

104. *Curved knife in a finely chased and beaded bronze case fringed with crotals made by the lost-wax method; once worn by a member of the Bagobo tribe in the Philippines.* PRIVATE COLLECTION

103. *Rare costume bells from Asia and Africa, purchased for the Traphagen Museum's collection:* Top left: *Amber and silver necklace from Nairobi, Africa, said to have been the property of the wife of the Mad Mullah of Somaliland and to have been on her person when she was decapitated with a sharp saber. Two of the large amber beads are split in two at the neckline.* Top right: *Silver prayer box from India, hung with silver bells and suspended from a necklace of amber and silver beads. Purchased in Mombasa, Africa.*

Bottom left: *Silver anklets purchased in Somaliland in 1928. Diamond-shaped pieces of silver are linked together to make flexible ankle cuffs, featuring a fringe of tiny silver bells; also, an Arabian sultana's silver chopines. The fringe of gold and silver bells is said to have kept the evil spirits away. Bottom right: Arabian hair ornaments of silver. Clusters of little silver bells tinkle on silver hairpins. Purchased in Zanzibar.* COURTESY OF THE TRAPHAGEN SCHOOL OF FASHION'S MUSEUM COLLECTION

105. *The old belief of like repelling like explains the use of these expressive "evil eye" crotals. Their bulging eyes supposedly repel whatever evil eyes are encountered in the natural world.* PRIVATE COLLECTION

Another kind of crotal, sometimes compressed, sometimes egg-shaped, seems to be commonly used as a charm in many areas of eastern Asia. These were at first believed to come only from Malaya and collectors called them evil-eye bells because, regardless of their variation in shape, each crotal appears to have a facial expression carved around a pair of bulging eyes and a widely slit mouth. Some are quite smooth except for the protruding eyes. Others are almost Chinese in feeling, with the eyes protruding from a geometric raised-pattern reminiscent of the ancient ogre masks. A small grouping of these, with no two "faces" alike, can prove quite amusing.

Still other types of bells from Asia are as varied as the characteristics of the countries that crafted them. Beautifully carved wooden bells are typical of Bali, as is a native brass prayer bell with its traditional four-pronged handle. This is used in an intricate Brahmanic ceremony. Seated cross-legged among his paraphernalia, the pedanda, a high priest, proceeds in a trancelike manner to purify the worshipers around him. After writing magic symbols in the holy water and dropping in flowers as he prays, he takes the bell in his left hand and strikes the clapper three times with a flower in his right hand. Holding the bell over incense, he continues ringing it louder and louder with quickened gestures as his prayers crescendo. Suddenly he stops, drops a final flower into the holy water, and all are now purified.

Burma, whose temple bells of Mandalay have been so familiarized through Kipling's words, is noted for bells of contrasting size—thunderous

gongs and lightly echoing wind-bells. One type of gong was formerly a military instrument, sounding into the hills for miles when used in battle. This is a very ancient drum form made of bronze and therefore classed with gongs. It is decorated with frogs, and is said to sound like an old bullfrog. Because of a belief that a frog's croaking brings rain, the frog-gong was often brought out and made to "croak" when rain was needed. Burmese wind-bells hang everywhere from gabled temple roofs. Their designs have been widely copied throughout Thailand and Cambodia. The graceful bo leaf attached to many a clapper symbolizes the great bo tree under which Buddha sat in contemplation for two years.

Although inexpensive and easily obtainable from importers, Burmese wind-bells are desirable little examples of *cire perdue* casting. Once considered a mysterious and little understood process, this lost-wax method is much more familiar today. American soldiers in Cambodia had ample opportunity to watch native workers using the method to fashion small bells and other objects. In more than one instance a soldier was so fascinated with the whole process that he collected a working sequence of molds used to make a small *khew*, or wind-bell.

Cambodian metalwork is distinguished by its rather heavy quality and symbolic ornateness. An example purchased in Cambodia prior to the Second World War illustrates these features. Really an oversized crotal in the likeness of a pomegranate, it hangs from a brass image of a phoenix rising from an encrustation of ashes. Suspended from the pomegranate on chunky

106. *Beautifully carved wooden bells typical of Bali craftsmanship. Twentieth century.*

107. *Wind-bells from Burma. Twentieth century.* PRIVATE COLLECTION

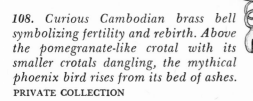

108. Curious Cambodian brass bell symbolizing fertility and rebirth. Above the pomegranate-like crotal with its smaller crotals dangling, the mythical phoenix bird rises from its bed of ashes. **PRIVATE COLLECTION**

brass rings are six small crotals. In symbolic language the phoenix represents rebirth, rising again from its own ashes; the small crotals are seeds bursting from the opened pomegranate, to indicate the number of one's descendants.

In the regions westward, nearing Arabia, fewer bells are used except for personal adornment and on animals. There is of course no tradition of their use for religious purposes under the Mohammedans; and the Turks abhorred them, even though they greatly enjoyed making music with cymbals, sistrums, and all kinds of rattles. However, there are ceremonial relics such as bells from the Armenian Church that on rare occasions turn up in Turkey or Iran (Persia). Persian metalworkers have designed

109. Old Cambodian gong.

110. Metalwork throughout Southeast Asia was greatly influenced by the ancient flow of religious and cultural influences from India and also from China. An Oriental influence is apparent in this gong from old Siam (Thailand). SMITHSONIAN INSTITUTION

a few very interesting small bells for decorative purposes. Their patterned traceries, to anyone at all familiar with Persian art, give them instant identity. Some are quite ambitious in their designs, copies of early Byzantine pieces and inset with simulated jewels.

OLD AFRICAN TYPES

Africa, that continent of strong contrasts, quite naturally reflects those contrasts in its creative expressions. If a bell collector were inclined to do so, he might find here a fertile field for assembling an African nucleus of amazing diversity—bells representing widely separated tribes that have developed independently of each other for thousands of years. The range would extend from the fragile silvery costume bells of old Somaliland to the crudest of iron gongs from the Congo. In between those two extremes there would be polished but primitive wooden effigy bells to choose from, as well as tiny Ashanti gold-weight bells. These are but a few of the many possibilities.

It is sometimes supposed that the concept of bells was introduced into Africa by Europeans such as Prince Henry and his Portuguese navigators, who in the fifteenth century landed on Africa's west coast with boatloads of red caps, small bells, Venetian beads, et cetera, for purposes of trade. Scholars have discarded such a theory, however, in the light of recent excavations in Northern Rhodesia (Zambia). Here in the Gwembe, or Middle Zambezi Valley, richly loaded graves have been discovered, dating back to the first millennium A.D. Among the objects uncovered were single iron bells having typological connections with similar examples from the Congo, and probably obtained by barter from that region. Apparently the idea of bells developed very early in Africa, and independently, just as it did in other parts of the world.

A seventeenth-century account published in Amsterdam, *Description de l'Afrique*, gives one of the earliest observations on the clapperless double iron bell (*ngonge*), known to have been produced before the fifteenth century not only

in the Congo but in many other regions of Africa. Here it was described as having the general shape of a horseshoe with two flattened brims to be struck alternately on the outside, thus giving two distinct tones. The *ngonge* was found to rank high among a chieftain's badges and was always used for all official announcements. Made locally by the village blacksmith, the double bell was as necessary as any weapon or tool, for it was evidence of the constant presence of power in the person of a chieftain. Although this seventeenth-century account of the *ngonge* makes no mention of its being used as a form of currency, later accounts record it as a frequent medium of exchange.

Musically, this same bell is still the most important of the idiophones featured in all West African orchestras of today. Sometimes as many as sixteen are used to maintain the beat set by the master drummer and to lend a rhythmic pulse of differing pitches. As a musical instrument, this bell is of course played by tribal folk of all ages. A letter from Nigeria that accompanied the sale of one double bell and one single bell of iron gives a picturesque description of their use in local villages:

111. The ngonge, *or double iron bell, from Rhodesia. It is an instrument known to have been made in the Congo and elsewhere in Africa as early as the fifteenth century.* COURTESY, STEELWAYS MAGAZINE

112. *One of the few remaining examples of these ivory double bells may be seen in the Brooklyn Museum collection. Made exclusively for the kings of Benin, these magnificent sixteenth-century carvings are unequaled among bell-like instruments. The carvings on the front of this larger bell depict a king and his attendants. On the other side a smaller bell shows a human hand in the mouth of a crocodile.* THE BROOKLYN MUSEUM COLLECTION

The double bell is used by the young girls in a sort of May Day dance when each section of the town tries to see how much better their dancers do than the other section. A little girl is trained to stand on an older girl's shoulder, and do a bit of dancing as they march along. She carries a feather in her hand, which she waves about as she sways from side to side. It is very pretty, but of course pagan. The girls wear their customary red beads and white cowry shells, with bunches of leaves. The red, white, black and green makes a lovely picture. Their black bodies are rubbed with oil until they shine. The girls in front beat these bells with sticks and the others sing, or chant, while the little girl on the shoulder dances. . . . The single bell is used by the Ibo men in the southern part of Nigeria. But the Ibos are the most aggressive people of the land and their old customs are changing.

Magnificent ivory double bells were carved in Nigeria during the sixteenth century. These, made solely for the kings of Benin, were struck with ivory wands in ceremonies of kingship, the tones being distinct but soft. The basic idea for these ivory ceremonial pieces derived from the iron double bell common at an earlier date throughout West Africa, but it was greatly modified by the guilds of skilled craftsmen working in ivory. The result no longer looks like a horseshoe but has more the appearance of a sistrum, with one large and one small bell attached to a single handle.

There are only five known examples of these sixteenth-century instruments. One was acquired by the Brooklyn Museum and another, the finest of the five, by the British Museum. The story behind the collecting of these instruments is a gory one. The Benin kings made increasing use of their ivory bells in designating prisoners for sacrifice. By the end of the nineteenth century, the human sacrifices involved in such royal ceremonies led to English intervention. The first British regiment sent to prevent the sacrificial ritual was massacred. Thereupon the great Punitive Expedition of 1897 was sent to destroy ancient Benin completely. It was then that these ivory instruments were collected from the royal courts.

The present Oba, or king, of Benin still uses a modern version of the old ivory bells at one of the important ceremonies held annually to renew the king's divinity. Elsewhere in Nigeria other sistrum-like idiophones are also still used for ceremonial purposes. One type is of carved wood with crotals jangling on the wires fitted into the frame.

Tribal chiefs are not the only ones who mark their rank with special bells. African witch doctors too are recognized by their special paraphernalia, including rattles and bells. Their rattles are made of whatever is handy—a snakeskin, shells, nuts; but more important are their clusters of iron bells on strings of blue beads, an unbeatable combination for warding off evil. The witch doctor is much attached to his paraphernalia, the badge of his official position in the tribe. As a result witch doctor's bells, like those of a chieftain, are not often found on the open market.

Nigerian tribal art is characterized by a fondness for masks, and this fondness has been translated into some curious bronze bell forms shaped to resemble horned heads. The first of these were uncovered by accident just prior to the Second World War. They were dug up southwest of the present city of Benin, a name known

113. A single iron bell from the Ibo people of southern Nigeria and a set of crude iron witch-doctor's bells from Ethiopia. PRIVATE COLLECTION

114. *Belonging to the Lower Niger bronze industry, these three bells in the form of horned heads were dug up southwest of the city of Benin.* COURTESY, THE LONDON ILLUSTRATED NEWS

115. *Various examples from an outstanding collection of African art in bell form.* Back figure: *Bambara iron scultpure with bell, eighteenth century.* Front row: *Bakongo carved wooden dog bell, nineteenth century; Balunda carved wooden dog bell, nineteenth century; Nigerian bronze twins, given on the birth of twins; Nigerian bronze bell; Benin bronze bell, cast in lost-wax method, seventeenth century.* OPPENHEIMER COLLECTION

116. *The work on this African bell is not only a superb illustration of Nigerian metalwork; it is also an unmistakable example of the expressive but abstract concepts used in African figural representations.* ESTHER OAKES COLLECTION

whether of wood or of brass, will have figural interest. Some collectors are little attracted to African carvings because by traditional standards of art they appear grotesque. Properly interpreted within the context of their own culture, however, the carvings can lead to an understanding of the whole panorama of African art.

The nature of the figures and of the workmanship differs from one tribe to another, but always the carvings must be considered in the light of their purpose. Here beauty has little, if anything, to do with art. From earliest days the African artist's main concern within his tribe has been to sculpture for religious purposes,

117. *A Dahomean figure from former French West Africa. It is less abstract and more realistically detailed than most African figures, even to the melonlike object that revolves between the boy's hands.* PRIVATE COLLECTION

the world over for its famous bronzes. Copies of these curious bells are made today by the same lost-wax method used since earliest time for all Benin bronzes. The copies are faithfully reproduced, even to the expressive scarifications that gave the originals their frightening but fascinating appearance. How such bells were once used remains uncertain; but like most ancient African art, they were undoubtedly ceremonial objects.

Sculpture is West African art par excellence, so it is to be expected that most bell forms,

which means for the purpose of influencing the spiritual powers themselves. To do this and thereby ensure the welfare of the tribe demands the combined efforts of both the living and the dead. Many of the figures in the form of a bell are ancestor effigies designed to summon the spirit of the dead person and bring it back to life. Others are used as fetishes. The uglier the fetish, the more effective it is thought to be.

The figures produced by tribal artists settled in the wide areas near the Niger and the Congo rivers are essentially abstract. Often they are exaggerated to the point of being caricatures, or so it would seem. Yet their apparent primitiveness should not be explained on the basis of cultural backwardness but, again, on the basis of the artist's purpose. In an African figure the proportions of the various parts express their relative importance. The head, for instance, may be exaggerated in size because it is considered the center of character. Not to distort this feature would be contrary to belief.

If ever there was an example of native sculpture capable of abolishing the label primitive as applied to African art, it is the silvery figure of a native boy crouching on a gracefully shaped bell, rolling in his upraised hands a melonlike fruit. Here the proportions of head to body, legs to torso, et cetera, are closer to the norm. The detailed workmanship is also in contrast to that on more abstract figures—the tightly woven cap, the pierced ears with dangling pink-beaded earrings, and even the striations on the melon.

The bell was made by an inland tribesman of Dahomey, formerly a part of French West Africa. It is typical of Dahomean figures in being considerably more sophisticated than those from other areas. The sculpturing here results from the same lost-wax method used elsewhere but employing a light aluminum alloy rather than pure brass or bronze.

Dahomean pieces differ from most African sculpture in being neither religious nor ceremonial in their intent. Therefore the subjects used are domestic and celebrate familiar scenes in tribal life: a balky domestic goat, a strutting cock, a man hunting, or a mother feeding her child. The figure on the bell described may well depict a juggler practicing for the king's court. He is a fitting illustration of one commentator's remark that Dahomey figures bounce with life and excitement.

The little Ashanti gold-weight bells from nearby Ghana are highly appealing but extremely rare. So called because they were used on a balance scale to measure gold dust, these gold weights were cast in many shapes to represent small creatures, household objects, or tribal figures—but rarely in the form of a bell. One, privately owned, is in the shape of a monkey with a clapper swinging between his feet. Another, also privately owned, shows two tiny turtles playing with a clapper swinging between them. These two bell weights measure only one inch high, though sometimes they are slightly larger.

Granting that the African artist's main function has always been to create for religious purposes, his artistic skills have been called upon in making dozens of objects for everyday use. The attractive feature of these artifacts comes from their blending of form and function, and here bells play a part. A chieftain's stool must not only be capable of taking great weight but must look as if it can do so. As his most prized leadership symbol, it must also look the part. So that none will mistake the chieftain's stool for another's, the craftsman who carves it often attaches a number of special bells.

Carved headrests for women are a sign of wealth in West Africa, and beautifully carved ones are found in the Congo. Curved to pillow the neck without disturbing a woman's hair style, they too are sometimes decorated with bells or perhaps jangling rings. These serve to warn the sleeper if she moves too much and is likely to disarrange her hair.

Among the nomad tribes in southern Ethiopia similar but less pretentious carved rests are used by both men and women. They call them wooden pillows. As with the headrests, bells or jinglets may be added at will. A letter

118. African aids to beauty include a wooden pillow from Ethiopia; a woman's necklace from Kenya, made from the metal of kerosene cans; and a man's heavy old brass armlet or anklet. PRIVATE COLLECTION

attached to one of these wooden pillows describes its use:

> One wooden pillow for nomads. It shall be put under the neck. The Borana, Wata and Somali tribes in southern Ethiopia all use it. You can meet these people everywhere out in the bush with a pillow like this in their hands, and when they drop down in a shadow under a tree they always put it under their neck. Don't seem to rest well without that.

A blending of form and function is also found in the anklets, bracelets, and necklaces worn by all ages. These brass ornaments are neatly devised and appropriately designed for the intended wearer. Because music is deeply rooted in the soul of the native African, he likes adornments that syncopate with his every move; and the tribal craftsman satisfies this liking by ingeniously incorporating suitable bells in his designs. Men wear chunky brass anklets with pellets rolling inside. Women wear bracelets and collars with little bells fixed to them. Children wear long strings of bright blue beads with a shrill bell attached. All such personal accessories not only please in a rythmic sort of way but also become amulets to charm the wearer against

harm; for here, as in other primitive regions, there is that old and widespread belief that noise will rout evil spirits. The children's amulets using blue beads supposedly assure added protection because of the magical qualities in blue beads.

Many tribal groups have special accessories peculiar to their manner of dress. Grown girls in the city of Benin wear aprons studded with tiny brass bells. Around Negelli, Sidamo, in southern Ethiopia unmarried girls wear strings of crescent-shaped little bells tied diagonally around their legs. Among the Makonde villagers in East Africa's Mozambique, dancers wear vests studded with dangling bells.

Where brass is not available, African craftsmen make good use of whatever metal comes to hand. In the district of Kyome, Kenya, East Africa, the silver-colored metal of old kerosene cans is used to make attractive collars of bells in the shape of half spheres, daintily prickmarked. With red yarn these are closely laced on a strand of rhinoceros hide, making a semi-flexible collar unique to this area.

One final type of bell is not to be overlooked, although outside the usual survey of African bells because it is used in the Christian church.

119. African bracelet with bells cast solidly to it. Originally purchased from a black World War I trooper whose family had prized it. PRIVATE COLLECTION

This is the Coptic handbell rung by young deacons of the church at several points in their service. It is a significant bell, an indirect heritage from the Christian culture of ancient Egypt that was founded during what is called the Coptic period. Art deriving from that culture is distinguished by interlacing geometric patterns worked as surface texture on metal and wooden

objects. These geometric patterns are said to have deep spiritual significance and are therefore highly suitable for working the surface of Coptic handbells, making them unique and very collectible from every aspect.

120. Typical Coptic bell used by young deacons in the Ethiopian churches. The geometric patterns are traditional in Coptic art. PRIVATE COLLECTION

4

European Favorites

BECAUSE OF THE NUMBER of countries producing them over the years and because of the number of uses to which European bells have been put, decorative as well as functional, the range of collecting possibilities here seems limitless. Within this vast range of possibilities, however, there are some categories that can help define different collecting areas and guide the collector while he pursues his personal preferences.

Certainly a large number of bells made of china deserve special consideration as a group. The word "china" is the general designation for all kinds of glazed earthenware, stoneware,

and porcelain, all of which have been used in producing table bells. Those of earthenware are made from any readily available clay and can vary considerably in content from one bell to another, from rough folk-art pottery to colorfully glazed faience. All are opaque. Those of porcelain, on the other hand, are of highly selected materials that give a hard finish and varying degrees of translucence when held to the light.

True hard-paste porcelain was unknown in Europe until introduced from China. The secret of its formula was not discovered until the

121. Early Meissen table bell, 1730–1735. Chinoiserie in the manner of J. G. Horoldt. RIJKSMUSEUM, AMSTERDAM

eighteenth century when the first porcelain factories were established by the royal families of Austria and Germany. The one at Meissen, Germany, which became the most important, has operated continuously as a royal and state manufactory since its beginning in 1710. The best period of Meissen work extended from about 1720 to 1815, and it is known that table bells were produced along with other pieces during that era, although most of the Meissen bells found by collectors are of a considerably later date.

The most famous pattern ever developed at Meissen, the blue onion, has been made continuously ever since its introduction in the mid-eighteenth century. It appears on bells either in the traditional pure blue underglaze painting on white or in polychrome on white. (*See* Color Plate II.)

The blue onion pattern is based on old Chinese designs and as a style of decoration is known as chinoiserie. Because Europeans admired many Chinese export porcelains being brought back by trading vessels of the day, it was inevitable that their artists would find inspiration in Oriental designs. The result was chinoiserie, an imaginative Western adaptation of Oriental scenes and figures on European and English wares. Oddly enough, the so-called blue onion pattern has nothing in common with onions. According to a letter from the Royal Porcelain Manufactory at Meissen:

> The fruits decorating the borders must be denoted as Japanese peaches and pomegranates. The center of the pattern is ornamented with a large aster and a branch twisted around a bamboo stem and copiously decorated with leaves and blooms. In the foot of the bamboo stem there are painted since 1890 our world famous "Crossed Swords," also in blue underglaze painting.

A quite different type of Meissen table bell dates to the Victorian period when floral decorations were popular. Molded and applied flowers and fruits of tiniest proportions cover the entire surface to create a bell that is not only distinctively charming but rare, since it was

122. *Early Meissen table bell, circa 1735. No mark. Mr. A. L. den Blaauwen, head keeper of the Rijksmuseum's Department of Decorative Arts, believes this bell was probably a replacement for a broken one of Du Paquier porcelain made in Vienna for August III of Saxony and his wife Maria Josepha of Habsburg. The Saxony-Habsburg arms are incorporated in the design.* RIJKSMUSEUM, AMSTERDAM

manufactured for only a limited time. It is thought that Meissen bells of this type were inspired by similar nineteenth-century bells created in France by Jacob Petit.

Too often there is confusion in the mind of the collector over the difference between Meissen and Dresden porcelain bells, for they are of somewhat similar size and proportion. Since the Meissen factory in the city of that name is located but a few miles from the large capital city of Dresden, Meissen is frequently thought of as Dresden, and vice versa. Yet there is a distinction. Porcelain was not originally manufactured in Dresden, but quantities of it were bought by firms in that city from nearby factories, then decorated and resold as Dresden ware. The term "Dresden," then, is the generic term for

123. Less recognized by collectors are the lovely early porcelain bells of Dutch make, such as these produced in Loosdrecht between 1774 and 1782.
A. Decoration is a young couple in elegant dress. She wears a rose gown, sleeves with "engageantes," and he a blue coat. She is holding a bird in her lap, showing it to her cavalier as he leans against a tree trunk.

B. Decoration, in brown, features a landscape with two men; to the right a tower, in the distance a river, hills, and a church; on the other side is a smaller landscape. RIJKS-MUSEUM, AMSTERDAM

every piece of porcelain decorated in or near the city itself, but there has always been only one Meissen factory.

This explains why there are only a few styles of genuine Meissen bells and many styles of Dresden-decorated bells. Naturally over a period of two hundred years there have been slight variations in the use of the crossed-swords mark that identifies Meissen ware, but the variations are always recognizable. Although famous marks like this serve as a guide, they do so only in confirmation of other known factors, however; unfortunately most of them can also be found on spurious pieces, for there have always been arch-imitators of Meissen and other great porcelains. Samson of Paris was one. There are even dark tales of how apprentices were hired to hide in barrels outside another pottery works to spy on secret formulas and decorative techniques.

Porcelain has seldom received more decorative importance than in Austria. It was in 1717 that a Dutch artisan, Du Paquier, established the Vienna porcelain factory that Queen Maria Theresa made a state industry under her reign (1740–1780). Here Viennese artists soon developed their own techniques for the "flower and figure" painting that was to make Vienna porcelain world famous. There are table bells of exquisite coloring to be found bearing the Royal Vienna beehive mark in underglaze blue. Some are decorated with conventional flower motifs; others, with elegant scenes and figures that may be either pastoral or courtly in style. Again, though, collectors need to be aware that the beehive mark has been imitated by various later and even contemporary factories, including Eichwald and Volkstedt.

France, too, had its Manufacture Royale de Porcelaine, established at Sèvres in 1756. There is little conclusive evidence of bells' being made by this factory, although imitations are known to exist. Quite the contrary is true of the Limoges factories, where small bells have been produced in considerable numbers since the late eighteenth century. Some, but not all, carry their maker's mark, and with the help of Thorn's *Handbook of Old Pottery and Porcelain Marks,* or a comparable volume, the collector can study these.

French porcelain bells, like those of Austria, are known for their elegant beauty; but very few are attributable. Among some bearing their maker's intitials are the charming table bells by Jacob Petit, who established himself as a potter at Fontainebleau in 1790. These are the bells thought to have inspired Meissen ones of similar design, with tiny molded flowers applied to the surface.

Considering the host of names among English makers of fine porcelain, the number of known bells produced is surprisingly few. For many years the making of high-grade porcelain was the closely guarded secret of European countries more cultivated in the arts than eighteenth-century England. But the discovery there of bone ash and its role in making fine china finally led to establishing such factories as Derby in 1750, and later Minton, both of which are still in full swing today, as are the somewhat later factories of Royal Doulton and Crown Staffordshire.

The Crown Staffordshire Porcelain Company has designed many attractive bone china bells

124. Miniature Limoges porcelain bell with its matching plate. The bell is only an inch and a half in height. Twentieth century. PRIVATE COLLECTION

bearing their mark. An early one was a figurine type in colorful dress honoring Jenny Lind. Later there were tea bells commemorating the accession of Elizabeth II to the throne; and others with decalcomania decoration—that is, a colorful overglaze that can be felt as ever so slightly raised. Royal Crown Derby's greatest, and perhaps sole, achievement in designing bells came with the issuance of five hundred table bells commemorating the investiture of young Charles as the Prince of Wales, at Caernarvon

125. Two views, left and right, *of the Prince of Wales investiture bell. Coloring is predominantly red, blue, and gold, with a border showing royal lions in red against flashed gold trim. From Royal Crown Derby. At center is a striking Nailsea bell in clear glass with swirls of cobalt, amber, green, and white.* PHOTO, COURTESY OF BERENICE DU BOIS

126. *Porcelain bell of rice-grain ware, by Friedl Holzer-Kjellberg; said to be the only one produced by this leading Finnish designer of rice-grain china. Twentieth century.* PRIVATE COLLECTION

Castle, July, 1969. The colorings and designs are richly befitting of the occasion, and each bell in its box of antique white satin is numbered and accompanied by a certificate.

Except for widely recognized bells of this sort and except as collectors come upon others that are marked, it is difficult to assess the types of bells that may have been produced over the years by any one company. As the present director of Royal Crown Derby states, the company assumes their investiture bell to be the first one made by them, never having seen any other in a museum or a catalogue; still, and to quote: "One hates to be too specific about what Derby has or has not made in the past, however, since the volume and variety over the years has been astronomical."

Similar guarded sentiments are expressed by the makers of Irish Belleek ware in venturing to state that to the best of their knowledge they have never produced bells. And so, taking these as examples, how should collectors look upon an Irish Belleek bell or an early Royal Crown Derby bell that appears to be authentic?

Unbeknown to present company officials, such bells may be quite genuine. They may have been

128. *Attractive German bell of fine quality jasperware that resembles Wedgwood in its decor. Nineteenth century.* RINGLAND COLLECTION

produced in very limited quantities, with all records of their manufacture lost or never written down. Then again, they may have been made as off-duty experiments by individual workmen who were either permitted to take home their experiments or who smuggled them out. Some experts scorn this theory so often used to explain the existence of otherwise unrecorded objects, yet it persists. Finally, even a bell that is properly marked can prove a counterfeit. Unscrupulous competitiors have always been prone to counterfeit famous trademarks as well as popular forms and designs.

127. Left and right: *Wedgwood bells of classic design, each with a bas-relief on either side.* Center: *Wedgwood's most recent bell, a black basalt miniature of the Liberty Bell, introduced as the brainchild of Philadelphian Charles B. Smith, to herald the United States of America's two hundredth birthday in 1976.* MYRL HUENE COLLECTION

The idea that a bell may have been made in very limited quantity, all records of its making lost or never written down, is an intriguing one to pursue. As in other artistic endeavors, there is a great deal of experimenting in bellmaking and sometimes a single experimental piece is the only one of its kind produced. Such is the true story behind a single bell in rice-grain china, the only one ever made by Finland's famous porcelain manufacturer. Wares in this pattern date from the Ch'ien Lung reign in China, and though much admired have been copied but rarely. They are made by a delicate piercing technique, the piercings being transparent rice-grain-shaped holes arranged in lacy patterns. Thirty years ago the Finnish designer Friedl Holzer-Kjellberg succeeded in perfecting a technique for rice-grain china, but not until years later was she challenged to try her technique on a bell. The task was too difficult, she concluded, so the bell was never mass produced. It is less than likely that the making of this one piece was entered in company records, yet the experimental bell does genuinely exist.

One particular event created an unprecedented stir among bell collectors in the early 1960s. This was the production of Wedgwood's first bells, jasper beauties in either pale blue or sage green with white cameos in relief; and in this instance the fact that none had ever before been made by the company seems conclusive, although for a time there was a degree of uncertainty even among experts. The uncertainty arose over a very fine quality old jasper bell, unmarked but decorated in the Wedgwood manner. This later proved to be of German make.

Nearly two hundred years earlier Josiah Wedgwood had enjoyed the patronage of George III, who was one of the first to own a piece of jasperware—then the latest achievement of that humble country potter who made several thousand experiments to perfect this special ware. Today, despite innovative additions in its china making, Wedgwood is still associated most often with its classical use of jasper, actually a white stoneware that is tinted before the bas-

reliefs are applied by hand. The beauty of the tiny raised figures ornamenting Wedgwood bells has no equal, and it is understandable that collectors are gratified over the company's choice of these classic cameos for ornamentation.

Undoubtedly the company likewise was gratified over the reception of its initial bells, for it subsequently issued a replica of the Liberty Bell in black basalt, thus giving bell collectors a representation of another of Josiah Wedgwood's major achievements. He perfected black basalt in 1768, but it was never used as a material for bells until the company agreed to issue these replicas of the Liberty Bell. The idea of making them originated with an American, Charles B. Smith of Philadelphia, who was seeking an exclusive sales item with authentic Philadelphia associations, one that might even herald the coming bicentennial of 1976. The resulting edition of black basalt bells was limited to one thousand. Each is impressed with a large M in addition to the usual Wedgwood mark. The three progressive trial bells are on permanent display in the United States at the Buten Museum of Wedgwood at Merion, Pennsylvania.

Although in England porcelain remained the favorite medium for the few types of bells that have been produced, a different situation de-

129. *Unusual German jasperware bell in the form of a decorated Christmas tree. In the foreground a tiny dog races around the base of the tree. Nineteenth century.* PRIVATE COLLECTION

veloped in Europe where porcelain never completely overshadowed the use of earthenwares such as faience. True, faience—or majolica, as it may be called—is often considered a second-rate product compared with fine porcelain. Yet it is not necessarily cheap, nor is it imitative of porcelain. It is simply different, and because of its versatile composition it has

130. *Various bells in colorful faience.* Above, left to right: *Swiss mosaic work on terra cotta, conventional design; French Quimper ware; Italian sgraffito decoration in turquoise glaze on natural clay; heavy Italian faience; German iridescent glaze with sanded majolica work on the raised flowers, all in shades of soft green, rose and lavender; Italian Spaghetti ware; Italian glazed terra cotta, its polychrome decoration patterned by pottery-making monks of Campo-Maldoli, circa 1900.* Below: *Large Italian betrothal bell showing the Easter flight of the swallows to Rome. Circling this, four variations of Della Robbia bells.* PRIVATE COLLECTION

been used to produce a variety of colorful bells. What these may lack in tonal quality is more than offset in their regional appeal, for the national characteristics of each country seem to be pleasingly revealed in faience bells.

Even the experts do not always agree on the origins of faience as a type of earthenware. The fact that it is also called majolica would seem to indicate an origin on Majorca, one of the Spanish islands. Actually, its more basic name of faience is, thanks to the French, traceable to Italian origins. Faience is the French name for the Italian town Faenza, where majolica was first made during the fifteenth and sixteenth centuries. The technique of its making had been practiced in the Middle East centuries earlier, and much of the ware imported by Spain. From there it was carried to Italy on ships from the island of Majorca; hence the popular mistake of thinking the ware itself was Majorcan.

Today the glazed pottery of many other European countries is referred to as faience, and nearly all its major makers have produced bells. Italy offers collectors the greatest variety of small colorful bells in this general class, and ranging into terra-cotta types. Top favorites are the Capo di Monte bells with their molded cupids and nymphs. Most of these collected today are of modern make and not of uniform quality, since they are produced at more than one location. Some, however, are extremely well executed and resemble early Capo di Monte so closely that even connoisseurs cannot tell the difference until they examine the marks.

The colorfully glazed terra-cotta bells in Della Robbia ware are also favorites. Their molded borders of fruits and flowers are patterned after wreaths made by Della Robbia in the fifteenth century to decorate shrines and altars. Another type of Italian terra-cotta bell, and one less commonly seen, is of sgraffito ware. Sgraffito is similar to the slip decoration but done, so to speak, in reverse. The entire surface to be decorated is covered with slip and dried. Then the desired pattern is scratched through the slip, exposing the clay surface underneath.

find a perfect specimen of Quimper, for the pottery chips and cracks very easily. In fact, this is so characteristic of old pieces that even modern reproductions are produced with faked cracks.

Bells of delftware from Germany and Holland, as well as those of Denmark's Royal Copenhagen ware, represent a high quality of faience. Interestingly enough, Holland's Royal Delftware De Porceleyne Fles Manufactory has never produced any bells in its more than three centuries of operation, or so the present manufactory believes. Dutch delftware bells continue to come in many shapes and designs from numerous other locations, but none from the Royal Delftware firm. The traditional German delftware bells with their blue-and-white windmill scenes are familiar to collectors. Some carry the crossed-pipes mark; some, the crossed-hayforks mark. These German delftware bells are especially porcelaneous and so illustrate well for the collector the close relationship between a high-grade faience and true porcelain.

131. Above: *Capo di Monte bell with modern mark.* WALTERS COLLECTION. *The German delft bell in blue and white bears a crossed-pipes mark.* PRIVATE COLLECTION

Favorite soft-paste pottery bells from France are those of Quimper ware. They were produced by Henri Quimper of Finistère, France, in a plant that supposedly operated from 1900 until the start of the Second World War. This operational span fails to explain the date '93 found on some Henri Quimper bells. It is difficult to

132. *Dutch delftware bell decorated in a variant of the blue onion pattern is marked* DELFT. WALTERS COLLECTION

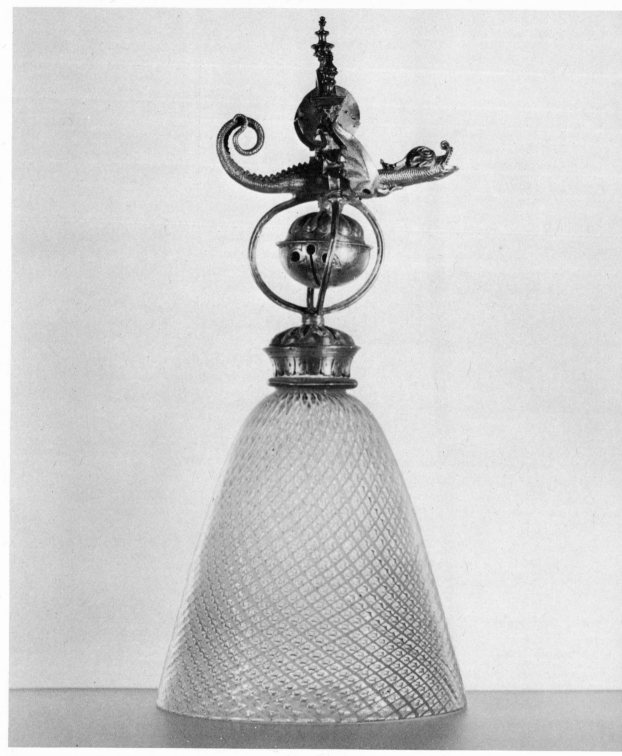

133. *Whistle glass of* vetro-di-trina *colorless glass with enclosed white threads and air traps. Venice or Northern Europe. The brass mount is dated 1673.*
THE CORNING MUSEUM OF GLASS

OLD WORLD GLASS BELLS

If scarcity of supply, beauty of coloring, and excellence of workmanship are criteria of collectibility, then it is easily understood why glass bells are so avidly sought. The large Nailsea and Bristol types with their jewel-like colorings are the ones most often pictured and discussed. There seems to be no agreement on whether these were made as a commercial venture or whether they were whimseys made as after-hour experiments by glasshouse employees, pieces designed to suit their personal whims.

Lacing together scattered statements from certain experts upholds the traditional picture of leavings in the pot being given to the glassblowers. These they used to satisfy their own creativeness and at the same time to improve their technique by blowing and shaping unusual objects such as canes, toys, bells, et cetera. They were free to use their creations as gifts or to exchange them for drinks at the local pub.

There are other experts who advise avoiding the word *whimseys,* even though it is customary to credit glass oddities to off-duty workmen experimenting for pleasure and profit. That theory, they point out, does not take into account the working conditions in glasshouses around the 1800s. Would a six-day week of ten to twelve hours daily over intense heat have left the workers enthusiastic about staying after hours in the dusky workrooms? And would the heavy tax on glass in England before 1854 have encouraged such promiscuous use of leftovers?

So far as bells are concerned, there is this additional question. Even granting that other offbeat objects might have been produced as whimseys, were bells really that much of an oddity? Apparently not, for there are bits of evidence that the production of bells was an early legitimate business venture at centers like Nailsea and Bristol. As early as 1738 when Prince Frederick and Princess Augusta visited Bristol, the pompous procession of city guilds was headed by glassmakers carrying their specialties—"some carried a glass bell which they rang lustily." The same is recorded of a similar procession of glassmen at Newcastle.

Other apparent evidence that glass bells were standard production lies in the uniform standard of workmanship in fine Nailsea specimens, for instance, and a certain homogeneous styling even though the bells display considerable variation in their combinations of transparent, translucent, opalescent, and opaque glass.

As a compromise to all the pros and cons there is yet one more viewpoint, a middle-of-the-road theory that a good many of the large Nailsea and Bristol type of bells were made as offhand orders, as a sort of sideline custom work. To accept orders for offhand pieces was common practice until the making of glass became specialized. Even after the turn of the century there were glassmakers in both England and America who would produce a half dozen of anything offhand, within the limits of the factory's equipment. This viewpoint of course implies a more limited production and would account for the scarcity of bells of this type.

Regardless of the time of day they were made, one thing is certain. Nailsea has become the rather loosely applied descriptive term for all bells of the type produced in the town of that name or in neighboring Bristol. This is acceptable terminology, for with so little documentary evidence it is difficult to be conclusive about which bells were actually made in these two centers and which were made elsewhere. It is a fact that similar ones, even some with loopings and color-twist handles, were made at Newcastle, Stourbridge, Warrington, Birmingham—and even by John Davenport of Longport, Staffordshire, who is better remembered for his pottery than for his colored glass. Very, very few of these are marked.

Within recent years a New York gallery offered a once-in-a-lifetime opportunity to view at close range a collection of glass bells, all presumably made at Nailsea during the first half of the nineteenth century. The collection had been purchased from an old family in the Nailsea district, and the bells were offered to collec-

134. *Bell of colorless glass decorated with three flat bands, three gilt masks, and three colorless knops with a blue bead. The handle has four ears. The lower flat band and the ribbed part of the bell are also gilt. The clapper is missing. Antwerp, seventeenth century.* RIJKSMUSEUM, AMSTERDAM

The usual handle is of clear glass, sometimes swirled or ribbed like the dome itself and sometimes with color twists blown in. Others may be opaque white or vaseline, pigeon blood, or apple green. The finials are topped with anywhere from one to seven knops, and occasionally a hand is molded at the very tip. Quite often the color of the handle is repeated at the base

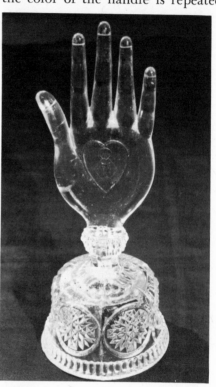

135. *Bell and handle all in one, colorless pressed pattern glass. Diamond registry mark in palm of hand indicates English manufacture of mid-nineteenth century.* PRIVATE COLLECTION

tors at prices ranging from $45 to $345. Only one bell was marked, bearing the name Chance Bros. and Company. The Chances were among the partners who founded the Nailsea glasshouse. A son was one of the purchasers of the glasshouse in the city of Birmingham that, after 1836, carried the name marked on the bell.

The steeple handles on these bells always attract special interest, and well they should. Forming them required the highest degree of adeptness and skill. When a glasshouse in Scotland experimented with an offhand order for eight large Bristol-type bells a few years ago, the director reflected afterward on the difficulties his glassblowers experienced in trying to shape graceful handles worthy of the bells, devoting far more time to this achievement than to fashioning the bells—and with only mediocre success.

of the dome in a thin border of enamel around the rim. More rarely the rim is stained to add a third color dimension. Clappers are usually of clear flint glass; but again, they may be swirled to match a handle or they may even be blown to show color loopings like those on the dome.

Though it is next to impossible to date and to attribute such bells with any degree of exactness, there are a few general observations that

PLATE I. *Mandarin hat-button bells. Bells one, two, and three in the foreground are from the Myrl Huene Collection; the others, from a private collection.*

PLATE II. *Collectibles in Meissen and Dresden bells, each clearly marked.* TOP ROW: *All except the one with gold striping are Meissen. The rarest are the figurine and the one with the applied flowers in the manner of Jacob Petit.* BOTTOM ROW: *The two Meissen bells here are in the onion pattern, also known as chinoiserie. One is in blue underglaze and the other in polychrome.* PRIVATE COLLECTION

PLATE III. *European glass bells in color.* TOP ROW: *Center bell of amethyst Spangle glass is by John Moncrief of Scotland. Typical Nailsea-type bell has white loopings. Typical Bristol-type has an expanded diamond pattern, sometimes called Venetian Diamond.* MIDDLE ROW: *The pink shaded cut glass bell is in Strawberry Diamond and Fan cut to clear.* BOTTOM ROW: *Bells of shaded pumpkin color and of mottled strawberry are by John Moncrief. Note the unusually deep ribbings in the green swirled glass.* PRIVATE COLLECTION

PLATE IV. *American glass bells in color.* TOP ROW: *The bells flanking the small Burmese bell have handle and dome molded in one. Made also in amber and green, by Imperial Glass Company, Bellaire, Ohio. Brief production was discontinued about 1958.* MIDDLE ROW: *Two bells at far left are a small one in Taffeta glass in Daisy Diamond pattern and a large one in Spanish Lace in opalescent Vaseline. Bell at far right is Custard glass, once a favorite ware for souvenirs decorated with local scenes. The scene on this bell is Harvey's Lake, Pennsylvania.* BOTTOM ROW: *Bell at far left is green Marble glass in Smocking pattern. To the right, a pink and white Spatter with opaque white lining, and a small Amberina in Daisy Diamond pattern.* PRIVATE COLLECTION

help. Color and pattern may offer somewhat helpful clues. Rightly or wrongly, diamond patterns are associated with Bristol just as latticinio work, or loopings, is with Nailsea. Bristol is also credited with perfecting its own special shades of red for its glasswares. This color was at first made with gold, which gave it a desirable rich purple-violet tint. Later the formula was changed, giving the red more of a ruby cast. There was also a cherry red color perfected at Bristol in 1765. These differences can be noted even in a small grouping of Bristol red bells made at varying periods throughout the eighteenth and nineteenth centuries.

Size may be a clue to age, for these glass bells apparently were made larger and larger with the passing years. Some late Victorian ones measure eighteen inches at the base. By the same token, very small Nailsea or Bristol bells are genuinely early nineteenth century. Perhaps the only other potential clue to age may lie in the handle. Cut glass was already being used in the 1780s and some of the early small bells were styled with cut glass handles. The combination at first glance appears incongruous, but in reality it gives reasonable proof that the bell may be an early one.

The fragile beauty of Nailsea-type bells has given rise to conjectural thoughts on how they were used. They are often mistakenly labeled "wedding bells," implying that they were produced chiefly as wedding gifts. An old print showing a tall glass bell holding a gentleman's wig once led to the notion that the bells were popular for such a purpose. Despite their fragile appearance, however, evidently they could serve as call bells on occasion. According to a historical account of Georgian England, by about 1810 "glass bells with a ruby red body, clear clapper and opal handle topped with a blob of peacock blue were being used to summon servants—although in all fairness, it must be said that such bells had been made at Bristol as early as 1755."

The bells could well have been used in these and other ways in many instances, yet prevailing opinion looks upon them as largely decorative. This would explain why Nailsea-type bells are frequently found in pairs. Popular pieces of Victorian furniture featured shelves framing a mirror on the top level. Even the simple country parson's fire grate might have such shelves over the grate. Glass and china objects were set in pairs on these shelves, one to each side of the mirror. In some cases, the pairs of bells were referred to as "lady and gentleman" bells and were companion pieces rather than identical pairs. They might match in body, for instance, but their handles would differ, the taller one being on the gentleman bell.

English glass bells, always beautiful to behold, are by no means the only ones that appeal to collectors. In fact, European countries were skilled in producing fine bells of glass long before England had mastered the art. In the Netherlands they can be traced to the end of the sixteenth or to the early seventeenth centuries. Mr. Paul Perrot, director of the Corning Museum of Glass, calls attention to the fact that in some of these earlier bells the sound is produced not by a clapper but by a metal bell in the handle, the bell vessel itself having been used as a glass. Some, rather than having bells only, also have whistles built in; sometimes, a combination of both.

These earliest European bells are of colorless glass; until about 1825, transparent colorless glass with engraved and cut decorations was the main product of glassmakers in most parts of Europe. There was no real European revival of the ancient Mediterranean techniques in colored glass until the 1820s, when the Bohemians first began to experiment with color. It was then that they invented their overlay glass, with patterns cut through the colored surface down to the clear base.

As most collectors are aware, Bohemian-type glass does not necessarily come from Bohemia. The techniques of glassmaking that originated there were more or less universally practiced all over Europe by 1830. Insofar as can be determined, however, the Bohemian invention of

136. An elegant six-paneled French glass bell, topped by an ormolu crown and orb, is heavily enameled with Oriental scenes in shades of pink and green. MOSLEY COLLECTION

overlay glass with a milk white layer over color, cut to a third layer of clear, suffered less competition than its later invention of flashed glass. This may be explained in part because overlay requires a more expensive operation, especially if the thick opaque white layer is enameled. Flashed glass has only two layers, with but a thin layer of colored glass to be cut through or etched. In any event, bells of milk white overlay glass are accepted as Bohemian, whereas examples of flashed glass are known to come from other countries as well as from Bohemia.

Examples of bells in flashed glass include those in the widely familiar deer-and-castle pattern. Originally produced only in ruby, the pattern is seen today in blue and in amber as well. In a few collections there are bells of the deer-and-castle pattern that bear a signature and the date 1876 etched in the glass, both of which marks appear to be genuine. Although documentation is lacking, it is reasonable to believe that these bells with the etched date 1876 may have come from the Bohemian-

Czechoslovakian exhibits at the Philadelphia Centennial in that same year. Many writers of the day stated that the Bohemian glass display "was superior to anything of its kind to be seen" at the centennial. Those exhibits were, in fact, credited with bringing Bohemia's fine colored and decorated glass its international fame.

Other colored glass bells were enameled with Mary Gregory figures, a type of decoration that is sometimes said to have originated in America. These are also made in several European countries, including Bohemia. They come in a variety of colors and their quality and their artistry vary considerably. (*See* Color Plate VII.)

Shortly after the Bohemians launched into experimenting with colored glass, the Venetians in Murano revived the color techniques that had once brought them fame during the Renaissance and the Baroque periods. Latticinio, with its threads of glass worked into fine patterns; millefiori, with its designs of little flowers embedded in the glass; and aventurine, with its spangles of metallic particles throughout the glass—all these became popular. They, along with Bohemia's experiments, encouraged the spreading taste for elaborate colored glass. Modern Venetian glass bells can be had in an amazing variety, for they are a popular Murano export.

With both Bohemia and Venice as models, French glassmakers began producing copies of all they saw. Not until mid-century did French colored glass become original and elegant in its own right, starting with the early Baccarat glass made by a firm founded in 1765 at Baccarat, France. Other famous names in French glassware evolved over the next one hundred and fifty years. These include Émile Galle and the Daum Brothers of Nancy, as well as the Schneider firm in Épinay-sur-Seine and the famous Lalique firm noted for its crystal with a lustrous satin finish. Bells were once designed in all the aforementioned types of French glass, and a few are being produced even today by firms that are still operating. Lalique crystal dinner bells are internationally advertised, and are appealing to collectors because of their ornamental handles. The current design shows a little nightingale of satin glass.

Collectors wisely realize that not all modern bells need be considered reproductions, for many of them have been made more or less continuously over the years. Yet there is sometimes a hesitancy to show such modern-day glass in a collection comprised largely of antique bells. A simple solution to the dilemma lies in keeping these contemporary bells in proper perspective, admitting they are collectible but not displaying them as antique. To deny them a place is to deny a collector the pleasure of seeing and touching a Bohemian overlay glass bell or a Venetian threaded-glass beauty perhaps made, in some instances, by the descendants of the very artisans who once experimented and developed the techniques for perfecting them. After all, early specimens of European glass bells are rarely found today outside of museums. Even examples of early twentieth-century bells from European glasshouses become more difficult to find with each passing year.

BELLS IN A SERIES

A few types of old European bells were made in a series, so to speak, and the challenge here is to acquire the entire set, if possible. A top favorite is a series of small flint glass bells, each with a different figure as the subject for its handle. Little is known about these except that they are French glass, some green and others amethyst. At first there were judged to be five or six subjects in the series; then collectors began speaking of a complete set of nine. Now at least thirteen are known, so there is reason to believe still more will eventually appear.

Though tiny, the enameled bronze handles on these bells capture their subjects with a precision and a wit reminiscent of the work on Vienna bronze miniatures. Each figure is unmistakable. Another delightful feature of these charming bells is seen in the clever coordination between each handle and clapper: a rabbit handle, a carrot clapper; a robin handle, a cherry clapper; or a cat and mouse combination.

More is known of the history and origin of at least one series in the little bells of Royal Bayreuth china. This is the sunbonnet babies series, designed from the "Infant Industries of the Week" oils painted by Bertha L. Corbett, a Minnesota artist of the 1900s. Miss Corbett had originated these figures to illustrate her book *The Sunbonnet Babies,* published in 1900. Later she was invited to collaborate with Eulalie Osgood Grover, and together they published in 1902 *The Sunbonnet Babies Primer* and its sequel *The Sunbonnet Babies Book.*

Those little babies with their faces never revealed became vastly popular. In 1904, J. J. Austen & Company of Chicago brought out a set of color cards taken from Miss Corbett's original oil paintings of the sunbonnet babies, and this series was among the first of the sunbonnet designs used by the Royal Bayreuth firm to decorate their line of children's china. The original six scenes show the babies busily at work on washing day, ironing day, mending day, scrubbing day, sweeping day, and baking day. This last scene is reputedly one of the rarest, not only on the bells but also on other pieces of the china.

The company decorated its bells with at least two other sunbonnet scenes, one showing the girls fishing and the other showing them on their way to church. The babies dressed in their dark winter outfits also appear on bells as the snow babies.

The nursery rhyme series of bells includes scenes involving such favorite characters as Jack and Jill, Little Boy Blue, Little Bo-Peep, Little Miss Muffet, and children dancing Ring-Around-the-Rosie.

Although not precisely in a series, there are also several floral and scenic styles of Royal Bayreuth bells in tapestry, a finish named for its resemblance to needlepoint tapestry. This effect was obtained by wrapping the piece in a coarse cloth before firing. The cloth was burned

137. *The coordinated handles and clappers are easily identified on these charming flint glass table bells in either green or amethyst. The bells above, conspicuously marked* FRANCE, *are from the Spear Collection. There are rumors but no firm information about a bell similar to these being also marked as Baccarat glass. (The other bells on these two pages are from the Moxon, Moseley, Vosburgh, Huene, and Torrance collections and a private collection.)*

138. *The set of color cards taken from Bertha Corbett's original series of oil paintings entitled "Infant Industries of the Week." These are the scenes Royal Bayreuth adopted to decorate their line of children's china. Verses based on the series* *are not consistent in assigning the babies their tasks on certain days of the week. The order shown here is taken from a verse copyrighted in 1907—washing day, ironing day, mending day, baking day, scrubbing day, and sweeping day.* PRIVATE COLLECTION

139. *The Sunbonnet Babies as they appear on little Royal Bayreuth bells. The last bell showing the girls fishing is not included in Miss Corbett's original series.* PRIVATE COLLECTION

the figure of a red devil. It is extremely rare and markedly different in shape compared with the other bells of this ware.

The lack of a mark on Bayreuth bells is not significant. For one thing, their form is an awkward one to accommodate the company's rather large crest. For another, much Bayreuth porcelain was sent out unmarked, or sometimes only one piece in a set would be marked. When it does appear the crest will differ from piece to piece, since it was frequently modified. Most of the blue marks were sent to America, whereas

away in the heat, leaving an unusual tapestry-like finish to be decorated. The rose tapestry pattern and the sunbonnet figures are two of Royal Bayreuth's most popular decorations.

In addition to all these, Royal Bayreuth china includes one bell among its pieces employing

140. *Bells from Royal Bayreuth's nursery rhyme series. Rarely do these have the rhyme on the reverse side, as on this Jack and Jill bell, from the Paul S. Fisher collection. The Little Boy Blue bell is from the Louise Dilts collection.*

141. *Royal Bayreuth bell in tapestry. The softly colored scene is of a fashionable lady standing beside her riding horse.* MOXON COLLECTION

the green marks went principally to England.

Current prices on Royal Bayreuth are spiraling, and it seems unbelievable that the little sunbonnet bells and other children's pieces once sold for a few cents in the five-and-ten. In view of the present heightened interest in bells of this porcelain, it seems equally unbelievable that as recently as 1960 at one of the nation's largest antiques shows two Bayreuth bells went begging at eleven dollars each. But no more! Today these little treasures sometimes sell for ten times that price.

From 1946 to 1959 a few novelty items were again made at the Bayreuth factory, but this revival of production proved too costly and all operations of this sort have been discontinued in favor of more functional creations. There is no firm information as to whether or not bells were among the novelties produced during this interval.

Sets of French bells ornamented with nautilus shells are seen in a number of collections. Of the three most popular designs, one has a gilded bird finial; one, a candle cup; and another has a small oval mirror flanked by twin perfume holders. It is this last variation that gives collectors a clue as to the original use of these bells. They obviously were designed for m'lady's vanity table.

Another set of French bells is similarly designed but with little reverse paintings on glass replacing the nautilus shells. The most common one of the set shows three scenes at the famous Grotto de Lourdes, the gilded finial being the figure of Our Lady of Lourdes. Scenes on other bells in this series are not necessarily French. One shows famous Holy Land sites.

Moving into the realm of European metal bells, a series of old German mechanicals introduces a bit of humor into the collection. Each is a sculptured head encasing a bell. Except for

142. *The extremely rare red devil bell in Royal Bayreuth porcelain has gold numbers on the money sack. Nearly six inches in height, it is considerably larger than other bells of this ware. The clapper, unlike those of rounded wood in the smaller bells, is of porcelain and wedge shaped.* RUTH ANDERSON COLLECTION

143. Above: *The two end bells may be part of a series designed around riding motifs. They are reputed to be trophies for polo matches. At center is a bell from a French series employing small scenic reverse paintings on glass—in this instance, scenes of the Grotto de Lourdes. Bell at far left is from the Myrl Huene Collection; others from a private collection. Below: Three bells from a French series designed around pearly nautilus shells. The bell with a mirror and perfume holders is from the Baxter Collection; others, from a private collection.*

the head of Satan, these bells usually represent familiar creatures of the animal world. A push on the nose or the beak or the tongue, as the case may be, releases the bell.

The large family of Hemony bells may be said to constitute another series of European bells, but unfortunately they also constitute an enigma of the first magnitude. The great majority of these are heavily embossed around the rim with the words F. HEMONY ME FECIT ANNO 1569. However, Franz Hemony, with his brother Pieter, was an illustrious bell founder in the Netherlands during the seventeenth, not the sixteenth, century. And there can be no thought of an error on Franz's part in casting the date. Being

the notedly conscientious workman that he was, he would never have permitted this to escape his attention.

Curators of European museums, particularly those in the Netherlands, therefore agree that the Hemony bells can in no way be attributed to that famous family of bellmakers. Rather, they are spurious castings from careless bellmakers wanting to capitalize on the name *Hemony*. To quote from a letter written by Dr. W. van der Elst, a foremost Hemony-connoisseur:

> The table bells you name are also acquainted in Holland. They are mystification of this century, made by an unscrupulous founder who did not know the just dates of our famous founder.

To compound the complexity collectors face in ascertaining facts on these bells, there are several puzzling variants; and even on the usual Hemony bells, at least on the smaller ones, the ornamentation almost defies interpretation. The wild characters in bottle-shaped reliefs must surely represent vestiges of some old custom, but an acceptable interpretation has yet to be given. Variant inscriptions such as this appear on bells ordinarily carrying the name Hemony: JACOVES SERKE HEFT MY GHEGOTEN A° 1370. Translated, this reads "Jacob Serke has cast me in the year 1370." Yet among the names of over five hundred Dutch bell-founders that of Serke does not appear!

And variant dates are no less confusing. Many such bells are dated 1569, but others are dated 1669. Collectors would like to feel that the 1669 date falls within Franz Hemony's lifetime and that he therefore might have cast certain of the bells bearing his name; but his life spanned only the years 1609 to 1667.

The variant dates on Hemony bells are easier to accept for collectors who are willing to acknowledge that they could be the result of slipshod casting and careless copiers combined. As an example, an imperfectly cast date of 1570 could well have been copied by later and careless founders as 1370. It is difficult on many of

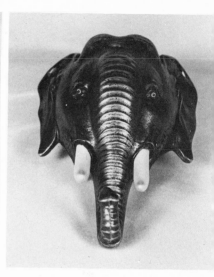

144. *Old German mechanical bells. Pressing the nose, beak, or tongue rings the bell. Cat bell is from the Cooper Collection; owl, the Ringland Collection; dog, the Breese Collection; the elephant, the Conard Collection.*

145. *One of the few German mechanicals depicting a head other than animal.* VOSBURGH COLLECTION

147. *The same "sad-faced queen" but with a very different ornamentation and inscription—an armorial shield showing a lion rampant and below this the name* ROELAND *heavily embossed.* MC KINNEY COLLECTION

146. *The "sad-faced queen" Hemony bell, ornamented with a deeply carved band of instrumental cherubs and the inscription* F. HEMONY ME FECIT ANNO *1569. Two indistinguishable maker's marks are impressed on the back.* PRIVATE COLLECTION

148. *Like others of the larger Hemony bells, this one has distinctive figures and scenes unique to its design. One man is seen leading a hound, while knights on horseback are jousting. Inscribed* F. HEMONY ME FECIT ANNO *1565. Handle features a Russian bear supporting a shield with the Russian emblem of arm-and-hammer in bold relief.* PRIVATE COLLECTION.

149. *Three Hemony bells with the usual decoration and inscription found on the smaller sizes. Only the dates vary. Figural handles are those of a turbaned knight, a wandering minstrel, and a crowned bear holding a shield showing a lion passant, as on the armorial crest of King Richard the Lion-Hearted.* MC KINNEY COLLECTION

151. *Detail of the young warrior in* 150, *who probably represents a member of the Children's Crusade of 1212. He wears a helmet, a tunic of chain mail, and high boots, and holds a club in one hand and in the other a shield with a heart-pierced-with-arrow in relief. A quiver attached to a shoulder strap rests against his side.* WALTERS COLLECTION

150. *Three Hemony bells of like decor and inscription, all dated 1669. The two end bells (flanking the young warrior) show a mythical bird or gargoyle and the upturned face of a man sporting a goatee. These two are examples of Hemony bells to be found with numerous variations in their features and in the proportions of their figures, thus suggesting that the bells were cast by many different makers.* PRIVATE COLLECTION

152. *Hemony bell with handle depicting ugly hooded head of undetermined significance. Dated 1370. Like almost any of the smaller bells in this category, this bell may be found either with the usual Hemony inscription or with the words* JACOVES SERKE HEFT MY GHEGOTEN A° 1370. *Among collectors, bells carrying this inscription are termed "Serke" bells to distinguish them from their "Hemony" counterparts.* MRS. STANLEY STEWART'S COLLECTION

153. *Uncommon Serke bell depicting scenes of Adam and Eve and Paradise. Handle is a serpent wound around a tree trunk. Inscription is the typical Serke wording but with the date clearly given as 1576.* MARION SPENCE COLLECTION

154. *Replica of the Great Bell of Moscow, showing its famous crack. Also seen are the figures of Alexis Michaelovitch and, in profiles above, Our Lord with the Holy Evangelists. Late nineteenth century.* RINGLAND COLLECTION

the bells to distinguish between a 5 and a 3. Similarly, the date 1569 could have been carelessly interpreted by some copiers as 1669, for it is also sometimes difficult to distinguish between a 5 and a 6 in the casting.

Regardless of their many puzzling features, Hemony bells continue to attract collectors because they present a series of most unusual handles. Some are stylized; others are realistic portrayals of a Russian bear, a bagpiper, a crusader or a mailed fist—to mention only a few. The fact that the figures on these bells represent different cultures has led many to believe they were cast in various European countries. This theory is substantiated by markings in some instances.

As to dating bells in this series, it is pointless to persist in trying to distinguish a copy from an original when obviously there never were any originals. Still no one can deny that some examples are far older than others and that the workmanship on some is far superior. Hemony bells began to appear in American collections at the close of the First World War. Several were brought back by soldiers at that time and were stamped either MADE IN ENGLAND or MADE IN BELGIUM. Shortly thereafter, advertisements for Hemony bells appeared in one or two American publications.

Interestingly enough, it is quite likely there are more Hemony bells in America today than in the Netherlands, which is supposedly the land of their origin. Following the Second World War, an American picked up in a London street-market one of these bells that collectors (for want of a correct epithet) laughingly label the "sad-faced queen." When the gentleman showed it to several Amsterdam dealers who handled hundreds of bells, they exclaimed they had never seen its like.

COPIES OF EUROPE'S FAMOUS BELLS

Replicas of world-famous bells lead to factual backgrounds so seldom available for most bells, and in this way they enliven the past for collectors. Certainly this is true of replicas made in the likeness of the Great Bell of Moscow. Popularly known as the Czar Kolokol, or King of Bells, and sometimes as the Czarina Kolokol, or Queen of Bells, this giant weighs nearly two hundred tons and measures nearly twenty feet high.

It was to have been heard for one hundred miles, but it never rang because, before it could be permanently placed, a large seven-foot section cracked off during the Moscow fire of 1737; the colossal bell plunged to the ground, where it lay for a century. Napoleon and his marshals must have gazed down on the fallen giant from the Tower of Ivan rising beside it. Napoleon was fond of the view from this tower, and history records that bells, wherever they might be, never escaped his attention.

Small replicas of the King of Bells are cast showing only a line to indicate the break in the

original; otherwise their tone would be impaired. All other surface features are faithfully duplicated, however, and this is all the more remarkable considering the high degree of artistic perfection in the lavish embellishments on the original.

Those embellishments are described best in the words of Auguste de Montferrand, the engineer who oversaw the raising of the bell to its present pedestal in 1836:

> Considered as a work of art, this bell is remarkable for the beauty of its form and for its bas-reliefs, which are of the schools of Bouchardon and of Coysevox. These bas-reliefs represent the portraits, at full length and of natural size, although not finished, of the Tsar Alexis Michaelovitch and the Empress Anna Ivanovna. Between these two portraits, upon two cartouches surmounted by angels, two inscriptions are dedicated, roughly sketched, of which only a few words without connection are legible. The upper part is ornamented by figures representing our Lord, the Virgin, and the Holy Evangelists. The upper and lower friezes are composed of palms, treated in a broad style, and with a great deal of art.

The Czar Kolokol now stands in the grand square of the Kremlin on an octagonal base of granite. Engraved in gold Cyrillic characters on the base is the bell's history in brief. On a few replicas, bits of this history are inscribed in Russian around the inside of the lip.

THIS BELL
CAST IN 1733, UNDER THE REIGN OF THE EMPRESS
ANNA IVANOVNA
AFTER HAVING BEEN BURIED IN THE EARTH FOR
MORE THAN A CENTURY, WAS RAISED TO THIS PLACE
4th AUGUST, 1836,
BY THE WILL AND UNDER THE GLORIOUS REIGN OF
THE EMPEROR NICHOLAS THE FIRST

Copies of the famous Kaiser's *Glocke* of Cologne Cathedral also exhibit artistic perfection in their details so faithfully reproduced. A victorious war gave the world this famous bell and a disastrous war destroyed it. The *Glocke* was cast in 1874 from twenty-two cannon captured from the French during the Franco-Prus-

155. *Singularly fine copy of the Kaiser's* Glocke, *which is seldom found with such a handsome mounting. Late nineteenth century.* HAMLIN COLLECTION

sian War; then in the First World War this beautiful old bell was melted down for German guns and munitions to use against the French.

156. *One of the most desirable copies of the Saint Peter's bell. When this replica is lifted, the full-bodied image of the fallen dove is seen lying in the center of the underplate. Late nineteenth century.* LA ROSE COLLECTION

The German inscription circling the top of the *Glocke* and each of its copies is translated to read:

THE KAISER'S BELL I AM CALLED,
THE KAISER'S HONOR I PRAISE,
ON HOLY GROUND I STAND,
I PRAY FOR THE GERMAN PEOPLE,
THAT PEACE AND PROTECTION
GOD WILL GIVE THEM

The nine-ton master bell hanging under the huge golden dome of Saint Peter's Basilica in Rome is considered by many the most beautiful bell in the world, so it is not surprising that replicas of it have long been desirable collectors' items. Here the desirability is based on a double consideration—again, a high degree of artistic perfection shown in the casting of the replicas and, in addition, the religious associations attached to the original.

Although they differ with respect to the styling of their finials, all replicas of the Saint Peter's bell show the Twelve Apostles around the skirt. The full-length figures stand in groups of three, each figure holding his ascribed emblem. For some it is the instrument of their martyrdom; for others it is the emblem of their office. The exact significance of the emblems is familiar to anyone versed in religious symbolism, though their exact origin is obscure. It is a reasonable assumption that they were introduced during the time of the Byzantine Empire, for apostolic iconography was popular then.

Like the original, the replicas display additional ornate figures and symbols above the heads of the Apostles. Here, hanging just under the shoulder of the bell, is a circle of pendent cathedral lamps signifying piety and wisdom or, in other words, spiritual light. Also just under the shoulder and on opposite sides of the bell are medallion busts of our Lord flanked by angels with uplifted wings, emblematic of the Church Triumphant.

Surmounting the top of the bell is a design representing the Pope's official headdress, or papal tiara. Supporting and encircling the tiara are serpents and four cherubs non-volant, who

157. *Two of the many variations among copies of the Saint Peter's bell. The variations appear only on the handle.* Left: *The cherub figures are seldom seen on replicas crowned with a cross. Here the artist has chosen to use a fleury cross.* Right: *Realistic modeling of the serpents and the supporting rope results in a handle of unusual interest. Late nineteenth century.* WALTERS COLLECTION; AND SPEAR COLLECTION, PETER WHITE MEMORIAL LIBRARY, MARQUETTE, MICHIGAN

are kneeling and pressing their hands on the heads of the serpents. Being combined as they are and symbolically antithetic, the cherubs and serpents illustrate the prophetic triumph of the Church over a world fallen through sin: IPSA CONTERET CAPUT TUUM, which is translated: "She shall bruise thy head."

In size and in finial design, replicas of the Saint Peter's bell vary considerably. The cherubs are absent on some, and there may or may not be a cross at the tip. Even when present, the cross may be one of several kinds. Occasionally the cross as a finial is replaced by an elongated handle of varying style. The most desirable of all the replicas, however, is the one resting on a matching plate. When the bell is lifted, a sculptured likeness of the fallen dove is revealed in the center of the plate, adding still greater significance to a bell already rich in religious symbolism.

Whether such replicas were cast before 1883 is not known; but at least collectors can be assured that some date back that far, for Sir Edmund Becket wrote of his model that year in his book *Clocks, Watches and Bells:*

I am told that the bell of St. Peter's at Rome sounds as ill as it ought to do from its extremely bad flower-pot shape; I have a model of it and it is loaded with ornaments in high relief, which are sure to injure the sound; but the shape is such that it is of very little consequence what the decoration is.

Reveling in the beauty of their own models, collectors are amused at Sir Edmund's lack of enthusiasm for his. Justified or not, so far as tone is concerned, his comments reflect the long-standing British prejudice against the slender flowerpot shape of many Italian and some Austrian tower bells.

According to official word from the Vatican Library, the most recent models of this bell were produced during the Holy Year 1950. It is logical to look ahead and hope that others will be issued commemorating the two hundredth anniversary of the final casting of the Saint Peter's bell. This accomplishment is attributed to the renowned Antonio Valadier in the year 1786, according to a copy of the official Vatican record stating: "La campana grande della Basilica Vaticana fu rifusa l'ultima volta nell' anno 1786 da Antonio Valadier."

158. A pair of Evangelist bells, larger than the average replicas of this type. The open-work carving adds to their beauty. The bells were originally suspended on a rod like a miniature shepherd's crook. Center bell is not a copy, but an old Armenian church chime newly mounted. A similar Armenian bell may be seen in the Smithsonian. PRIVATE COLLECTION

159. Lustrous porcelain copy of the 1936 Olympic Games bell shows all the decorative features of the original: the Reichstag building, the imperial eagle, and so forth. MOSLEY COLLECTION

Still another preeminent church bell that has been widely copied is the Evangelist type. This one is appropriately named, for it displays in relief the names of the Evangelists and their apocalyptic symbols: an angel for Matthew; a lion for Mark; for Luke, an ox; and for John, an eagle. There are conflicting opinions as to the origin of these symbols, most authorities crediting them to writers of the second century who based their selection on the opening content of each Gospel.

It is uncertain just which original is being copied in this case, since an Evangelist bell is attributed to cathedrals in both Belgium and France. A replica that was hand carved at the close of the First World War bears this inscription around its base:

THE BELL OF BRUGES CAST FROM THE PROPELLOR OF H.M.S. "VINDICTIVE" ZEEBRUGGE OSTEND APRIL 1918

At the same time an inkwell bell, also an Evangelist type, bears this inscription under its handle:

REIMS L'DAREL 1670 INF

Without a doubt there have been more rep-

licas made of the Evangelist bell than of any other great bell, and apparently they have been produced in several European countries. They can be found in assorted sizes and with assorted handles. A favorite among figures used on the handle is that of Saint Thérèse of Lisieux. There are also variations in the spelling of the Evangelists' names, depending on the country where the replicas were cast; but the most distinctive variation lies in the carving of the symbols. Some are in crisp relief on solid brass, but others are carved in part or in whole as open-work, giving a three-dimensional effect.

Small models of Europe's famous bells are not limited to copies of old ones. Many collectors show porcelain models of the Olympic Games bell and the Freedom Bell, both originating well within the present century. The Freedom Bell was dedicated in 1950, when it first rang from West Berlin's town hall as a symbol of the Crusade for Freedom on behalf of people behind the Iron Curtain. The Olympic Games bell has an especially memorable and, at the same time, regrettable story. When Germany organized the games for the XI Olympiad in 1936, this bell sounded the opening event. Suffering the vicissitudes of war, it never rang again but does stand on a pedestal as a memorial

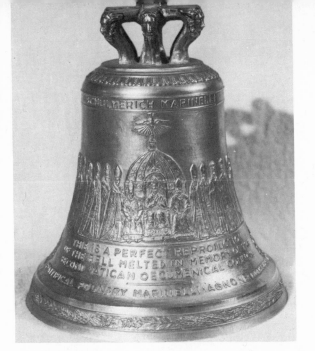

160. *Replica of the Second Ecumenical Council Bell, 1964, Vatican City, Rome. One of only twelve replicas cast by Marinelli in Agnone, Italy, from the metal of the original used at the council. Commissioned to be cast by Schulmerich Carillon, Inc., of Sellersville, Pennsylvania.* WINSTON JONES COLLECTION

at the south entrance of the Olympic stadium in Berlin. The lustrous porcelain replicas were limited in production to one for each participant in the 1936 games.

Neither are copies of Europe's famous bells limited to copies of large ones. There are two or three small table bells said to be copies of like ones created by Benvenuto Cellini, Italy's flamboyant master goldsmith of medieval days. Few collectors are in possession of an original bell from this master artist in gold and silver, but the copies give a glint of the superlative detailing that characterized his bells. The eminent English novelist Horace Walpole was fortunate in owning an original Cellini bell, and he wrote of his pride in acquiring it:

> One of the pieces in my collection which I value the most highly is the silver bell (made by Benvenuto Cellini) with which the Popes used to curse the caterpillars—a ceremony, I believe, now abandoned. Lahonton, in his travels, mentions a like absurd custom in Canada, the solemn excommunication of the turtle-doves, which greatly injured the plantations. For this bell I exchanged with the Marquis of Rockingham all my Roman coins in large brass. The rilievos, representing caterpillars, butterflies, and other insects, are wonderfully executed.

SOME ECCLESIASTICAL TYPES

The use of various small bells to punctuate religious services is an ancient custom dating back to the early centuries of the Church. These were only crude handbells at first. Then, as worship became more ritualistic, Sanctus bells were placed upon the altar. Starting with three short rings to punctuate the opening words *Sanctus, Sanctus, Sanctus,* the bells were used at several points throughout the Mass. From a functional point of view the Sanctus bell could be, and often was, a plain and unadorned bell resting on the altar. But because early artisans were obsessed with the desire to symbolize every aspect of church life, iconography characterized even the simplest of religious objects. Many of the Sanctus bells are loaded with symbolic images, and therein lies their appeal for the collector.

Three early examples are recognized and seen in collections, for although their originals are

161. *The stork bell in fine old silver, with an underplate. Note the slender profiles of the storks whose outspread wings form the skirt of the bell. Other symbolism is noticeable in the scallop shell motif (emblematic of Jesus' baptism) and in the fish forming the handle (in Christian art, emblematic of the Christ).* PRIVATE COLLECTION

162. *Two small but significant altar bells.* Left: *The bell associated with Martin Luther, whose symbol was the swan (Latin,* cygnus). Right: *The Crucifixion bell, showing in relief four ladders (associated with the Passion) and four creatures of Latin name associated with Christ's nature: pelican (sacrificial); lion (kingly); eagle (soaring, heavenward); lamb (suffering).* PRIVATE COLLECTION

163. *Old altar bell representing the Four Gospels (in the four bells under a single handle) and the harmony of those Gospels (in the singing birds on top). Bells are tuned, have multiple clappers, and are very melodious.* PRIVATE COLLECTION

164. *Two old Spanish altar bells.* Left: *Bell with matching plate and a cross pattée for its handle. Under the handle is an embossed eight-pointed star (associated with the idea of regeneration or baptism).* Right: *Eighteenth-century bell of exceedingly fine grained brass. Busts in high relief around the skirt are likenesses of saints.* PRIVATE COLLECTION

unknown their ornamentations have been quite commonly copied. One is the Crucifixion bell, so called because of the ladder repeated in the relief work around its surface. This was an early symbol associated with the Passion. Superimposed upon the ladders are four creatures representing the fourfold attributes of Christ. One is the pelican, symbol of Christ's sacrificial nature because the bird was believed to give its own lifeblood to nourish its young.

The most beautiful of these three early examples is the stork bell representing the legend of the stork at the birth of the Christ Child, when it plucked feathers from its breast to make the manger soft. The beauty of the bell lies in the designer's use of two bird figures to form the entire skirt with their outspread wings. The significance of the bell is strengthened by the use of other symbols associated with Christ, the most noticeable being the two fish forming the handle.

The third example shows in high relief two pairs of floating swans. Here the symbolism is based on illustrations from the medieval bestiaries that show swans singing even with their dying breath. In like manner the Christian martyrs sang their heavenly praises to the last. This particular bell is often associated with Martin Luther, since the swan came to symbolize his name. When John Hus was burned at the stake in the early fifteenth century he prophesied: "It is easy for you to burn this goose but the swan is coming whom you cannot burn." This prophetic utterance was applied to Luther by friend and foe alike; and his symbolic association with the swan was all the more respected because the coat of arms of the Elector of Saxony was a swan and Luther enjoyed the protection of this wise ruler.

With the development of European metal arts came the idea of multiple bells on the altar, some of them tuned. One of the most musical sets is Italian in origin, consisting of four bells suspended from a single handle. The handle is of bronze sculptured to resemble the branch of a tree, and at each of the four points where an arm of the branch holds a bell, a bird lifts its head in song. Symbolically the four bells represent the four gospels, and the birds, the harmony of the gospels. The bell is rung with a twisting motion of the wrist, and does indeed ring with a musical harmony indescribably beautiful.

The design of this altar bell supposedly derived from an earlier version having multiple bells suspended under a shell of pierced brass. Some very handsome specimens have been located in England, Germany, and Spain, indicating a rather widespread use of this particular type of altar appointment. Although a few of the piercings seem to follow a pattern, the work on the brass shells can also prove highly individualistic, the styles of the crosses and other emblems of the church evidently selected at will.

A third type of Sanctus, or altar, bell was introduced when artisans began designing a matching underplate for each bell. This not only enhanced the beauty of the bell but could also be used as a receiving plate for offerings. Particular attention was directed to altar bells of this description by the late Frank Miller, whose collection for many years graced the rooms and gardens of California's famed Mission Inn. Mr. Miller found a number of such altar pieces still in use throughout Europe, but observed that often the bell and its plate had been separated. His observation is all too true, so matching sets that have survived are naturally to be treasured.

Something quite different in the way of ecclesiastical bells appeared when the sacring bells on wheels came into use. Wheels of bells, designed to be rung at the elevation of the Host, were known elsewhere in Europe as early as the fifteenth century. One mounted on the walls in the German Abbey of Fulda carried one hundred and fifty bells. However, the smaller and portable sacring wheels were used primarily in Spain and to a lesser degree in Italy. These were the sacring wheels the Spanish padres brought with them to Mexico, much to the delight of their Indian converts. There is some basis for believing the wheel, as a religious object, commemorates Saint Catherine's martyrdom. Saint Catherine of Alexandria, patron saint of bell founders, was tortured on a wheel before being beheaded.

Still another ecclesiastical type is seen in the ornately beautiful bells on brackets. These are

165. *From Granada, Spain, a wheel of bells boasting a religious lineage dating to 1760, the year it was made. Originally mounted on a monastery wall, the wheel was salvaged when the monastery was demolished. Later, nuns rang the bells for a time, to lend a spirit of gaiety on their festive days. The notes are remarkably clear. Observe the wrought iron crank that operates the wheel. Total height of frame: 27 inches. Diameter of wheel: 16 inches.* RUTH ANDERSON COLLECTION

166. *The ornate Saint Mark's bell with its bracket. All parts are finished in silver. Two bands of Latin inscription suggest its former function to initiate prayers and sound the benediction.* PRIVATE COLLECTION

iage, and a stylized griffin ornaments the bracket. Incised around two smooth bands is a twofold Latin inscription, which when translated reads:

> OUR FATHER WHO ART IN HEAVEN
> THE LORD BE WITH THEE AND WITH THY SPIRIT

Most ecclesiastical bells afford the collector an opportunity to increase his appreciation of religious art as applied to metalwork. So many guides to religious symbolism are presently in print that it is a simple matter to find, for example, that choirs of angelic musicians encircling a bell were intended to symbolize eternal praise to God or that the eight points on a Maltese cross represent the eight Beatitudes.

Inscriptions are a study in themselves. Often they constitute a clue to the former function of an ecclesiastical bell, as they do on the Saint Mark's bell—clearly indicating that it was used to mark the moment for prayer and to signal the benediction. Other inscriptions may be merely dedicatory, honoring a particular saint, or may exhort in some way. In the dispersal sale of the Knowlton collection of some years ago, a large Sanctus bell had this appropriate but unusual inscription chased around its rim: SATANUS VADE RETRO (Satan, get thee behind me).

On very old Sanctus bells, however, attempting to decipher an inscription can be frustrating. Early founders, whether working with Latin or with their mother tongue, were sometimes ignorant or careless in the matter of spelling, and many eccentricities can be found on small

associated with European monasteries and are characterized by Latin inscriptions and heavy rococo decorations, often involving allegorical figures from the medieval bestiaries. A noted example of this type and one much sought after by collectors is the Saint Mark's bell. Deeply carved musical figures decorate the body of the bell, intermingled with profuse scrolls and fol-

167. *Three old brass ecclesiastical bells.* Left: *Ornamented with a choir of angelic figures and, interspersed with Maltese crosses, a beautiful Latin script that says* GLORY TO THE FATHER, THE SON, AND THE HOLY SPIRIT : : FOREVER AND FOREVER, AMEN. Center: *Eighteenth-century altarpiece with four bells under a pierced shell.* Right: *Inscribed* QUI ME TANGIT : VOCEM MEAM AUDIT (*Who rings me : hears my voice*). PRIVATE COLLECTION

168. *A pair of* rimonim *hung with bells, formerly used as finials on the two rods holding the Torah scroll read in the temple.* THE HEBREW UNION COLLEGE MUSEUM

bells as well are large. HALLELUJAH may appear as HALALUGEVA; or the letters may be quite jumbled according to no rule at all, as on an altar bell with a cock for its handle and these Latin words around the base: SANC IRT EP IT. They are meant of course to spell SANCTI PETRI.

Why, no one seems to know, but bell founders occasionally reversed the order of their inscriptions. If completely baffled over a translation, collectors might try reading the letters in reverse. Then a meaningless line like this falls neatly into place:

6261: IN : IM : OD : ON : NA :
ANNO DOMINI 1626

One other use of small religious bells in the Old World should not be overlooked, and that is on the principal religious objects in the Jewish synagogue. The Torah, or scroll containing the books of Moses, is bound on two rods topped with carved silver finials. The finials are termed *rimonim* and are often elaborately decorated with bells. Sometimes carved crowns hung with bells substitute for the *rimonim*. In either case

169. *Hebrew spice box ornamented with bells. Silver filigree. Warsaw, circa 1860–1870. Signed: I. Perlman.* THE JEWISH MUSEUM, NEW YORK

170. *Ancient Dutch bell, wind-mill form; designed by R. M. Lancelot.*

the use of bells here is considered more ornamental than symbolical. Some Jewish scholars feel that their use can be traced back to the biblical admonition decreeing bells for the high priest's robe; but most look upon them as decorative devices designed to give a royal importance to the Torah that it may be heard as well as seen when it is carried into the synagogue.

On rare occasions *rimonim* and also Torah crowns are offered for sale at leading galleries, but most of them have long since found their way into museum collections. Interested private collectors are more likely to find one of the bell-decorated Hebrew spice boxes. These of course belong in the home, where for centuries they have been used with other religious objects in observing the Sabbath.

ODD AND ELEGANT SILVER BELLS

Bells of silver enjoy what might be looked upon as a royal heritage. One of the earliest mentions of decorative handbells is found in an inventory of personal effects belonging to Charles V of France and dated 1380. Listed among those effects is one "little silver bell which had been the property of Queen Je-

171. *English dinner bell of swirled crystal with silver-plated handle and overlay. These three pieces are held together by a long screw from which is suspended a clapper of silver plate. Bears the London hallmark for the years 1897/98. Reverse of handle is shown. Obverse has a space for a monogram where the bird is shown here.* WALTERS COLLECTION

banne." Another royal inventory mentions the ill-fated Mary Stuart possessing a "silver bell which stood upon her majesty's table." Until the end of the seventeenth century, in fact, small silver bells were rarely possessed by other than royalty. In 1650 the knowledge that a lesser nobleman had a silver bell upon his desk was cited as proof of his eccentric conceit!

Among the finest of early European silver bells are those from Holland. In a country noted for its famous silversmiths from an early date it is not surprising that some turned their talents to designing beautiful table bells. A most desirable specimen is a silver Dutch windmill in bell form, dating back to the period of Ostade and Teniers. It is a faithful depiction, even to the figure of the miller toiling up the steps.

For many centuries glassworkers have enhanced their works of art with mountings of silver, the glass article at first being made to the desired shape and the silver mount then fashioned to fit its form. In 1884 a German artist patented an easier means for encasing glassware, whereby the glass could be blown directly into open metalwork ornamentations, which could then be plated with silver. A number of English firms took out patents that more or less duplicated the German method, and soon metal-mounted glassware was being universally produced. Silver-encased glass bells were numbered among the pieces. The mountings on some are of the same pattern used for matched place settings on the table—the knives, forks, and spoons.

In addition to these more sizable silver bells favored by collectors, there are any number of silver tintinnabula to be sought. Among these are the little good-luck bells from the Isle of Capri, with an engraving of a four-leaf clover; tiny silver tokens in the shape of Canterbury bells, the flowers named for the bells Chaucer's pilgrims wore on returning from their pilgrimage to Canterbury; or small John Newbery bells, though these can easily go unrecognized. Known best today for the children's book award in his name, John Newbery, the British book publisher, was best known to children of his day for the small bells and pincushions he gave as presents to his young customers.

Small silver bells have long been the prerogative of church dignitaries, as they once were of royalty. A cardinal's silver bell still rings in the Vatican each mid-morning, summoning "bearded patriarchs and red-sashed prelates" to the world's most unusual coffee break.

The miniature silver bells once worn or carried by priests are referred to as 'Tantony bells, or more properly Saint Anthony bells, derived from the fact that this saint was usually represented with a small bell at the end of his staff. Sometimes it was suspended instead from the neck of his strange companion, a pig. With the help of his bell Saint Anthony was reputed to have a most singular power over spirits of evil. This virtue was often extolled in medieval art and literature. In a sixteenth-century comedy one of the characters comes on stage proclaiming:

> Good Christian people, I am come hither verelye
> As a true procture of the house of St. Anthonye.
> Lo, here is a belle to hange upon your hogge
> And save your cattell from the bytynge of a dogge.

OLD INSTRUMENTAL BELLS

For those who are attracted to bells used as musical instruments, the collecting possibilities are limited; yet each instrument acquired is certain to have some distinctive quality, and this fact alone compensates for the scarcity of such pieces.

Some percussion instruments are related to bells simply by virtue of having metal bars tuned to a definite pitch. The celesta with its light silvery tone is one of these, played by means of hammers controlled from a keyboard. The early celesta was often a very elegant little instrument suitable for tabletop playing, in a case inlaid with shell and pearl. Composers of the day considered it an instrument worthy of their musical efforts, and Tchaikovsky took the lead in writing solo passages especially suited to its elfin tinkle.

First cousin to the celesta is the glockenspiel, a frame of tuned bells to be held aloft and struck with two hammers. Sometimes metal bars substitute for bells, even in the early glockenspiel, but always of a metal that gives an appropriate bell-like sound. Mozart included parts for this instrument in his works.

Forerunners of the glockenspiel were the sistrums, but these were usually untuned and far less musical. They were not indigenous to Western European cultures but were used principally in Turkey, and at a relatively late date. Now and then one found its way into another country.

A most dramatic use of instrumental bells is found in one other Turkish musical device, one popular with their bands as they toured Europe in the eighteenth century. Each Turkish band boasted at least one schellenbaum, meaning "bell branch" or "bell tree." Fascinating to look at, the schellenbaum was also fascinating to hear. A gentle shake would set the bells tinkling and the jingles clashing lightly. It made a splendid addition to the already colorful Turkish military band, and in its way helped to create the craze for Turkish music that swept over Europe.

The strange-looking schellenbaum consisted of a carved pole about five feet long. On the top was a metal ornament shaped like a crescent and decorated with bells. Farther down came another ornament resembling a Chinese hat, with bells and jingles all around the edge. Sometimes there were other ornamental "branches" carrying bells and also long plumes of horsehair.

Carried by the bejeweled and beturbaned Turkish military bands, often on horseback, the

172. A type of schellenbaum carrying brass stars, crescents, and bells. Center rod slips into a sliding handle of wood. Europe, nineteenth century. MISSION INN, RIVERSIDE, CALIFORNIA

schellenbaum was looked upon as the most exotic instrument Europe had ever seen. It was widely imitated and here and there given other names such as the *chapeau chinois* (Chinese hat) or, in England, the jingling **Johnny**.

173. An objet d'art fashioned by Carl Fabergé, court jeweler to the Russian czars. The bell exemplifies the type of luxurious bibelots peculiar to the last years of imperial Russia and synonymous with the name Fabergé. Its pink and black rhodonite base enhances the beauty of the gold dome, decorated with acanthus leaves and foliate sprays above a border of filigree openwork. The bell push is an amethyst cabochon; the inner lining is of brass to give required pitch and volume to the bell. SPAULDING COLLECTION

174. Rivaling the work of Carl Fabergé, this Russian bell in ormolu is inlaid with seventy-two lapis lazuli gemstones. Surmounting the handle, cherubs support the crown and cross. CONARD COLLECTION

OTHER EUROPEAN TYPES

An almost endless array of other European bells can be counted from one collection to another. High on the list of favorites are bells of Russian origin. Choicest of these, of course, are bells from the nineteenth-century workshop of Carl Fabergé, eminent jeweler to the Russian czars; but there are others of undeniable beauty bearing the mark of jewelers working elsewhere in Russia. Like Fabergé, they admired the old Byzantine pieces and some of their bells are not unlike them in appearance, with restrained yet rich ornamentations.

Less glamorous but interesting in their own way are the heavy wheels of bells once used on ponderous old doors of a Mediterranean villa; the curious mechanical bells from German toymakers; and all manner of small bells having literary and sometimes historical associations.

175. An all-brass wheel of bells attached to a simulated rope issuing from a lion mascaron. Wheels of this sort decorated gates and entrances to villas of Southern Europe, a fact that contrasts oddly with the artist's conception of such a fierce and inhospitable lion. PRIVATE COLLECTION

Even the ordinary handbell has meaning if its use can be documented. It may be proven a family heirloom, rung fifty years ago by a child on Oranges-and-Lemons Day at Saint Clement Danes Church in London; for on that day, by ancient rite, Danish children rang handbells as they gave oranges and lemons to all youngsters at the church. Or the bell may have inscribed on it the initials of one known as the local muffin man or the postman. So many street vendors were using bells by 1850 in England that Parliament was forced to pass an edict prohibiting their use, yet vendors continued "ring-

176. *Three small brass bells of exceedingly detailed workmanship. Left: Desert scenes, sometimes interpreted as those from the Destruction of Sennacherib. Handle is the cloaked figure of a nomad standing on guard, dagger in hand. Center: Exceptionally fine-textured brass, resembling gold, in a bell with decorative features of classical connotation. Right: Although of English make, this is sometimes pointed to as a Cellini-type bell. Typical of London-made objects is the lion sejant affronté (that is, facing front and supporting a cartouche).* PRIVATE COLLECTION

177. *German designers never lacked for originality, as evidenced in such unusual tap bells as these. Left: Satan sits in an acid bottle in a wicker basket. The word* VITRIOL *is strung in bold letters across the front. Around the base a serpent twines, head biting tail. Satan's head pops up automatically after tapping device is depressed.* MC KINNEY COLLECTION. *Right: Expressive masks decorate this box-like bell that at first glance looks more like a bank or a music box. End panels show urns of flowers. Only wording is the German* DER MUSTER, *front and back.* MYRL HUENE COLLECTION

Handbells marking the epochs of war have a less happy association with history. Still, since wars are known to destroy many fine bells, both large and small, it is promising to realize that sometimes other bells are produced as a result of these same wars—either directly or indirectly. These can help to perpetuate memories of the events. Each British air-raid-precaution bell from the Second World War carries the initials A.R.P., and its blackened surface is mute evidence of the stories it could tell. Several companies cast them but those from Gillett & Johnston are the most sought for by collectors now

178. An angelic trumpeter forms the handle on this lavishly ornamented German pewter bell. Symbols surrounding the focal point of the date 1900 include an hourglass, a horn of plenty, and clasped hands with the words EAST, WEST, SOUTH AND NORTH. *Inscribed around the date, in German:* BLESSINGS ON YOUR HOME : : PEACE BE YOUR FIRST CONCERN. *Another inscription, in Latin, follows the rim of the bell.* RENICK COLLECTION

ing" their wares or their services well into the present century.

There are earlier handbells that reach the auction sales, documented as once the possession of a bellman, and as such they are part of a picturesque past that has appealed to poets and artists alike. The bellman was none other than the night watchman with a new title given him in Elizabethan days after a law was passed requiring him to carry a bell. At first he used his bell in a businesslike way to help proclaim the hours; but in true Elizabethan fashion he soon was waxing poetic and chanting his messages in rhythmic rhymes to the accompaniment of his bell, adding his own blessings and even personal salutations for his more noble masters.

179. Handsome silver and gilt bell with conventional design in studwork. Cameos on either side picture a man's and a woman's head in Teutonic armored headgear. Of uncertain significance. Signed: L. Ostermayr, Nurenberg. PRIVATE COLLECTION

180. *The V for Victory bell features the profiles of the leaders of the Allied forces in the Second World War: Churchill, Stalin, and Roosevelt.* PRIVATE COLLECTION

that this old company is no longer in existence. They can be readily identified by these marks:

A. R. P.
G & J
1939

It is almost traditional that in the aftermath of war certain patriotic groups start salvaging metals with a view to casting commemorative bells. The Royal Air Force did just that in designing what is called the V for Victory bell.

With three profiles in relief around its circumference, those of Churchill, Stalin, and Roosevelt, it commemorates that renowned triumvirate of leaders for the Allied forces. Around the base the inscription reads:

CAST WITH METAL FROM GERMAN
AIRCRAFT SHOT DOWN OVER BRITAIN
1939–45 R.A.F. BENEVOLENT FUND

181. *Included in this English town crier's paraphernalia is a neat leather holder for carrying his bell.*

5

The Search for Americana

EVEN WITHIN THE CONFINES of a single collectible like bells, the search for Americana can take many directions. Much depends on individual inclination. But regardless of the direction, whether it leads to early glass bells or to crudely crafted cowbells, those bells that represent the work of a known maker hold a special place of value in any collection of Americana.

To search intelligently for such pieces, at least a superficial knowledge of makers' names is required, the names of men and women whose chosen career was to design and make the bells once needed in America's schoolrooms and church sanctuaries, on its dining tables and desk stands. There were also those who specialized in making bells for livestock and horses, but they merit a chapter of their own.

It is uncertain just when the first small bells were cast in America. Colonial founders were primarily preoccupied with the demand for something larger to fill the empty belfries of America's churches and schools. But judging from a few of the earliest advertisements, there were founders who also cast whatever type of bell the customer wanted. Dated June 5, 1738, one such advertisement states that

> A Bell Founder, John Whitear of Fairfield, Conn., makes and sells all sorts of bells from lowest size to two thousand weight.

For the most part, however, the production of small bells did not get under way until the early nineteenth century when a host of specialized industries sprang up in the picturesque Connecticut Valley. The hub of activity here was in East Hampton, often called "Jingle Town, U.S.A" because of its reputation for supplying 90 per cent of the small bells used all over the world.

William Barton set the bells ringing in East Hampton when he established the first foundry there in 1808. His first product, a cowbell, rests today in the cornerstone of the town's Congregational Church. Before long he was branching out and making not only animal bells but other kinds as well. As business prospered, however, he soon began having formidable competition, first from Bevin Brothers, established in 1832; then, in succession, from the East Hampton Bell Company, Starr Brothers Company, Gong Bell Manufacturing Company, and the N. N. Hill Brass Company—this last firm not organizing until 1889.

These, then, were the major bellmakers of East Hampton; but all together more than thirty firms flourished there at various times, not to mention numerous others elsewhere in Connecticut. However, the demand for many of their inventions dwindled as the twentieth century progressed, and one by one East Hampton's bell factories closed, until today Bevin Brothers alone remains.

In their heyday the total output of the Connecticut companies resulted in an amazing va-

182. *Nineteeth-century handbells from East Hampton, Connecticut. Bell with wooden handle is double-chiming type patented by Ezra G. Cone and made by Gong Bell Manufacturing Company in several sizes (medium size shown). Diameter: 4 inches. The pair with brass handle and body cast in one are marked Barton & Starr.* PRIVATE COLLECTION

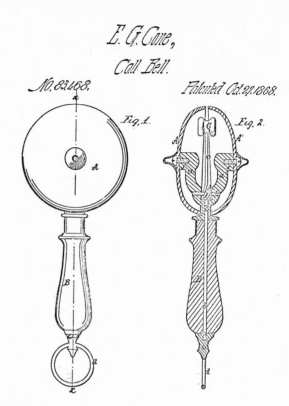

183. *Patent design submitted by Ezra G. Cone for his double-chiming bell.*

riety of utilitarian bells. And where are they now, collectors wonder. That is a fair question, considering the quantity in which they were made for the better part of a century. Nevertheless, for one reason or another, very few survive.

Unfortunately for the collector, even fewer bear their maker's name. Collectors wise enough to have acquired old catalogues from these companies—and others, too, for that matter—are of course in the best position to trace the make of whatever bells they may acquire from the Connecticut foundries.

Even with the help of a primary source like a catalogue and even when a bell is marked, it may still present a baffling identity. To illustrate: one such bell known to collectors is a solid brass handbell with a perforated brass handle marked Barton & Starr. To those familiar with East Hampton's history this mark is puzzling, inasmuch as the Bartons and the Starrs were competitors and veritable archenemies, as one historian expresses it. Subsequent research through a descendant of the Starrs, however, reveals a marriage tie between the two families; and although it still seems unlikely that the two ever actually collaborated in bell production, it is possible that some one of the five

Starr brothers and a Barton experimented with the idea. This might explain the BARTON & STARR mark; yet even if true, this conjecture still leaves the bell unique in the annals of East Hampton manufacture, and very likely places it before the year 1874 when the Barton Bell Company closed.

Sometimes a collector is fortunate in finding a dated specimen of a bell that ordinarily carries no marking. An exact date coupled with patient searching may lead to original patent papers; and when it does these will give undisputable facts on the who, where, and why of the bell's production—disillusioning facts sometimes, but indisputable nevertheless.

So it was in the case of the double-chiming handbell popular with collectors. This had long been accepted as a type belonging to the colonial town crier. Only recently were two of these found to have stamped on the handle the date Oct. 27, 1868. When patent records were located, they revealed that the inventor was Ezra G. Cone of East Hampton. This would

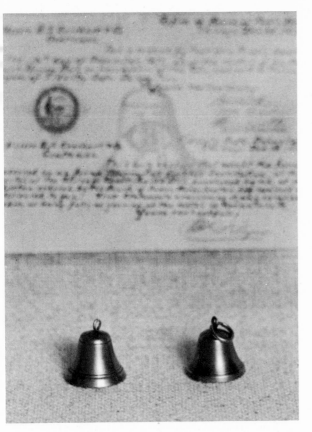

184. Tiny charms cast from the metal of the old Chicago courthouse bell, fallen in the Great Fire of 1871, are shown against their certificate of authenticity, written in a script difficult to decipher. PRIVATE COLLECTION

assign production to the Gong Bell Manufacturing Company of which Mr. Cone was an official; and, in his words, the bell was produced "for calling persons to their meals, having a more melodious sound than bells for the same purpose heretofore constructed."

Obviously this melodious handbell must have been used by any number of different persons, by schoolmarms as well as by street vendors and kitchen maids, but just as obviously the colonial town crier was not among that number. Surprisingly, this latter fact has had no adverse effect on the steadily climbing prices being asked for these double-chiming bells. Like others who have shared similar experiences, a past president of the American Bell Association used to enjoy recounting how, through an advertisement, he paid five dollars for his bell of this type, then watched subsequent advertisements climb to fifteen, thirty-five, and fifty dol-

lars. To cap his story, an over-the-counter sale was seen in a Vermont antiques barn recently where the same bell sold for one hundred dollars.

Bevin Brothers are known for their custom work in bellmaking, and from time to time they have been called upon to design and make memorial table bells. One that is highly prized is the Paul Revere memorial bell cast in limited quantity for Dr. William H. Vail in 1941. Dr. Vail issued a descriptive leaflet authenticating the fact that each bell contains particles from a shattered Paul Revere bell cast about 1798 for the Minot Ledge Lighthouse on Boston Bay.

After the Chicago fire of 1871, Bevin Brothers acquired from a manufacturing jeweler of that city a piece of the old courthouse bell that had fallen into the flames. They recast it in the form of tiny bells suitable to wear as charms. These are treasured because some of the metal in the old courthouse bell had come from the cannon used in defending Fort Dearborn in 1832, at the time of the famous Indian massacre.

A Chicago candy merchant for a time gave one of these miniatures in each box of his candy, and occasionally today one can be picked up for a modest price if it has become separated from the original certificate that accompanied each of the bells. With its certificate, however, the little bell brings a price well into two figures.

COMMEMORATIVES

Commemorative bells have a special way of keeping history alive for the collector. Events that seem far away when measured by the flight of time become real and vivid in the presence of bells designed for specific occasions in our nation's history. In this connection, the major fairs and expositions held all around the country years ago have proved a great boon to bell buffs. Each was commemorated in one or more bell forms, all of fine-quality workmanship and a few of quite ornate design.

The first of these events was the Centennial Exposition of 1876 held at Philadelphia's Fair-

185. *Miniature commemorative from the Centennial Exposition of 1876 shows crack, as in the Liberty Bell. It is suitably dated 1776 and 1876. Within the little supporting "beam" is a view of Machinery Hall on the Exposition grounds.* PRIVATE COLLECTION

mount Park, and here various small replicas of the Liberty Bell were sold. To correct a common misconception, none of these contains any particles of the Liberty Bell itself. The few replicas having grains of metal from the original bell had been made years earlier when workmen bored into the bell after it cracked, hoping to forestall further damage.

On May 1, 1893, the World's Columbian Exposition in Chicago opened and found itself in the grip of a collecting craze. The craze for historical glass was especially strong, having been generated by the many Liberty Bell items in glass at the Centennial of 1876. Two historical glass bells commemorate the Columbian Exposition. One has an etched design and the lettering WORLD'S FAIR 1893, with the additional lettering

WORLD'S COLUMBIAN EXPOSITION 1893 around the base of the frosted, swirled handle. Its companion has etched scenes of the landing of Columbus but no wording either under the clear, swirled handle or on the bell itself.

Because of their exceptional quality, these companion bells are often assumed to be from the glassmaking house erected on the exposition grounds by E. D. Libbey to publicize his company. In the light of expert opinion, however, there are two very good reasons for believing these are not examples of Libbey glass after all: (1) glass souvenirs made by the Libbey factory at the World's Fair, or sold there, were always inscribed with the company name, and (2) there is no evidence that Libbey ever made any glass bells commercially.

Indirectly the Columbian Exposition was responsible for the casting of perhaps the most handsome American commemorative bell known to collectors, and certainly one with a unique parentage. This is the Columbian Liberty Bell. The original of the same name, standing six feet tall and weighing more than six tons, had been purposely cast for the exposition at the special request of the Daughters of the American Revolution. Wishing to use the bell in promoting peace, members had asked that it be cast in the likeness of the Liberty Bell and appropriately inscribed with words of their own choosing.

As a patriotic gesture, people all over the world were invited to send contributions for the metal from which the bell would be cast. Silver

186. *Two colorless glass bells commemorating the World's Columbian Exposition of 1893. Both are often mistakenly identified as Libbey glass. Their manufacturer is unknown.* PRIVATE COLLECTION

PLATE V. *Animal bells from East and West. At left of the large Tyrolean cowbell is a llama bell on a colorful fur chain, from Peru; at right is an old Hindu cowbell on blue and white beads, from India. Headband of pear-shaped crotals, worn on a bullock's forehead between the horns, is also from India. Helmet-shaped water buffalo bell of shiny brass, profusely etched, is from Java. Wooden buffalo bell from Bali is painted with head of the Garuda bird, Indonesia's chosen symbol.* PRIVATE COLLECTION

PLATE VI. *Figurine bells in porcelain and pottery. Jenny Lind in ruffled skirt and poke bonnet* (FOREGROUND) *is the only one identifiable by name and the only one with a maker's mark. All date after 1940 except ladies in yellow stripe and in black polka dot dresses* (TOP ROW); *lady with cockatoo, Mr. Wizard, and Jenny Lind* (BOTTOM ROW). PRIVATE COLLECTION

PLATE VII. *Colorful modern glass bells available to collectors.* TOP ROW: *Two end bells are Venetian enameled glass; center is an American reproduction.* MIDDLE ROW: *Two center bells are Czechoslovakian Mary Gregory-type glass with enameled figures; bell at far left, also Czechoslovakian, has deer and castle etched design. Bell at far right with frosted ribbon stripe is Venetian.* BOTTOM ROW: *Gold filigree panel glass, Czechoslovakian; two Venetian bells in a diamond quilted pattern with white lining; white overlay type of glass, Czechoslovakian. (In modern parlance, Bohemian glass is often referred to as Czechoslovakian.)* PRIVATE COLLECTION

PLATE VIII. *Danish plates designed with bell theme.* TOP: *Small Royal Copenhagen Christmas plates, 1925.* BOTTOM: *Three Bing & Grondahl plates: regular series, 1934; jubilee issue, 1920; Easter, 1927.* PRIVATE COLLECTION

spoons by the hundreds and thimbles by the peck went into this peace bell. Many objects were historic. There was a copper kettle that had been Thomas Jefferson's, a surveyor's chain used by George Washington, and keys to the Jefferson Davis house. Said Chester Meneely, whose famous foundry at Troy, New York, cast the bell: "It came out all right although we were plenty skeptical when all those patriotic old relics started melting and became just so much lead, copper, silver and gold . . . to dull the tone."

The bell served its purpose on the exposition grounds; but when the Daughters of the American Revolution decided to take it on a patriotic tour, there was no bell to be found! Impossible as it may seem for a six-ton bell to disappear, no trace of it has ever been found.

Despite its disappearance this historic bell lives on in its commemoratives, each inscribed SOUVENIR COLUMBIAN LIBERTY BELL 1893 and each cast from the same molten metal that went into the original. As is customary while casting important bells, a quantity of the metal was kept out. This was acquired by the McShane Bell Foundry of Baltimore to cast the souvenir bells requested by the Columbian Liberty Bell Committee. The committee sold these to schools and issued a primer with each, suggesting appropriate use of the bell on various patriotic occasions.

As those who own this commemorative know, the bell is unusual, not only for its traceable and

187. One of the most handsome and storied of American commemorative bells, known as the Souvenir Columbian Liberty Bell, was cast in 1893 by the McShane Bell Foundry of Baltimore. FALCONER COLLECTION

historic background, but for its mounting with yoke and wheel in the manner of large turret bells, and for its disciplined tone. The McShane Bell Foundry, now well past its century mark and still operating, has always been noted for the fine tonal quality of its bells.

Both the Buffalo Pan-American Exposition of 1901 and the St. Louis World's Fair of 1904 are commemorated in sturdy brass bells made from historic metal of a different sort. The inscription on each coinlike handle tells the story. On the

188. Bells commemorating America's fairs and expositions. The bells with eagle finials commemorate the Centennial Exposition of 1876. The two suspended in frames, the California Panama–Pacific Exposition of 1915. Bell with coinlike handle, from the Saint Louis World's Fair, is made from metal recovered from the battleship Maine. PRIVATE COLLECTION

189. *One of the fifty bells cast in the 1840s to commemorate a special run on the Boston and Maine Railroad. The eagle finial depresses to ring the bell under a shell representing the rock-bound coast of Maine, above a circle of thirteen flag shields.* PRIVATE COLLECTION

St. Louis bell the obverse and the reverse sides are inscribed as follows:

THE BRASS IN THIS
BELL
WAS RECOVERED FROM
THE WRECK OF THE
MAINE
DESTROYED IN
HAVANA HARBOR
FEB. 15, 1898

and

REMEMBER
THE MAINE
DESIGNED FOR THE
WORLD'S FAIR
ST. LOUIS, MO.
1904

Probably California's Panama-Pacific Exposition of 1915 offered the greatest number of commemorative bells in the widest range of designs. Several of them incorporate the figure of the California bear.

Aside from those made specifically for fairs and expositions, there are of course bells commemorating other events. One of the rarest, because only fifty were cast, is a presentation bell with the initials *B & M* in high relief. The initials, of course, stand for the Boston and Maine Railroad. Although there are no clearcut records, some collectors believe these bells were cast in 1846 and presented to notables on a special run commemorating the first passenger train on that railroad. Others believe they were cast two or three years later and given to invited guests on the railroad's famous mile-a-minute run between Boston and Lawrence.

Although present-day commemorative bells are often of a flimsy quality, there are pleasing exceptions. The Seneca Glass Company of Morgantown, West Virginia, issued a fine crystal bell for their state centennial in 1963. It is etched with a map of the state and the appropriate dates.

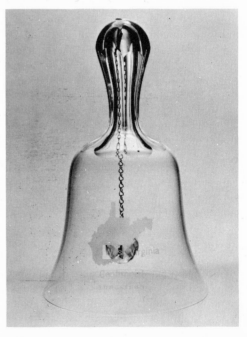

190. *Crystal bell produced in 1963 to honor West Virginia's centennial is suitably etched with map of the state and inclusive dates.* COURTESY OF THE SENECA GLASS COMPANY, MORGANTOWN, WEST VIRGINIA

TABLE BELLS OF PORCELAIN AND GLASS

Any discussion of American-made porcelain bells is of necessity brief, for they are few in number. Among those that can be documented is one that has several areas of appeal. It comes from New Jersey, where a good deal of early porcelain was produced and where "American Belleek" was perfected in the late nineteenth century. It is not only an example of this lovely, lustrous ware but is designed in the likeness of the Liberty Bell, complete with simulated crack and inscription, plus a view of Independence Hall. The decorations are all of a bright underglaze blue that enriches the creaminess of the Belleek. Also in underglaze blue is the rather ornate company mark of the Columbian Art Pottery, established in Trenton in 1876. From every aspect, a bell like this makes an important addition to any grouping of American historical china. Collectors who own the bell and who enjoy ·delving into historical background will want to learn how "American Belleek" came to be. In his pictorial account, *Handmade in America,* Sigmund Lavine relates the story in very readable fashion.

Quite different, yet also of historical interest, are the small imported porcelain bells showing either hand-painted views or tranfers of American scenes. Many are marked GERMANY and may or may not be stamped with the name of the importing firm or the individual who sold them as souvenirs. Apparently these souvenirs were most popular with merchants in the East, as the scenes are frequently of New England: a

191. American historical china bells. Left: *"American Belleek" from the Columbian Art Pottery, Trenton, New Jersey. Designed to resemble the Liberty Bell, it has a view of Independence Hall in bright underglaze blue. Circa 1876.* Right: *Blue lusterware, German, with hand-painted scene of Robert E. Lee's Gettysburg headquarters and an inset of the general himself. Circa 1890.* PRIVATE COLLECTION

historic belfry, a lighthouse, or perhaps a town crier. Souvenir china was at the height of its popularity in the 1880s but was generally popular from 1865 through the early 1900s.

Closely related to bells in that category are those imported as blanks from such countries as Germany, Bavaria, and Austria and then hand-painted by American artists. Like all pieces from the era when hand-painted china was in vogue, the bells are individually decorated to reflect the taste of the artist.

Occasionally sets of dinnerware by important American manufacturers have included a matching table bell, but this practice has now been largely discontinued. One of the last came out about 1950 when Syracuse China advertised porcelain bells of a simple classic pattern matching one of its table settings.

192. China bells hand-painted by American artists. Each has its matching plate. Bell on left shows quaint country scenes overhung with branches of mistletoe. Signed and dated 1897. PRIVATE COLLECTION

193. *One of the few bells, and perhaps the only one of its kind, known to have been made at the old Boston and Sandwich Glass Company. Scene shows a stork standing near cattails in a marsh. This bell was made by the present owner's great-uncle, Charles E. Wright, a decorator in the Sandwich factory. (Information by courtesy of the Sandwich Historical Society.)* DAVID F. WRIGHT COLLECTION

American glass has become probably the most thoroughly researched of all the antique-collecting fields. Much has been written, and authoritatively, on correct terminologies and on the complex techniques of producing colorful art wares in American glasshouses. Yet despite all the writing on the subject, the documenting of individual pieces remains extremely difficult. Designs were often exchanged and formulas sometimes copied. Workers tended to move about from one glasshouse to another, taking with them their specialty; thus identical, or nearly identical, patterns and colors and finishes appeared in widely separated localities. Then, too, European glassblowers emigrated here and turned out imitations of their native country's glass objects. A collector can easily mistake a Waterford-like glass bell made in New Jersey for its Irish original.

So far as bells in particular are concerned, there is one other consideration to be faced. Although metal bells of nineteenth-century America are represented in old catalogues to some extent, glass bells are less commonly described in this way. A few types, especially in pressed glass, were made as a commercial venture; but it is questionable whether as many of the art glass types were produced commercially in America as in England. Life in the New World did not create any great demand for such decorative luxuries as fragile glass bells, and there is evidence that many of the loveliest museum examples were made as offhand orders or as experimental pieces by certain glassblowers. Consequently, compared to utilitarian objects like vases, bells were not widely advertised.

When obstacles to attribution can be overcome and a bell established as made at a certain glasshouse, it naturally assumes greater value and interest. On the other hand, lack of attribution need not lessen a collector's pleasure in the various types of glass that can be assembled in a collection of bells. After all, the bells originally must have been cherished mainly for their aesthetic qualities.

From the early 1800s when glassworks were able to gain a foothold in America, their key word was "experimentation"; they constantly attempted to imitate imported glasswares from the Old World. The blown three-mold glass appearing shortly after 1800, for example, was one ingenious invention of craftsmen in the early Republic in response to the demand for imported cut glass. But bells as a feature of this experimentation do not appear in any number before the heyday of pressed pattern glass, after the 1860s, when quantities of such ware were being produced inexpensively with little or no handwork involved.

Because the Boston and Sandwich Glass Company not only perfected the techniques for pressed glass but was a primary source for it, pieces of pressed glass are often referred to as Sandwich glass. Yet by 1879 there were seventy-five glass factories in Pittsburgh alone—and at least a third of them were engaged in making tablewares. It is reasonable to assume that many of the bells in pressed pattern glass originated in the Pittsburgh area.

Bells do not appear to have been made in even a fraction of the innumerable patterns created during the years such glass was popular. Those that are known to collectors include Currier and Ives, Inverted Thumbprint, Daisy and Button, Daisy Diamond, Smocking, Thousand Eye, Hobnail, and Tree of Life. Although bells in these and probably other patterns may have been made in appreciable quantities and sold "for a song," today they are becoming increasingly rare and their prices are soaring. It is the exceptional collection that can boast a fairly complete assortment of patterns in pressed glass bells.

Realizing that pattern glass has been reproduced in volume, the novice sometimes hesitates to pay the price for a pattern glass bell lest he be picking up only a reproduction. Unfortunately this can happen, but without any blame attaching to the dealer. Reproductions of one pattern or another have been made for well over thirty years, many from the same molds used originally; and it is often next to impossible to distinguish an original from a reproduction. The best assurance lies in buying a bell that has a proven history of ownership, yet this is very seldom possible.

Cut glass bells of the Brilliant Period are apparently the least understood and appreciated

194. Treasured specimen of the pressed glass pattern known as Tree of Life, patented by William O. Davis of the Portland Glass Company, Portland, Maine, 1869. The pattern has the name Davis interwoven in the complicated vinelike tracery. Handle is of blown glass. Coloring throughout is a rich gold-amber. RENICK COLLECTION

among glass bells, yet their brilliant sparkle on lighted shelves is unsurpassed. From around 1880 until 1915 (the Brilliant Period) cut glass was much in demand, and pieces were produced

195. Bells of colorless pressed pattern glass. Left: A popular pattern with frosted leaf motif. Center: Inverted thumbprint border; a small bell-shaped perfume bottle is the clapper. Right: Daisy and Button pattern. PRIVATE COLLECTION

196. Cut glass bells of American make, all from the Brilliant Period. Bell in foreground is a signed Hawkes specimen in American strawberry diamond and fan cut. Cuttings on the other bells feature hobstars and splits. PRIVATE COLLECTION

197. Crystal bell with flute cutting. Production was discontinued in the 1940s. COURTESY OF STEUBEN GLASS

in many grades and by many cutting houses. Bells are among some of the finer deep-cut pieces, their patterns consisting chiefly of arrangements of stars, splits, hob-stars, and American strawberry diamond and fan scallops. Any with pinwheel patterns are definitely dated as twentieth century, since this motif was not cut earlier.

Cut glass was never an inexpensive product. It was always a luxury glass because it had to be made of highest quality ingredients. Lead was costly but essential for perfect crystal purity. Moreover, fine cut glass must be cut by skilled hands.

Two eminent names in the cutting trade were those of Henry Clay Fry and Thomas G. Hawkes. Fry cut glass, known for its brilliance, continued in production at Rochester, Pennsylvania, until 1929. Much of the glass carries an acid-etched trademark: the name FRY in a shield. It was Hawkes who cut entire table services for President Cleveland and millionaire families like the John Jacob Astors. T. G. Hawkes & Company opened about 1880 in Corning, New York, the community destined to become the center of the glass-cutting industry, with at least a score of shops employing over one thousand cutters. Their output was sold to well-known

retailers like Tiffany's in New York and Marshall Field's in Chicago. But the era ended for all time with the closing of the Hawkes Company in 1963. It was the last of the fine old Corning glass-cutting shops.

For a trademark Hawkes ordinarily used just a single H or two hawks in a shamrock. Presumably all his pieces after 1895 were marked. Most of the cut glass bells from his factory are marked in a different way, however, having the word *Hawkes* etched on the handle. This, it should be noted, is a much later mark of T. G. Hawkes & Company.

Signed and unsigned, a cut glass bell in the Russian pattern is highly desirable because of the associations this pattern has with the history of American glassmaking. The Russian pattern was designed by a cutter for Hawkes, patented in 1882, and assigned to the Hawkes Company. This was the pattern used for the table service of fifty-dozen pieces cut by Hawkes for the White House during Cleveland's first administration. The pattern proved so popular that makers of pressed glass brought out their Daisy and Button pattern in imitation of it.

The tradition of pure crystal glass at its finest has been carried forward in the present century by the Steuben Glass Works, originally founded by Hawkes and his friend Frederick Carder of Stourbridge, England. While Mr. Carder remained in charge from 1903 to 1932, a number of glass bells for table use were designed, and they continue to be designed today.

Heisey glass became an almost instant collectible upon the closing of the company of that name in 1954. Although scarcely considered collectible up until that time, Heisey crystal remained of high quality, always handwrought since the day the firm was founded in 1895. In fact, it was the firm's refusal to turn to machine-made glass that contributed to its closing. The company prided itself on a staff of master cutters and engravers, but in later years found it increasingly difficult to secure apprentices.

The Heisey Glass Company was one of the first such companies to adopt a trademark.

About 1902, many of their pieces were showing the letter *H* inside a diamond, the company founder having used his fraternity pin as a model for the design. Among the crystal bells from this Newark, Ohio, glasshouse is a graceful one of simple colonial design showing that trademark on the handle. The only ornamentation is a wreath engraved around the base.

The introduction of American art glass in the 1880s widened the choice of bells for today's collectors. Examples may be few in number but they are found in a diversity of colors, textures, and shapes, all resulting from new techniques and a great deal of creative experimentation in the leading glassworks of that period.

Of the various kinds of art glass exemplified in bells, the shaded wares evoke special interest. The success of shading one color into another depended upon clever manipulation of the heat that produced various color tones from metallic oxides; the necessary techniques were developed first at the New England Glass Company in Cambridge, Massachusetts. The whole idea, in fact, stemmed from this company's efforts to produce something new and so to meet competition from the Midwest and the Pittsburgh area, where a cheaper glass was being made.

Amberina was the name given the first bi-colored glass with its shadings from rich red to pale amber. As the creator of Amberina, the New England Glass Company held the patent but later licensed Hobbs, Brockunier & Company of Wheeling, West Virginia, to make the same glass. Beautiful blown-molded bells of large size were made by this Wheeling company and are today considered museum pieces. Interestingly enough, however, the smaller Amberina bells in pressed patterns, though not so artistic as those in blown glass, are considered equally rare.

Prompted by Amberina's popularity, the Mt. Washington Glass Company at New Bedford, Massachusetts, came out with a translucent glass called Burmese, in colors ranging from salmon pink to lemon yellow. As with Amberina, it was the soluble gold in the mix that caused the rosy

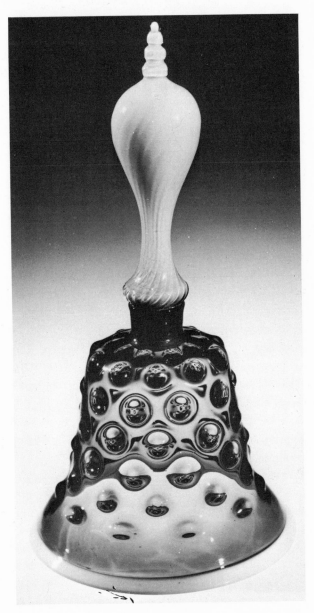

198. *Bell pattern-molded of cranberry-colored and opaque yellow glass was blown by J. A. Klumpp for the Thomas Evans Glass Company, Pittsburgh, 1898. Presented to the Corning Museum by the Klumpp family in 1952.* COURTESY OF THE CORNING MUSEUM OF GLASS

color to appear when the yellow glass was re-heated. Burmese was made in either a glossy or a dull acid finish. Most bells of this glass have a glossy surface which, oddly enough, is considered the more rare of the two finishes. Perhaps the

199. Left: *Webb Burmese glass bell,* Right: *Gunderson bell of Peachblow glass. Made at the old Mt. Washington plant during the period it was operated by Robert M. Gunderson (1938–1952). Coloring shades from deep rose to frosted white, with very little suggestion of blue. Soft matte finish.* HAMMOND COLLECTION

most unusual rarity in a Burmese bell was a very small one offered for sale a few years ago in the Midwest. In addition to being so small—only four inches tall—the bell was unusual in having a dual finish, dull on the outside and glossy on the inside, with a handle of camphor-satin glass.

This and other early Burmese bells are quite likely not of American make, actually. Authorities claim there is no evidence of bells in this glass ever being made at Mt. Washington. However, shortly after the company introduced Burmese they patented it in England and licensed Thomas Webb & Sons to produce it at their Stourbridge glasshouse. Fine bells of this glass are looked upon as Webb Burmese, though some later reproductions are of less certain origin and a few are thought to have come from American glasshouses. (*See* Color Plate IV).

Encouraged by the immediate success of Burmese, several companies brought out another art glass with shaded rose colorations. It was named Peachblow, in the wake of publicity over

an antique Chinese vase auctioned in New York for ten thousand dollars. The vase was the color of peach blossoms.

At the Mt. Washington plant almost all this glass was given an acid bath resulting in a soft matte finish. Apparently the few existing Peachblow bells in matte finish did not originate here, however, during the two years the glass was made. Instead, they can be traced to the 1940s when Robert M. Gunderson succeeded to the Pairpoint Manufacturing Company, originally the old Mt. Washington plant. He is known to have made a few pieces of Peachblow from an old formula he supposedly found in the buildings, and it is an accepted fact that on special order he produced a few table bells in Peachblow. These show shadings from soft rose to frosty white but lack the touch of light blue-gray seen in the color gradations of the old Mt. Washington Peachblow.

Bells of varying sizes, shapes, and colorings represent still another of the best-known art glass introductions, the Tiffany iridescents brought out by Louis Comfort Tiffany, son of the famous New York jeweler. His greatest contribution was the technique of satinizing glass through the use of gases and oxides. Tiffany iridescent glass is often called and sometimes signed FAVRILE—a trade name derived from an old Saxon word meaning "handwrought."

Some of the most eye-catching Tiffany bells show the influence of art nouveau, that contemporary European art style Tiffany is credited with introducing to American designers. It is a style characterized by simplified natural forms and curvilinear lines. Although short-lived as a style of decoration it had a wide effect on the arts, and other bells than those from the Tiffany Studios show this effect.

Immediately after the successful introduction of Tiffany iridescents, the Northwood Glass Company of Wheeling, West Virginia, countered with a cheap imitation they called Taffeta glass. It is sometimes nicknamed "poor man's Tiffany." When it did not prove overly popular, the company began disposing of its surplus to carnivals, where it was given away as prizes. So today the name Carnival glass, rather than Taffeta, is used commonly, although the latter seems much more appropriate for the charming little pattern glass bells of this texture.

If not signed, a bell of Quezal glass might well pass for a Tiffany piece. Quezal is also an iridescent and a very superior art glass. It was produced by the Quezal Art Glass Company of Brooklyn for only a few years, prior to 1920. A genuine Quezal bell is a rarity, but readily identifiable from the signature engraved on its handle—a favorite spot for trademarks and signatures on glass bells.

Spangled and Spatter and End-of-Day are terms used, sometimes with confusion, to describe bells of variegated glass. The name Spangled glass is correctly reserved for pieces showing spangles—that is, flakes of mica or other metallics. Spatter glass has no metallic flakes embedded in it. It was made simply by breaking pieces of colored glass, gathering them up, then warming them into the content of the object being made. The color could be controlled, resulting in a pink and white Spatter glass, perhaps; or it could be variegated. The variegated pieces came to be called End-of-Day, an unlikely name that implied odds and ends left in the pot at the end of the day were mixed together and somehow resulted in a beautiful article of glass. This idea is just an old canard. Both the idea and the term itself have fallen into disuse today among knowledgeable collectors of old glass. Bells of either a single color or a varicolored Spatter usually have an opaque white lining that adds to the clarity of the colors.

The terminology for opaque glass bells, mostly in pressed patterns, also needs some clarification. Aside from those of milk-white color, wrongfully called Milk glass, there are others in a creamy yellow appropriately called Custard glass; and occasionally some in opaque pink, blue, or green.

Although rare, bells of Marble glass are among the most distinctive of all opaque types. The technique of mixing white with swirls of color came into use about 1872 and, whether true or not, is said to have been inspired by the technique used in marbleizing papers for the end pages of leather-bound books. Since purple was the most popular color for medium-priced glass of that day, purple Marble glass was naturally a favorite. But most bells seen in this glass are of the more rarely found soft green color. Marble glass in shades of green was produced chiefly by Challinor, Taylor & Company of Tarentum, Pennsylvania, between 1870 and 1880, so these bells may have been made by that company.

Marble glass has too often been referred to as "slag," a misnomer if ever there was one, implying a haphazard glass made from the leftover dross in the pot. As an authority on pressed glass terminology, Ruth Webb Lee was always outspoken in her dislike of the term:

"Slag" seems like an ugly and inappropriate name for such attractive glass. Actually great difficulty was encountered in the making of Marble glass, in fusing the white of the

200. *Three strikingly beautiful bells from American nineteenth-century glasshouses.* Left: *Bell epergne filled with blown glass grapes in clear and cobalt. Attributed to Phoenix Glass Company.* Center: *Exquisite hand-painted roses in shades of yellow and soft rose on a green glass bell. Tentatively attributed to the Phoenix firm.* Right: *Outstanding example of South Jersey glass has yellow loopings. Handle is of Fry cut glass.* MOSLEY COLLECTION

mixture and making it adhere to the colored part.

Marble, rather than "slag," is the term now accepted by most students of glass to give this ware the dignity it deserves.

Besides these larger categories of art glass there are many miscellaneous types, each with its own special appeal. Like all art glass, these miscellaneous types were used to make decorative objects of every description. Included here are bells that range from a two-inch miniature in Crown Milano to a twelve-inch beauty in Spanish Lace.

Crown Milano is sometimes included with shaded art glass, but it is not a two-toned glass. Its pastel tones on a satiny cream background have been carefully traced and painted. Crown Milano bells, really little cabinet pieces, were made at the Mt. Washington Glass Company for a period of about ten years near the close of the century.

Bells of Rubina Verde glass are imitative of those in Amberina, but with two differences: one of the bicolors is flashed on—that is, added in a second coat of glass; and though some Amberina bells are of pressed pattern glass and some of blown-molded, all those seen in Rubina Verde glass are blown-molded. Much of this particular glass is credited to Hobbs, Brockunier & Company.

Bells of South Jersey glass with their opaque white loopings and those attributed to Nicholas Lutz, with their threaded effects, are all reminiscent of the Venetian influence. Crackle glass, too, owes its invention to the Venetians, and bells of this material are distinctive in a collection because no other glass gives a similar effect. Crackle glass is produced by plunging red-hot glass into cold water, then reheating and reblowing it and thus producing an unusual outer surface that appears to be covered with tiny cracks. The interior surface remains smooth.

Although not exclusive with that glasshouse, Spanish Lace is the descriptive trade name given an opalescent glass of that design made by the Beaumont Glass Company of Martin's Ferry,

201. *A unique bell decorated with cigar bands. Names of the Presidents appear near the base in an arrangement of arcs. This is one of more than a hundred unusual glass bells in the permanent collections of the Butler Institute of American Art, Youngstown, Ohio. Of all sizes and types, these were originally gathered by Mrs. Fanniebelle McVey Trippe.*

202. *Tap and twirl bells designed with a double chime, thus doubly melodious. Left: Bell revolves when twirled. Center: Bell was cast on a saucerlike base; patented in 1863. Right: Of Britannia ware, the bell supposedly owned by President John Adams.* PRIVATE COLLECTION

Ohio. It is quite unlike any other art glass—and altogether beautiful in a large bell of canary opalescence.

Whether the idea is simply a myth or not, earlier writers on the subject of American glass felt that artists-in-glass became preoccupied with surface finishes on their wares as a concession to the Victorian fondness for plush, velvet, and satin fabrics. Even if unfounded, such a line of thought proves interesting, for soft matte and satin finishes distinguished glasswares of the period. Satin glass was brought to perfection in America by Joseph Webb from Stourbridge, England, where the process for this finish was being used by the famous Webb glaziers. Webb settled in Beaver Falls, Pennsylvania, and it was here under his guidance that the Phoenix Glass

Company produced the first such glass in this country. Satin is a versatile finish and many variants occur. The choicest of all bells in such finishes are those with mother-of-pearl iridescence and those known as Cut Velvet. Both are usually of a diamond-quilted pattern. The Cut Velvet glass is constructed of two laminated layers of glass with the inner casing of white giving it a textured depth, like velvet to the touch.

TO TAP, SNAP, TWIST, AND TWIRL

Ordinarily bells that are sounded mechanically by manipulating a knob are considered more or less utilitarian and are likely to be lacking in artistic design. There are exceptions, of course, none more striking than the fine glass specimens mounted either with silver or with gilded brass. An art glass known as Wavecrest was used this way on a footed brass base, the bell suspended under the opaque glass shell and rung with a light tap on the brass finial. Wavecrest glass was decorated and distributed by the C. F. Monroe Company of Meriden, Connecticut; it enjoyed great popularity over a twenty-year period ending with the First World War.

204. *A study in silver- and shellwork, showing bells that snap, tap, and twist. Left: From Rogers Smith, Meriden, Connecticut. Has continuous ring once knob is twisted. Center: A type to be placed on floor and snapped by foot. Patented, 1859. Right: Lustrous abalone shell encases a tap bell fitted underneath.* PRIVATE COLLECTION

203. *Old Sunday school tap bell, valued because it came from Little Pigeon Creek Church in southern Indiana, which Abraham Lincoln attended while living nearby. Figure of the goddess Minerva decorates bell. Dated 1840.* PRIVATE COLLECTION

Bells of this delicately decorated ware, usually in pastels, were probably intended for use on a dressing table.

The silver industry was attracted to styling a good many silver-mounted cut glass objects. One was a tap bell, a shell of brilliant cut glass fitted to a footed silver mount covering the bell. Although mentioning this fact anticipates a coming chapter, the silver industry's innovative use of the tap bell in tableware designs merits some recognition here, for these pieces are in a class by themeslves in representing a unique phase of American craftsmanship. Literally dozens of different silver pieces for the dining table cleverly incorporated a tap bell in their design.

Although tap bells were favorites and were easy to ring at the slightest pressure of the finger, others required a firm pressure to snap the spring-based clapper against the outside edge of the bell. Some snap bells could be set on the floor under the dining table and sounded by pressing the foot on a spring to release the clapper. Still other compact little bells needed a quick twist of the finial to ring them, and they gave off a sound more akin to a musical buzz. Under related nomenclature were the twirlers with their melodious ring. These might be styled with a double chime that revolved not once, but twice.

Bells made to tap, snap, twist, or twirl can be found in silver, but the vast majority are nickel over brass. Most of them are unmarked except for a patent date; 1855 is considered an early date on bells in this category, most of them bearing dates around 1865. Since they were made largely for utilitarian purposes, only one in twenty is likely to show imagination in its design; however, when that one is found it may prove to be exceedingly unusual. A figure supporting the bell or otherwise incorporated in its design is always of interest, and sometimes the base of the piece is out of the ordinary.

Tap bells and their kind have another characteristic that makes some of them collectible regardless of their plebeian appearance. As functional everyday objects, they were much in de-

205. *A twirler of uncommon design, resembling the old ordinaries or high-wheeled bicycles of yesteryear. Bell rings when miniature pedal is twirled. The figure is posed.* PRIVATE COLLECTION

mand a century ago for schools, hotel desks, stores, and so on. It is reasonable to expect that many have had a direct association with historical personalities. When this can be documented, the bell of course adds an irreplaceable bit of Americana to any collection.

The most highly prized of all, naturally, are bells combining significant historical association with a degree of style, as in the tap bell brought back from England in 1788 by John Adams, later the second president of the United States.

The bell is made of a new metal then popular in England—Britannia, a superfine grade of pewter originated in Sheffield in the mid-eighteenth century. Britannia was found to take a high and lasting polish, and it is only surprising that more bells were not made of it, for it gives a fine melodious ring. The mounting on the John Adams bell is a neatly turned oakwood base with pewter feet. When found in an old mansion, the bell bore a yellowed sticker on the underside of the base authenticating purchase in England in 1788. This was the year when Adams, at his own request, was recalled as minister to England. It is assumed that the bell may have gone with him to the White House when, as its first resident, he moved in during the fall of 1800, only four months before his term ended.

206. *From the Gorham Catalogue, 1888.* COURTESY OF THE GORHAM COMPANY

MISCELLANY

High on the list of favorites from the wide assortment of miscellaneous types are the dainty silver tea bells of Victorian days. Many of these date from the period when art nouveau flourished in America, just prior to 1900. The Gorham Manufacturing Company's designs in bells are considered the finest expression of this decorative style with its curving lines and arabesques. The Reed & Barton catalogue of 1900 also shows a partiality to art nouveau. Ten different bells are illustrated, decorated with swags, flutings, and naturalistic floral designs.

Silversmiths like these and International Sterling frequently made tea bells to match their various patterns of silverware. Whiting Manufacturers offered a bell in Lily of the Valley to match their table settings of that name.

The all-time favorite in Victorian table bells from American silversmiths is one whose manufacture predated the introduction of art nouveau in America by a number of years. It is a Gorham bell cherished for its beauty and for its heritage as well, for the company that made it dates back to Jebez Gorham, who began working as a silversmith in 1818.

The bell is a copy of a fine old Florentine masterpiece. Details of its production by the company are outlined in a letter from present-day Gorham officials:

. . . concerning a bell marked: "Old Florentine 042 Gorham" our records show that this is a silverplated bell, the base metal being bronze, which was a reproduction of an old Florentine bell originally made of bronze. These were first made by us in 1884 and were continued in production until 1916. Our records indicate they were very popular around 1900. It is impossible for us to tell how many were made because of the number of years that these were in production. However, when an item is in production that length of time it indicates that it did have considerable sale so we may assume that a goodly number of them were made.

Our records also indicate that many of these were made with an ivory handle . . . with the rest of the parts made in Gorham silverplate or it may have a silverplated handle on it.

Other silver table bells are known to have been made about 1890 by James Tufts at 33 Bowker Street, Boston; and about the same time J. H. Johnston at 17 Union Square, New York, was advertising solid silver bells with handles depicting either Rip Van Winkle or Peter Stuyvesant.

Aside from bells for table and desk, all sorts of doorbells were being patented in Victorian days. Some, like the shopkeeper's bell, bounced on a long spring as the door was flung open. Others were more elegantly encased to ornament

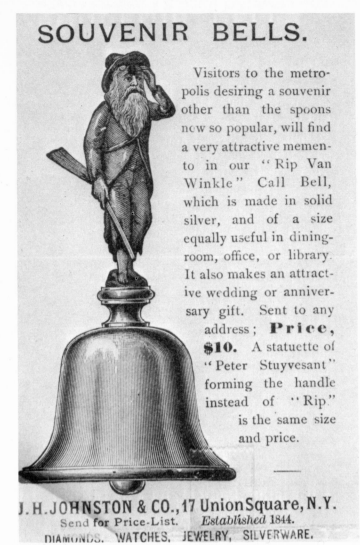

208. An 1891 advertisement.

A.	1868	[symbol]	1885	[symbol]	1903	[symbol]	1920
B.	1869	[symbol]	1886	[symbol]	1904	[symbol]	1921
C.	1870	[symbol]	1887	[symbol]	1905	[symbol]	1922
D.	1871	[symbol]	1888	[symbol]	1906	[symbol]	1923
E.	1872	[symbol]	1889	[symbol]	1907	[symbol]	1924
F.	1873	[symbol]	1890	[symbol]	1908	[symbol]	1925
G.	1874	[symbol]	1891	[symbol]	1909	[symbol]	1926
H.	1875	[symbol]	1892	[symbol]	1910	[symbol]	1927
I.	1876	[symbol]	1893	[symbol]	1911	[symbol]	1928
J.	1877	[symbol]	1894	[symbol]	1912	[symbol]	1929
K.	1878	[symbol]	1895	[symbol]	1913	[symbol]	1930
L.	1879	[symbol]	1896	[symbol]	1914	[symbol]	1931
M.	1880	[symbol]	1897	[symbol]	1915	[symbol]	1932
N.	1881	[symbol]	1898	[symbol]	1916	[symbol]	1933
O.	1882	[symbol]	1899	[symbol]	1917		
P.	1883	[symbol]	1900	[symbol]	1918		
Q.	1884	[symbol]	1901	[symbol]	1919		
		[symbol]	1902				

207. Gorham Year Marks, as they appear on old silver hollow-ware by Gorham and also on articles once a part of the company's regular ecclesiastical line.

209. Small silver tea bells. Left: Bell with silver overlay, art nouveau decor. Center: Gorham's Old Florentine bell, with ivory handle. Right: Heavy silver bell in pineapple cut, the same pattern favored by President Monroe's wife for her silver tea service. PRIVATE COLLECTION

210. Ornate little automatic alarum. Point is designed to be set against the door at an angle. If anyone opens the door, this point is pushed down and sets off a furious ringing. Winds by turning the front dome. HALPERIN COLLECTION

211. *From the Try-Me Burglar Alarm Company, this bell was found in the original cloth-covered box, with label and directions for use. Oddly shaped weight is designed to lie on the doorknob over which the bell hooks. When the knob is turned, the weight falls and triggers the bell. Winds with key.* PRIVATE COLLECTION

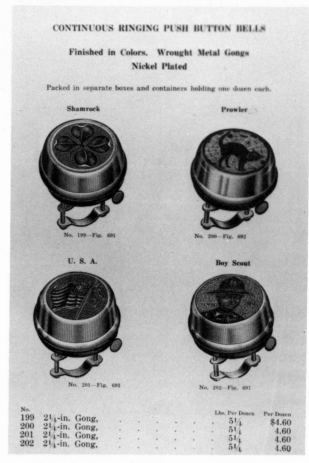

212. *From Bevin's catalogue of bicycle bells, 1926. Dozens upon dozens of different designs and styles are shown.* COURTESY OF BEVIN BROTHERS MANUFAC-TURING COMPANY

the front door and were sounded either by turning or by pressing a lever. Considerable attention was also given to inventing alarum bells to be placed on entrance doors. The Try-Me Burglar Alarm Company of 145 North Eighth Street, Philadelphia, was a leading inventor.

Seeking old stagecoach bells or the later bicycle bells and reading of their use give the colletor interesting sidelights on bygone customs of the road. The cyclist had dozens of bells to choose from, judging from the fact that entire catalogues were issued on bicycle bells alone. The nicest ones were enameled in gay colors to accentuate their designs. If a little page of proper rules for using the bell was not given free with its purchase, the serious cyclist could invest in a

handbook outlining proper etiquette while cycling:

> When riding should he meet an excited horse and should the animal show signs of fright at the sound of his bell, the cyclist should dismount without delay, roll his machine out of sight, and offer to lead the excitable animal onward.

Curiosities in bells, as well as the customary types, were a part of the American scene one hundred years ago. There were little raindrop bells looking ever so much like mousetraps. They were designed for the windowsill, where unexpected raindrops during the night soaked loose a band of blotting paper and thus released a spring to sound the bell. This alerted all but the soundest sleepers to hurry and close the window. Then there were "chestnut bells," the most popular novelty ever introduced by the Gong Bell Manufacturing Company. These resembled midget yo-yos and were sold for men to

213. The conductor's punchbell that so fascinated Mark Twain. Patented March 18, 1884. SPEAR COLLECTION, PETER WHITE MEMORIAL LIBRARY, MAR-QUETTE, MICHIGAN

wear on their lapels, with instructions to "ring the little bell on every old joke and your life will be prolonged." Other curiosities included conductors' punchbells that rang with each punch of a ticket. These so fascinated Mark Twain that he couldn't resist composing a ditty about them, with this rollicking refrain:

Punch, brothers, punch, punch with care!
Punch in the presence of the passenjare!

Streets and alleys of our land once echoed to the clang and chink of handbells; and delving into records of their use can lead one down trails of interesting commentaries on American life of an earlier day. Auctioneers, perambulating advertisers, railroad crossing guards—all these and others used bells freely in performing their duties. Lively street vendors crying their wares and services ding-donged their way through city neighborhoods. Among these were butchers, vegetable men, and tin peddlers, garbage men, and dustmen.

In a few rare instances the image of these criers has been preserved for us. More than a century ago one Nicolina Calyo executed a series of thirty-six watercolors depicting the streetsellers of New York City as he saw them in 1840. His muffin-and-cracker seller is shown ringing a bell. And there are descriptive references to the butter bean man "driving his white horse and sulky cart up and down the street . . . crying 'Butter beans, butter beans' and ringing his big old bell." In the Edward Arnold collection at the Metropolitan Museum of Art is a quaint old oil painting on cardboard entitled *Potpye Palmer with Garbage Cart and Bell, 1805, East Side, corner of Elizabeth and Pump Streets.*

Many collections show a handbell known to have been used by a particular street vendor or perhaps an official town crier. These deserve to be cherished; for common as they once may have been, bells that were owned and used by private individuals are often handed down in the family as valued heirlooms and are not for sale at any price. There are even tales of such bells being buried with their owners lest they fall into disinterested hands.

The town crier with his clangorous bell cut quite a dapper figure as he swung along the streets proclaiming good news and bad. "See how he uplifts the bell in his right hand," wrote Hawthorne, "and shakes it slowly at first, then with a hurried motion, till the clapper seems to strike both sides at once." Thus commanding attention, the crier went about shouting warnings against Indians, announcing a Gr-r-h-and Co-h-once-ert To-ni-gh-t, or giving notice of a missing child. Louisa May Alcott once told of being lost when a tiny girl and waking from a sound sleep to hear the town crier's bell and a voice shouting, "Lost, a little girl with a green dress and red shoes. Reward twenty-five cents."

The use of small bells as altar appointments was not characteristic of the colonial church in America. Except in the Episcopal and the Roman Catholic churches, puritanical attitudes forbade the use of such ritualistic objects; but

214. *Williamsburg's town crier holds antique bell of the type cherished as a symbol of vigilance. Silversmith holds silver replica awarded Winston Churchill in 1956.* COLONIAL WILLIAMSBURG, WILLIAMSBURG, VIRGINIA

by the late nineteenth century, heavy tuned altar chimes were being advertised by bell-makers. The 1899 catalogue from Bevin Brothers shows several types. The J. C. Deagan Company of Chicago manufactured tubular church chimes of fine quality brass mounted between musical staffs. These indicated appropriate notes for playing the chimes at four places in Roman Catholic services: Offertory, Sanctus, Consecra-

215. *A genuine and ingenious piece of Americana—town crier's bell combined with a wooden rattle. When all was well, the bell was rung. When danger lurked, the rattle was sounded.* ELSIE SIMMERS COLLECTION

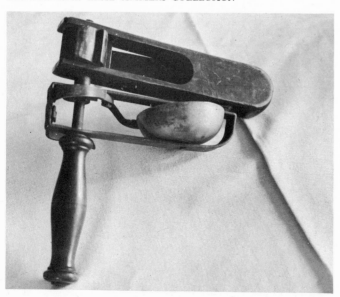

tion, Benediction. The Gorham Company, best known for its silver hollowware, also made tubular chimes and a variety of other types in bell metal and brass. One of the most elaborate and most expensive Gorham pieces shows definite European influence in its design and symbolic ornamentations. Six bells are suspended under a two-tiered shell decorated with angelic faces in relief and cameos emblematic of the Evangelists. Pierced work on the shell features the symbolic trefoil and the beautiful trinity cross with its fleur-de-lis tips. The trefoil motif is repeated in the handle. Interestingly, Gorham religious articles are back-stamped with the same year marks the firm used on its silver hollowware, starting in 1868. The articles are, of course, readily dated through these marks.

Old sales records show that most of the altar chimes produced were sold to Roman Catholic, Episcopal, and Lutheran churches. Sales for such articles remained brisk until the First World War, then slowly declined. When large altar chimes finally began falling into official disuse at mid-century, they oftentimes found

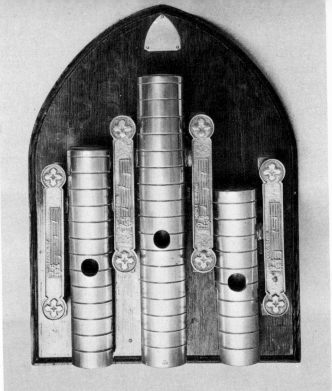

216. *Large, handsome chime manufactured by Gorham as a part of the company's regular ecclesiastical line. The pipe symbol included in the back-stamping indicates this particular chime was produced in 1911. It was still in production in 1916, and priced then at $42.* PHOTO, COURTESY OF BERENICE DU BOIS

217. *Heavy church chime, manufactured by J. C. Deagan, makers of tubular carillons and chimes. Musical notes embossed on brass bars indicate the proper tune for Offertory, Sanctus, Consecration, and Benediction. Very resonant. Brass presentation plate reads* TO RT. REV. T. CORBETT FROM SISTERS OF ST. BENEDICT : : CHRISTMAS 1910. PRIVATE COLLECTION

their way into local antique shops, where collectors were quick to acquire them. Now, a generation later, they are more difficult to find.

A set of tuned bells that undoubtedly accompanied a great deal of hymn singing was patented March 2, 1875, by B. Schoninger of New Haven, Connecticut, expressly for the Cymbella organ manufactured by his company. The distinctive feature of this organ, and the one from which it derived its trade name, was the upper register stop called a "cymbella." This stop controlled the built-in attachment consisting of two and one-half octaves of graduated, cup-shaped bells neatly nested on a metal rod. The first Cymbella organ was completed especially for the Centennial of 1876 and was played for the first time on July 4. With so much planning and patriotic sentiment involved in manufacturing his organ, surely Mr. Schoninger could not have foreseen the day when collectors would be lifting out and salvaging the bells that formed such an integral part of his invention.

218. *Set of tuned bells from a Schoninger's Cymbella organ.* PRIVATE COLLECTION

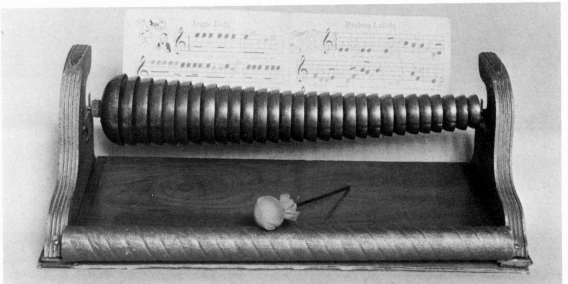

MADE IN AMERICA: 1900–1950

Although the demand for bells steadily decreased in America after 1900, there were artisans who helped keep alive the craft of bell-making. A foundry unique in the annals of the industry was the California Bell Company founded in the early 1900s by Mrs. A. S. C. Forbes, the world's first woman bellmaker.

At that time Mrs. Forbes was working zealously to restore California's El Camino Real—known as the King's Highway—which had once connected Father Serra's chain of Spanish missions. Appropriate road markers were needed, and so the now-familiar bell posts were designed and cast in the foundry Mrs. Forbes established. The first markers, placed in 1906, sparked the start of a new career for their originator. Californians wanted small replicas of the road markers, and in supplying these the California Bell Company was launched. It eventually developed into a world business for Mrs. Forbes, who found herself casting a wide range of bells;

yet her greatest interest lay in creating copies of old bells, large and small, from the Spanish mission era of the early West. It is these, of course, that collectors of Americana particularly want. One of the most difficult to locate because only a modest number were made is Mrs. Forbes's miniature copy of the earliest sacring wheels with wooden bells.

Some years later a Midwesterner found himself casting bells of another sort. While on a world cruise in 1936, George E. Tucker of Kansas City, Missouri, began collecting bells and studying ways in which they were made from country to country. On returning home he set up his own studio, where he started designing and producing many types of call bells, in an effort to keep alive an art that was disappearing in America. Some of his designs were influenced by European bells he had collected; others were distinctly his own—but all exhibited a handsome rubbed finish and were of heavy casting. His bells are readily identifiable from occasional catalogue pages issued by him until the Second World War brought his work to a close.

219. Modern bells made by George E. Tucker, under the trade name of Kay Studios. The high quality of his workmanship is evident. PRIVATE COLLECTION

220. One of the early advertisements for this unusual bell produced at Provincetown, Massachusetts. COURTESY OF MRS. WILLIAM F. BOOGAR

sea bell

whose tone recalls the harmonics of long point bell buoy—

at boogar's bronze foundry

and nowhere else in the world

465a commercial st.

adjacent to flagship

Farther east, a Cape Cod metal artisan decided he would try to capture the sound of the bell buoy in bronze. The result was a hanging bell of most unusual tone, shaped like a half-opened scallop shell, with a dangling seahorse figure acting as the clapper. There are not too many bells as artistic as this little scallop being made today, and popular demand keeps them still in production at Boogar's Bronze Foundry in Provincetown.

For those who collect contemporary as well as antique bells and who enjoy ferreting out the unusual, there are other enterprising craftsmen who can be found working with bell forms in all mediums: alabaster, clay, spun glass, wood, silver, even tin. Obviously some of their creations are more decorative than functional, but to the collector it is interesting to see the perennial appeal of the bell as an art form in almost any medium, even in ultramodern America.

SHIPS' BELLS AND OTHER BIG ONES

Too often, and for reasons not always clear, ships' bells, locomotive bells, farm bells, tower bells, and others of comparable size are looked upon as the stepchildren among collectible types. Yet those who have enough space to display toscins such as these claim several special satisfactions in collecting them. They are, for instance, truly functional bells once closely intertwined with local history. Most of them boast a well-defined past, and viewers can readily identify with them because they once rang on the old engine that passed Grandpa's ranch every day or they called children to their lessons back in the village where Aunt Alice taught school.

There is also the satisfying knowledge that each acquisition in this category is genuinely old. With only one known exception, these more sizable bells have not been reproduced. There is evidence, however, that the No. 1 farm bell is being made, rather surreptitiously, and sold as antique. The names and dates of early makers appear on the yokes of these bells and help to deceive unwary buyers.

Pleasantly enough, collectors are not deterred from buying these bigger bells because of their unreasonable prices. Dollar for dollar, they usually feel they are getting more of a bell for their money than they do when buying in other categories where the size is small in proportion to the price.

Finally, there is the satisfaction that comes in documenting a large bell. Not all are marked with the name of the manufacturer, but a high percentage are. Many can be traced to famous old firms like the E. W. Vanduzen Company of Cincinnati, Ohio, or the Meneely Bell Company of Troy, New York, both known for fine tower bells as well as ships' bell; some of them for Uncle Sam's naval vessels. Thousands of old farm and plantation bells made from steel alloy bear the name of noted manufacturers, such as the C. S. Bell Company of Hillsboro, Ohio, a firm still doing business today. Several individual studies on each type of tocsin are also a tremendous asset in documenting.

Ships' bells have been used by the United States Navy since Revolutionary War days, made always according to exact specifications. Most of these big navy bells and those from other giant ships, once they are retired, are acquired by museums or they are given places of honor in public locations. Equally interesting and somewhat more collectible are the bells from smaller vessels. There is usually a certain relationship between the size of a bell and the size of the ship on which it was once used, though sometimes big bells were carried by modest-sized boats.

The one with the largest recorded diameter is permanently displayed, along with some thirty other ships' bells, at the Mariners' Museum, Newport News, Virginia. It measures slightly over forty inches across the mouth and once belonged to a Mississippi River steamer built in 1895 and called *Kate Adams III*. For those who are statistically inclined, this and other significant ships' bells are detailed in the 1964/65 winter and spring issues of *Inland Seas: Quarterly Journal of the Great Lakes Historical Society*.

221. *Handbell and small ship's bell once used by Mark Twain, both obtained at an auction of his effects. Corner card verifies original ownership.* PRIVATE COLLECTION

Regardless of their size, many small ships' bells nevertheless gain stature from their historical associations. This is evident in the carefully documented collection at Mystic Seaport in Connecticut, where a number of small and medium-sized ones are exhibited. The eight-inch bell Mark Twain used on his Mississippi riverboat is further evidence. It was one of his proudest possessions. Between St. Louis and New Orleans, where he was licensed to navigate in 1850, rivermen knew the sound of his bell. Though Mark Twain's prowess as a pilot was sometimes questioned, no one questioned his ability to activate his signal bell when he wanted to rouse the roustabouts at river landings.

Traditionally there is also a relationship between the size of a ship and the tone of its bell. For example, vessels from twenty-six to sixty-five feet in length use A flat; those over sixty-five feet use A natural; still larger vessels, over one hundred tons, like destroyers, used B natural; tugboats use D flat, and so on. Thus, the tone of the bell shows the size of the vessel so that the boat may be distinguished in a fog.

It is apparent that such information on size and tone enables a collector to make an educated guess as to the size of the ship where a certain bell was once used, even when no historical data is available.

As to acquiring a ship's bell, there are dealers who specialize in nautical antiques and there are always auctions as another possible source. A very special source not to be overlooked lies in large salvaging operations. However, in an operation where a bell has been found on a sunken ship, collectors will find themselves competing for it with the diver who found it. Customarily he is entitled to keep any bell he can manage to salvage. In instances where a ship is being broken up for scrap, persistent searching will sometimes uncover its discarded bell lying in the rubble.

Procuring a locomotive bell is another story. Auctions and scrapyards seldom yield one of these. There was a time when an individual could purchase a discarded engine bell by applying directly to certain railroads. In some cases officials would even obligingly hunt through their accumulated bell stock to find one of the particular make sought by the customer. That era more or less ceased when the Southern Railway initiated the idea of donating its retired bells to churches and civic groups. Other roads were quick to adopt this gesture of goodwill, and today their supply of bells has dwindled after years of dieselization. Those few remaining are tagged for special donations. Consequently, unless collectors were fortunate in securing such bells years ago, most must content themselves with reading about them or viewing them in long-established collections.

222. *Ship's bell from the U.S.S.* Cleveland *(1903–1929). One of the most unusual bells ever carried by an American warship, it displays an elaborate basrelief of Perry's victory on Lake Erie in 1813. Now in the permanent collection of Western Reserve Historical Society, Cleveland, Ohio.* WESTERN RESERVE HISTORICAL SOCIETY

223. *Old engine bell in ornate hanger closely resembles the bell that rang on the Union Pacific locomotive during famous Golden Spike ceremonies of 1869.* ELLIOTT COLLECTION

Railroad Magazine, in its September 1949 issue, carried a comprehensive article on old locomotive bells. Highlights of the article focus on the manner in which each old-time foundryman devised ways of putting a special tone into his bells. Formulas differed, and there was a competitive spirit to see which railroad achieved the finest tone and greatest volume. Some roads cast their own bells; others bought theirs from manufacturers like the Buckeye Bell Foundry of Cincinnati, Ohio. The sizes varied but slightly, since the sizes of the engines themselves were fairly well standardized. Big steam engines carried bells about eighteen inches in diameter; smaller ones, about thirteen inches.

The artistic yearnings of early locomotive builders found expression in the ornate mountings for the bells, and experts who have made a study of the subject claim there are certain earmarks that distinguish the hangers of individual builders. The most artistic of all were made just prior to the Civil War, sometimes so elaborate that the bell itself was all but hidden. Later the mountings became plainer and purely utilitarian.

Historical collections of old engine bells are excellent starting points for anyone who would delve into the intricacies of learning how to identify the tone and the workmanship of each railroad's bells. One of the largest collections stands in a parklike setting in Northfield, Minnesota, where forty locomotive bells from forty different roads are arranged around a bronze Statue of Liberty replica at the Schilling Hobby House.

Old farm and plantation bells were part and parcel of rural American life a century ago and well into the present century. Usually of steel alloy rather than bell metal, they were made locally by many foundrymen as well as by specialty firms like The Goulds Manufacturing Company of Seneca Falls, New York. Never noted for their tonal quality, as compared with that found in bells of bronze or brass, they nevertheless served a purpose and were sold not only to farms and plantations but to schools, fire stations, and even some churches. Bells of steel alloy weighed only half as much as those of equal size cast from bell metal, and they were therefore easier to transport and mount. Too, they were much less costly.

The complete story on the making of these bells has yet to be written, but in due time the first chapter at least will be completed. Arnold H. Barben, a veteran employee of Goulds, now retired, is presently assembling material in booklet form on the farm bells once made by the various pump manufacturers of Seneca Falls. Meanwhile, old catalogue advertisements from those firms give the collector a fairly detailed description of the bells they produced—often referred to as the morning glory type because of their shape.

Every major founder from colonial days onward has striven for perfect tonal quality in the bell metal he used to cast tower bells for churches, schools, and other prominent buildings. This quality, not to mention the historical associations in such bells, often prompts a church or a school to keep its old bell as a relic long after it has been retired, thus making these bells scarce from a collector's standpoint. Locating big ones of this sort today is mostly by chance, according to James H. Baker, whose specialty is finding, preserving, and studying big bells from America's past. From his observations he has concluded that the collector who seriously seeks a fine example of a tower bell needs to

224. Old advertisement for two types of farm and plantation bells made in Seneca Falls, New York. Above: 1885–1905. Below: 1870–1889.

225. Old advertisement for one type of farm and plantation bell made in Seneca Falls, New York, 1862–1869.

become an opportunist as well as a master in the art of friendly persuasion. Upon hearing of a church or a school being demolished, he should make immediate inquiry about its bell before it is stored away and forgotten, or is sold for scrap. Bell metal is valuable even as junk. However, a competitive offer from an individual has been known to change a board's mind even though other plans for a bell had already been made. Incidentally, warns Mr. Baker, collectors ought always to obtain a receipt when buying big bells, so that no one can claim they were stolen.

That tower bells of historic worth can still be found, by chance, was evidenced only a few years ago when a Kansas man working with a ground crew in California unearthed an old Spanish mission bell. It proved to be a close duplicate of the priceless bell in San Miguel Chapel, Santa Fe, New Mexico, the oldest mission bell in America.

As many collectors have discovered for themselves, the old Spanish mission bells of the early Southwest hold a charm all their own. A little leaflet called *Your Guide to the Spanish Mission Bells in New Mexico* is helpful in studying the workmanship on early specimens. It is written and illustrated by Jane Howe, a leading exponent of Spanish history as it pertains to the mission bells in America.

Largely because of the space they and their mountings require, there are only a limited number of collections that feature large bells to any extent. One that is privately maintained but open to interested visitors belongs to the Oliver Elliotts of Tarentum, Pennsylvania. As an extension of their large general collection inside, the Elliotts keep their mounted bells here and there in a spacious grove surrounding their home, called Bell Haven. There are tocsins of every type: a crude iron one from Revolutionary War days; a splendid Spanish mission bell dated 1834; fire engine and ships' bells, also a canal bell from the Andrew Fulton Foundry of Pittsburgh (1828–1860); and several church bells, one a colossal example weighing over two thousand pounds. Thirteen railroads are represented. One of the most interesting locomotive bells (*see* Ill. 223) has an ornate hanger and closely resembles the one used on the Union Pacific when the Golden Spike was driven in Utah, May 10, 1869, celebrating the completion of rails connecting East and West.

In all there are eighty large outdoor bells in the Elliott collection, each carefully documented and fitted into its proper historical niche.

227. *Detail of the 1859 church bell showing the band of decorative reliefs. Figures of cherubs alternate with inscriptions pertaining to the bell's manufacture.* ELLIOTT COLLECTION (News and Dispatch Photo)

226. *Bell cast in 1859 by the C. W. Coffin Company of Cincinnati. Once used in a Toledo, Ohio, church.* ELLIOTT COLLECTION

228. *This Minnetaree chieftain leading the frenzied Dog Dance shows how Indian rattles from deer hoofs were once used. (Painted in 1833 by a young Swiss artist, Karl Bodmer.)*

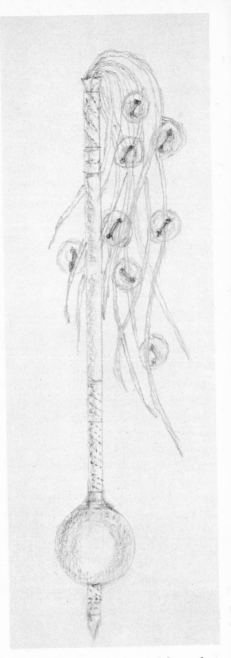

229. *Gourd rattle filled with sand or grain gives a swishing sound, accented by the tinkle of little Indian trade bells decorating the leather fringe. Beautifully beaded handle. Kiowa. Circa 1880.* PRIVATE COLLECTION

AMERICAN INDIAN RATTLES

Collectors do not usually associate the American Indians with cultural groups employing bells to any great extent. Yet they adopted the white man's sleigh bells, given in trade, with avid delight. Wisconsin historical records show the high trade value placed on such tintinnabula. In the winter of 1804/1805 Malhoit was pricing "forty small sleigh bells at a value of three beaver skins"; and in 1821 the American Fur Company inventoried to one of its traders for the Milwaukee area "½ doz. sleigh bells @ $3.83."

These the Indians wore on their wrists, their ankles, or on their long plaits of hair. They also had a special fondness for using them as peripheral ornamentation on wearing apparel or on other objects like cradles. It is old items of this sort, decorated with Indian trade bells, that especially appeal to collectors, although even single archaeological specimens of early Indian trade bells are now considered museum material.

An item from a museum shop listing of the 1950s is typical of the bell-decorated Indian apparel sought by collectors:

B124 INDIAN BELL NECKLACE, Wishram Indians; a very early mid-nineteenth century necklace of large Hudson's Bay trade beads and trade bells; these old cast brass bells are a distinctive type traded in the Northwest and probably date around 1850; this necklace, one of several heirlooms purchased from a local Indian family, has 29 red glass beads with yellow centers and 24 rare brass beads, all about ½″ diameter; also five old brass trade bells, each 1″ long overall. Rare $25.00

Aside from adapting the white man's sleigh bells to his own purpose, the American Indian devised bell-like ornaments distinctly his own. These are the cone-shaped tinklers he rolled

230. *Northwest Indian rattle in the shape of a doughnut. Note the resemblance to the doughnutlike horse bell known to the Japanese (Ill. 233). Nass River, British Columbia.* MUSEUM OF THE AMERICAN INDIAN

from a triangular piece of copper or tin. The Plains Indians were especially adept at fashioning these bell-like tinkles in great quantities. They made a melodious fringe for leggings, skirts, and other apparel.

The rhythmic clicking and tinkling of such tintinnabula was an indispensable feature of Indian ceremonial dance, an aid to continued movement, and a constant incentive to vigorous performance. Costume tinklers alone did not satisfy these needs, however, and so a variety of large hand rattles came into play for greater rhythmic accent.

Generally speaking, these rattles may be divided into two main classes: those in which ob-

231. *Indian effigy rattle of copper. Alaska.* MUSEUM OF THE AMERICAN INDIAN

jects of approximately equal size are strung together on a stick or a thong and those in which small pebbles or seeds are enclosed in a hollow container of some sort. In private collections the most commonly seen examples of these two classifications are the hoops strung with deer hoofs or perhaps bird beaks, from tribes of the Far West, and either gourd-and-pebble rattles from the Plains Indians or tortoiseshell rattles from the Iroquois.

Whatever the type, the Indian's own handmade rattles were looked upon as symbols of prestige, as important accompaniments to all dance ceremonies and shamanistic rituals. Along with other ritualistic paraphernalia, they were supposedly endowed with magical powers, including the power to awe evil spirits. They were therefore sacred objects.

Collectors acquiring their first American Indian rattles and making even a superficial study of their use are amazed to find a degree of resemblance between some of these and certain types of bells from distant cultures. Indians of the Northwest, for example, used a doughnut-like rattle that in shape closely approximates the Japanese *ba rei* familiar to collectors. They also made a goblet-shaped rattle resembling the traditional bell form used in Europe's earliest handbells.

Most of these were of wood, only rarely of copper. But they all pose an interesting question: If metal had been more readily available to these skilled Indian carvers of the Northwest, would they perhaps have become our first native American bellmakers? Though there is not enough evidence to make any sweeping evaluation of their role in this respect, there is merit in the thought. After all, using materials at hand, some tribes even mastered the technique of fashioning free-swinging clappers. They hollowed out the horns of mountain sheep and fitted them with clappers of the same material.

For the bell collector of catholic tastes there is a very fertile field here for a fascinating study of Americana, as yet barely touched upon by the majority of collectors.

6

Beast of Burden Bells

IN THE WORLD OF ANIMAL BELLS, those used on horse trappings claim widespread attention from collectors; and because of their venerable heritage and their varied styles they are deserving of this attention. As already observed, the Lurs and the Israelites and almost all early people employed horse bells of one kind or another. Each culture evolved its own style of belled trappings, but the reasons for their use, real or imagined, remained fairly constant: they frightened off any evil spirits lurking near the horse's path; on narrow, winding trails they warned of his approach; and they instilled confidence, even courage, in the animal himself, especially in warfare. On special occasions they also added pomp and gaiety to ceremonial processions.

One way to visualize early fashions in horse bells is to study historic equines in statuette form, like the curious Haniwa horse figures from ancient Japanese burial mounds. These provide an accurate record of the actual bells horses wore in Japan because such terra-cotta figures were modeled from real-life subjects. All during the long span of years between the second and the eighth centuries it was customary to pose realistic figures of persons and animals on Japan's burial mounds; and because the horse was virtually worshiped in that country, many of the statuettes are of him, fully caparisoned and usually with bells.

An unusual and much later type of Japanese horse bell is one that is unique to that country.

It is a doughnut-shaped object of cast brass with rolling pellets enclosed, and it is called a *bo rei*. Since it is a type found in many sizes, some as large as a saucer, Japanese collectors are fond of assembling a graduated set for display in much the same way American collectors like to assemble a graduated set of sleigh bells.

Horses the world over have always played a prominent part in the legendry of each land,

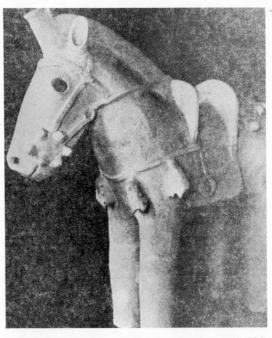

232. *Illustration from* Haniwa *by Fumio Miki, translated by Roy Andrew Miller and published by Charles E. Tuttle Company.* COURTESY OF CHARLES E. TUTTLE COMPANY

233. *The Japanese country doctor who, according to legend, invented the doughnutlike object that was later adopted as a horse bell (bo-rei) in Japan. From an old print.*

234. *Pair of very old and rare Mongolian stirrups. Sixteen heavy one-inch crotals on each add considerably to the weight.* RANNEY COLLECTION

and in some instances even their trappings are the subject of mythical tales. The Japanese *bo rei* originates in a typical Oriental legend about an old country doctor who traveled about from village to village and who one day was met on the road by a tiger in great pain. The tiger requested the old doctor to cut from its throat a growth causing the pain. This the doctor could not do unless he had some way to hold open the beast's mouth. That night he made an iron doughnut-shaped ring of the type later worn by horses. Meeting the tiger again the next day, he stood the ring in its mouth and operated through the hole. Afterward, such rings became a part of each wandering doctor's equipment and were called "tiger stretchers." Carried and twirled on the fingers, they announced his coming in each village.

Minus any myths, there is still much conjectural romance attached to many old sets of horse bells. An ancient pair of heavy bell-fringed stirrups may have spurred on a Mongolian horseman to victory—or a Roman soldier. Even more romantically, they may have been worn by a medieval knight like Parzival's antagonist on whose feet "the stirrups with golden bells rang true." An old strap of carefully preserved Mongolian pony bells could have been worn by the mount carrying some Chinese princess beyond the Great Wall, as the unwilling bride of a distant Khan in order to keep peace in the kingdom. And from Russia come moving tableaux of horses' troika bells frightening off wolf packs from sleighs speeding through dark forests.

A number of European countries are credited with certain horse bells of a style not seen elsewhere. The muleteers' conical bell towers used

235. *Spanish muleteers' strange wooden bell-towers, used on lead mules climbing the Pyrenees in the Basque country. Each cone is pierced to accommodate three tiers of bells.* MOSLEY COLLECTION

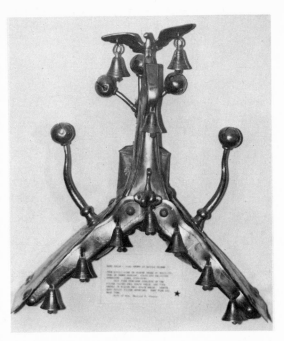

236. *Saddle chimes (hame bells) from Sicily. Used in dress parades, they originally belonged to nobility. Circa 1820–1840.* WINSTON JONES COLLECTION

237. *Back-pad of tuned bells, once popular with Swiss horsemen on festival days. The spring-mounted clappers are activated by the slightest vibration.* PRIVATE COLLECTION

in the Basque country are unique to that region, and so unusual that surely there is a "story" underlying their origin, if only it were known. For festival days in southern Italy and Sicily it is traditional for horses to wear towers of bells festooned with colorful streamers. Supposedly the height of the tower is commensurate with the owner's wealth.

Switzerland is known for the musical quality of its animal bells—and fortunately so, for the sake of spectators at such festivals as the annual spring Sechseläuten, where bell-laden horses perform at a thunderous gallop. The highlight of this April day is the burning of winter, person-

ified by a giant snowman. To help swell the noise and ring in the spring, village boys run around shaking all the unused harness bells they can find.

One set of Swiss horse bells not often seen anymore, but once popular for such festivals, is a graduated arrangement of tuned bells mounted on a tough leather back-pad decorated with colored fringe. Mounted upside down—that is, with the open mouth turned up—each bell has its clapper fixed to a spring so that the entire set rings at the slightest jiggle. On a galloping horse the sound is best described as a carillon gone wild.

238. *Elegantly mounted brasses and fliers with colorful cockades; used by nobility. Royalty seen in the portrait brasses are Queen Victoria, King George V and Queen Mary, and King Edward VII.* PHOTO, COURTESY OF BERENICE DU BOIS

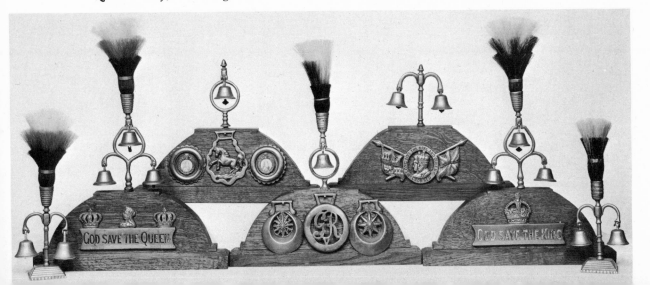

239. *One of some eighty-six different styles of swingers on permanent exhibit at the Municipal Museum, Hull, England.* MUNICIPAL MUSEUM, HULL, ENGLAND

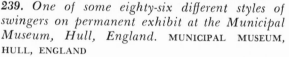

240. *Set of latten bells with graceful, decorated leather hood. Particularly well matched bells.* MARION SPENCE COLLECTION

Less vibrant are the lightly jingling fliers so characteristic of English horse bells. Also called swingers, these carry one or more brass bells swinging freely in a little upright frame topped by a cockade, or brass socket holding a stiff plume of dyed horsehair. The largest flier ever found carries eight bells and a brush. An excellent overall view of these little swingers awaits visitors to the Municipal Museum at Hull, England. Eighty-six different styles are exhibited, along with all sorts of ornamental horse brasses.

Fliers were worn largely for ornamental purposes on festive occasions or by fashionable carriage horses bearing the local gentry from tea party to tea party. They were fastened either between the ears or on the saddle. When not in use they could be set in low boxwood stands especially designed to hold them. When the day for using such fliers had passed entirely, small groups of them were permanently retired to their boxwood stands and kept in the manor

house as ornamental reminders of England's colorful old coaching days. Occasionally a collector is fortunate in locating such a mounted set, but only after a long wait. He is more likely to acquire what he wants one by one, and then arrange to have them mounted individually.

Out of the great welter of English-type horse bells, there is one other of unusual distinction that is highly desirable in a collection. This is the wagoner's set of latten bells suspended in an iron frame fitting into sockets on the horse's collar. Warning of his approach on narrow country lanes, the bells saved the driver a great deal of back-up time. Their ring could be heard for miles, giving oncoming drivers time to pull aside for the massive hay cart or wagon piled high with sheaves.

Such sets are called latten bells because of the mixed metals in them; or they are called "box bells" because of the boxlike leather hoods under which the four to seven bells hang. Although they were introduced for utilitarian purposes on large draft horses, these sets are not lacking

241. *Small horse bells from five lands.* Left to right: *Tibet, India, Scotland, Japan, Belgium. Little bell from India, in punch-work design, is common on horse-drawn tongas in the Kashmir.* PRIVATE COLLECTION

in appearance. The leather hood is often studded with brasswork, sometimes using agricultural motifs. Although the bells have not always been assembled in uniform size, nor in perfect gradation, usually they have been selected for tone so that ringing together they give off a pleasing chord.

It is not surprising to find bells of this type so musical, for many were cast by the same founders who made England's church bells. One of the most prolific founders, whose initials *R. W.* appear on both latten bells and large packhorse crotals, was Robert Wells (1764–1799) of Wiltshire.

OLD CONESTOGA WAGON BELLS

It was only natural that bellmakers in the New World pattern their horse bells after the multitude of styles known in Europe and England. This explains why old catalogues are filled with pictures of Russian troika chimes, Swiss shaft chimes, Norwegian rump bells, and the like. But there are other types of early team bells never pictured in manufacturers' catalogues because they were either made or hand-

assembled by local blacksmiths. The Conestoga wagon bells on their gracefully turned iron hoops are among these.

Historians who have made lifetime studies of the Conestoga wagon all agree that the bells, as a standard part of its equipment, were purchased in bulk and turned over to any local blacksmith. He mounted them on the required

242. *Conestoga wagon bells. Iron bow is typical of the style used on teams pulling these great covered wagons.* MARION SPENCE COLLECTION

243. *Mules equipped with bells demonstrate how mining freighters were once hauled. Operated by Horace C. Lewis of Ketchum, Idaho, until about 1905, this was one of the largest outfits in the West. Complete with original bells, it remains in excellent state of preservation.* COURTESY OF CAMERA SHOP AT SUN VALLEY

hoops with pointed prongs that would slip into staples on the harness hames. Mr. Howard C. Frey, the foremost present-day Conestoga historian, leans toward the theory that the best bells were German imports or were cast in the colonies by German immigrants. But whether of welded iron, brazed iron, brazed brass, or cast brass, none has ever been found with a distinguishing mark to show where or by whom it was made. For that matter, no two identical sets of Conestoga bells have ever been found. The iron bows vary as much as the bells themselves. Some are covered with dogskin tanned with the hair on. Others are wrapped in cloth, or they have long tails of fur decorating them.

Collectors can only theorize on the making of Conestoga bells, but they can turn to a great deal of descriptive material on their actual use. The teams for the wagons were selected and hitched in pairs according to size, strength, and intelligence. The front ones, called the lead team, were the smallest and nimblest and most knowledgeable; the middlers, or swing team, were larger; those next to the wagon were the wheelers and were the largest. A full set of bells consisted of two five-bell hoops for the lead horses, two four-bell ones for the swing span, and a three-bell hoop for the right wheeler. The nigh wheeler seldom wore bells, since the driver rode saddle there.

His beautiful six-horse teams were the Conestoga wagoner's joy—these and the bells they wore. But if he had trouble along the road and needed help from another driver, he was required to forfeit his bells. Naturally it was every wagoner's wish to return home, literally, "with bells on" so that all could see he had successfully overcome the hazards of the road. Many a driver

244. *Not all horse bells were used in workaday situations. Some very fancy ones were designed for dress parade.* WHITMAN COLLECTION

in trouble would go to great lengths to avoid forfeiting his bells, even slyly breaking his wagon tongue so passing drivers could not help him and claim his bells.

Named for the Pennsylvania valley where they were made—the valley of the Conestoga Indians—these wagons once ran in fleets numbering three thousand daily between Pittsburgh and Philadelphia. Little imagination is needed to visualize what so many chiming bells added to the majestic scene of all those red and blue wagons moving along under their white homespun tops.

Most sets of the bells were eventually broken, and today very few collectors—or even museums—can boast a complete and original set. But even one hoop in a collection can bring to mind bits of the historical romance connected with these bells. Someone, somewhere, perhaps owns the arch of bells George Washington mentions buying at Leesburg on September 1, 1784. Or perhaps someone owns an arch of bells from one of the Conestoga wagons that carried supplies to Washington's men during their hard winter at Valley Forge.

Later when the Far West opened up, similar arches of bells were a "must" for the freighter teams hauling ore and borax. Freighting schedules in those early days called for travel by night as well as by day, and in the mountains heavily loaded freighters picked up considerable speed on the treacherous downgrade. Bells were imperative as a warning device to upcoming teams.

One of the largest mining freighters ever built remains intact with its bells in the state of Idaho today. Team bell enthusiasts in the West were privileged to see this freighter driven before the grandstands during the Sun Valley Rodeos of 1937 and 1938. As had been customary, the freighter was drawn exclusively by mules except for the wheel team of large draft horses.

The use of bells on horses in a semiofficial way did not end with the passing of large-scale freighters, for the horsecar came on the Ameri-

245. *With its swish of horsehair plumes and musical two-tone chime, this fancy set of horsebells enlivened many parades. Nickel-plated throughout, and highly polished. Eagle finial of excellent detail adds patriotic touch.* MAYER COLLECTION

can scene in major cities about 1850. Each horse pulling a passenger car wore a bell prominently marked with the name of the local railway company employing him. The earliest bell dates from 1832 when the first horsecars for passengers began operating on wooden rails in New York City.

By comparison with the graceful and musical wagon bells, horsecar bells are nondescript and toneless. Their greatest merit lies in their historic worth and their challenge to the collector wanting to display the names of as many street railway companies as possible.

SLEIGH BELLS FROM CONNECTICUT

As in other lands, the horse in colonial America was the prince of animals—generally as a working creature wearing heavy brass bells, but sometimes as a participant in parades and other special events, where he was decked out with fancy bells that might be of silver or gold. Carriage horses employed to buggy the family to church often wore fliers or small arches of chimes with pinwheel clappers bouncing on the outside.

247. *A chiming pony bell, American; a five-bell swinger, English; and a strap of ancient Mongolian pony bells. Strap is covered with old red wool and bells are embossed with rosette motifs and Chinese characters. Very high pitched but musical.* PRIVATE COLLECTION

246. *Proud horses once wore these stately bell pieces. The softly colored horsehair plumes are crowned with pinwheel-clappered bells.* MARION SPENCE COLLECTION

But whether they were workaday bells or fancier types, the full medley of their music was at its peak in winter. There was added traffic then, for that was the ideal time to haul heavy loads on smooth, snow-packed roads. Though he might have only one wagon, a farmer often owned two or three sledges loaded and ready to move after the first snowfall. So many sledges and sleighs speeding silently along created a public hazard, and laws were soon passed requiring the use of bells.

Manufacturers rose to the need and brought out the greatest assortment of sleigh bells ever made. In order to adequately describe the various kinds he may acquire, today's collector must familiarize himself with a whole new vocabulary of terms long since fallen into disuse. Saddle bells; hame bells; fliers; shaft, or thill bells; rump bells; collars, and body straps—all were used and available in an undetermined number of shapes and combinations to please every driver.

The popular globular sleigh bell was made in twenty numbered sizes, the largest (No. 18) measuring nearly four inches in diameter and the smallest (No. 00) measuring less than one inch. The largest often hung singly on a collar and was called a "pung bell" after the one-horse sledge of that name. When used on a span, one on each horse, large bells of this or any other kind could be had in pairs carefully tuned to produce a pleasing sound.

These globular sleigh bells of graduated size were individualized by each maker—compressed, elongated, or expanded into different shapes and in single- or double- or triple-throated styles; that is, the bells had a single slit cut to let out the sound or cross slits or six slits in the Scandinavian manner. Their shapes gave rise to fanciful catalogue names such as tulip, apricot, or acorn bells. The acorn-shaped ones are special favorites with collectors. They were one of Ezra G. Cone's patents, and were being produced by

248. *Three types of bells for the working horse: ordinary saddle chimes, nickel over brass; rump bells, yellow brass on polished red leather; and a single horsecar bell from Louisville, Kentucky, marked* CENTRAL PASSENGER RR CO. PRIVATE COLLECTION

the Gong Bell Manufacturing Company in the mid-nineteenth century.

Sleigh bells were given a further stamp of individuality with embossings and engravings. In the early days when they were cast and not merely stamped out of brass, they often bore the manufacturer's initials. These are a welcome clue to the collector, indicating not only the maker but the relative age of the bells. Nine out of ten sets of initials will prove to be those of Connecticut Valley bellmakers. Though the making of sleigh bells was by no means exclusive to that area, the Connecticut Valley—and East Hampton in particular—soon gained a reputation as the sleigh bell capital of the world.

The original credit for this honor goes to the same William Barton who pioneered the entire bellmaking industry in East Hampton. With true Yankee inventiveness he devised a method that would speed the production of sleigh bells.

249. *One of the oldest existing straps of American sleigh bells. The name* J. HANKS *is marked on each bell. Hanks is known to have established a bell foundry in the colonies as early as 1700.* CRANNELL SADDLE SHOP, BROADALBIN, NEW YORK

Up until that time they had been cast in two spheres, then soldered together after inserting a pellet. Barton's idea was to cast them in one piece, around a pellet in a ball of sand that could later be sifted out. Most of the early bellmakers sent their apprentices to Barton; and since they were free to copy what they learned, his new process was soon in effect throughout the area.

Grandfather Barton would have been gratified knowing that East Hampton maintained its worldwide reputation in the sleigh bell market long after the peak year of production was

250. Left: *Stamped figure of small horse and initials* W E B *stand for William E. Barton, grandson of the first William.* Right: *Initials* W B *mark bell as one made by William Barton himself, the man who speeded up sleigh-bell production in East Hampton.* PRIVATE COLLECTION

251. *Shaft chimes, also known as thill bells, with heavy duty clappers.* PRIVATE COLLECTION

reached in 1887. The company with the longest continuing record is the well-known Bevin Brothers, still in operation after nearly a century and a half of bellmaking, with sleigh bells a specialty.

Indicative of names once famous in the industry are these initials on sleigh bells attributable to East Hampton manufacturers:

W B	for William Barton himself
H B	for Hiram or Hubbard, his sons
W E B	for William E. Barton, his grandson
J S	for John Starr of Starr Brothers Bell Company, established in 1882
V B	for Veasey and Buell, a company well known about 1850
N S	for Niles & Strong, another of East Hampton's early bell factories
W H	probably for one of the Hill family, who continued in the industry until recent years

A fine place to see long straps of initialed sleigh bells is the barn at Sturbridge Village in Massachusetts. Some of them are marked with full names, such as C. N. SMITH, E. HAMPTON, CT., or SMITH & PARSONS, E. HAMPTON, CT. These were made by Clarke N. Smith and his onetime partner Phil Parsons.

The Crannell Saddle Shop of Broadalbin, New York, owns a nine-bell strap with each bell marked J. HANKS. This is conceded to be one of the earliest recorded straps of American sleigh bells, Jonathan Hanks having established what was possibly the first recognized bell foundry in the colonies in the 1700s. More than the usual interest attaches to these historic bells, since Jonathan Hanks was ancestor to Abraham Lincoln's mother.

Occasionally a collector will come upon a string of sleigh bells with somewhat offbeat inscriptions, requested apparently as the personal wish of the purchaser. A decade ago a string with decidedly unusual wordings was offered by a dealer in upstate New York—a string that may once have belonged to a circuit rider of philosophical persuasions. As described:

On this string are bells # 1, 2 and 3. The inscription on the back of the bells marked #1 reads REFORM IN ALL THINGS; on the bells marked #2, TRUTH FOR EFFECT, BUT LOVE TO DIRECT; and on the bells marked #3, ALL FORCE IN MAN IS GOVERNING, UNPHILOSOPHICAL.

The manufacturers, of course, could either rivet or toggle their sleigh bells to straps, but great loads of them were simply sold by the pound as loose bells to harness and hardware distributors. The Bevin family still has the little old trunk in which William Bevin carried his sleigh bells when he traveled by steamer to New York to sell them. The price of a finished strap varied from one to eighteen dollars, depending on the quality of the leather used, and also the quality and number of bells on it. A leading antiques magazine making an editorial excursion into the subject of sleigh bells in 1950 found straps in most antique shops averaging fifty cents a bell. The asking price today is, of course, considerably more.

This increase is due, in part, to the growing demand for straps of sleigh bells even among those who are not collectors. The decorative possibilities here have captured the attention of many; for others, there is joy involved in owning a strap of such bells merely for sentimental reasons in recalling the past. Poets and song writers alike have waxed nostalgic over the silvery sound of sleigh bells. It was their rhythmic staccato heard on the streets of New York that inspired Clement Moore's classic "'Twas the night before Christmas/When all through the house/Not a creature was stirring/Not even a mouse."

CATTLE BELLS

The lowly cowbell, also reminiscent of an earlier day, is collected for its sentimental associations as well as for factual data on its making. In an age when woodlands and open meadows are disappearing, it is pleasant to glance upon a row of cowbells, to lift one and listen to its hollow echo as Thoreau must have when he wrote:

> That cheap piece of tinkling brass which the farmer hangs about his cow's neck has been more to me than the tons of metal which are swung in the belfry.

Surprisingly enough, there is more extant factual data relating to the cowbell than one would suppose. Several quite lengthy European dissertations have been published on the subject. And in this country the New England Dairy and Food Council maintains a file of published research as well as a traveling exhibit of cowbells from around the world.

Strange as it may seem, the first recorded bells of the type used on cows were the handbells used by Saint Patrick and other missionaries to Ireland about the fifth century. These were cut from sheets of iron, the corners cut, and the sides then bent together. As the art of working metal progressed, cowbells were more easily made by stamping them out with a press; and the finest of all were cast in a mold. However, because the American frontier was always in motion, its arts were transient and remained crude well through the nineteenth century. Thus many

pioneers further west continued to cut and bend their own cowbells by hand, as Abraham Lincoln is known to have done. Moreover, the handcrafting of such bells continued to occupy tinsmiths and blacksmiths on the frontier long after livestock bells were being mass-produced in factories.

In fact, it was possible to prosper well on the sale of livestock bells alone, for they were an absolute necessity for early settlers and those moving west over vast unfenced lands. Only by the sound of their bells could roving livestock be easily located, and there is more fact than fiction to the idea that their sound scared off four-footed, and sometimes two-footed, marauders. One Midwesterner who so prospered and who was known far and wide for his handmade livestock bells was Orson Starr of Royal Oak, Michigan, whose father before him had been making livestock bells in Ontario County, New York.

When Orson moved to Royal Oak in 1831, the cowbell factory he established was that community's first industry; he continued to operate it for nearly fifty years. His bells were made in eight sizes, and at first had his name O. STARR in raised letters. Later a seven-pointed star was substituted for the name. Due to careful brazing and a generous coating of brass, Starr bells have a remarkable tone that can be heard for two miles. At the peak of Orson's success, a wagonload of his bells had an exchange value equal to that of a large farm. He gladly made the exchange, and so acquired a much-needed larger home for his family without endangering his savings.

Many who are interested in this area of collecting try to complete a numbered set of Starr cowbells. Others prefer looking for examples with original labels representing all different makers, such as Holstein bells by Blum Manufacturing Company of Collinsville, Illinois; Hereford bells by M & M Manufacturing Company of Yoakum, Texas; and either Long Distance or Kentucky Improved styles by Bevin Brothers.

252. *Where cowbells were cast in the city of Chicago over a century ago.* COURTESY OF THE CRANE COMPANY

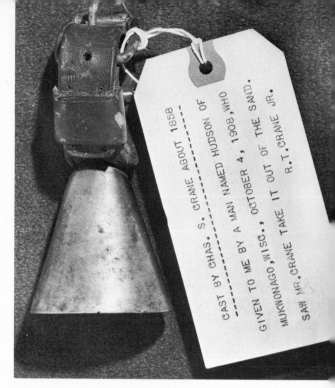

253. *The only known example of a Crane cowbell.* COURTESY OF THE CRANE COMPANY

As with other collectibles, there can be disillusioning experiences in buying even an ordinary object like a cowbell. Both dealers and collectors have frequently been deceived by the heavy brass cowbell dated 1878 and embossed with the maker's name, CHIANTEL FONDEUR, and the Swiss canton where he worked, SAIGNELEGIER. This is a beautifully toned bell available in at least ten sizes, and a genuinely old specimen is much to be desired. However, too many newer specimens are overrated and overpriced. The fact that they are all dated 1878 does not mean they were all cast that year. They have been made continuously in Switzerland and exported in quantities. Years ago two American firms acquired molds for these same bells, and they too made hundreds upon hundreds of them, all of course dated 1878. Up until the Second World War, Sears, Roebuck and Company had been selling these intermittently since 1900, purchasing over the years a grand total of fifty-five thousand from one firm alone. With such statistics in mind it is quite obvious how many such bells are in circulation.

Unfortunate experiences in collecting—perhaps paying too much for bells that are not what they seem—are sometimes outweighed by exciting experiences of discovery. Not too many years ago a collector was surprised to see in a Chicago merchant's catalogue the quaint old picture of a heretofore unknown bell foundry. Borrowed from a memory album, the picture showed a little wooden building topped with a prominent sign reading:

R. T. CRANE
BRASS & BELL FOUNDRY

Apparently no one, not even the present-day Crane Company, knew anything of the foundry's history. There was excitement enough among company officials and collectors alike when one surviving livestock bell was found as proof of the foundry's early work. And so another illustrious name was added to the list of those who supplied our pioneers with livestock bells.

Cattle bells from other parts of the world differ in their shape, size, and tone according to the resources and the artistic mores of the country. Many of Switzerland's large cowbells are of cast brass and are classics of their kind, so beautifully toned that over the mountains they sound like a distant carillon. And indeed, many are made by the same founders who cast the village church chimes. The smaller tinkling sizes used on calves are the very same kind used by the Swiss bell-ringers.

The pageantry associated with the use of cowbells in the Swiss Alps has been well celebrated

254. *A noted type of Australian bullock bell that has been in production for more than a century.* COOPER COLLECTION

255. *An excellent example of the odd wooden bullock bells native to Thailand and Cambodia.* LA ROSE COLLECTION

in pictures and stories. During the semiannual trek to the mountains and homeward again, each cow wears a bell proportioned to her size. The leader, or queen, may wear a twenty-pounder so heavy that she finds it impossible to graze with the other cows and must be hand fed by the herdsman. These larger bells are seldom available to collectors, for they quite often bear a family crest and have been kept as heirlooms for generations; and even the smaller sizes oftentimes display artistic designs, names, and pretty sentiments hammered on by special craftsmen.

Austrian cowbells from the Tyrol region are also of a comparatively large size, often with colorful painting on their bulbous surface and with beautiful straps stitched and fringed in color. A great deal of pride goes into decorating a large strap worthy of a Tyrolean cow-queen's bell. As all who have priced them are aware, the straps alone cost eight or ten times as much as the bell.

A rather odd cattle bell is now and then mentioned in Australian literature as a Condamine bell. An original label on one of these identifies it as a "Genuine Jones" Condamine Bull Frog Bell. The word *Condamine* refers to the name of an Australian river flowing through the cattle and sheep country of south-central Queensland, where such bells were first made during

the 1860s. The words *Bull Frog* supposedly have reference to the deep and hoarse tonal quality of the bells, as in the case of Burma's froglike gongs that are made to "croak" for rain.

The maker of these bells, a Mr. S. W. Jones, was a blacksmith who knew well how to rivet, braze, and peg a bell that could be heard six or seven miles distant. The bells were popular for use on bullock teams going into unsettled areas. The true Jones bells were stamped on the tongue, and these are greatly prized when they can be found.

Mr. Jones hired several assistants to help him keep up with production, and many learned how to make good Condamine bells; but only one learned the secret of the Bull Frog Bell. That was Mr. Alf Ormand, who became Jones's successor in 1912 and is today the only man alive who knows the secret. He is privileged to label his products Condamine Bull Frog Bells. All others are simply Condamine Bells.

In the Fast East, cattle bells of quite original shapes are often made from wood, bamboo, or bone. Bullock bells used in Cambodia and Thailand are strange contraptions made from which-

256. Heavy and ornate old brass collars once worn by India's sacred bulls. Full-bodied images of sacred bulls decorate the clasps. PRIVATE COLLECTION

257. Double supporting ears and intricate brass embroidery give individuality to these cattle bells. Of uncertain origin but judged not to be brassware from India. PRIVATE COLLECTION

ever of these materials is at hand. They consist of a hollow cylinder with hinged clappers knocking against either side. The bells range in size from heavy ones a foot high to miniatures only an inch high, the small ones being used on goats and other small animals.

On the Indonesian island of Bali, where the venerated cows of India do not thrive, water buffalo are used to harrow the rice paddies. They wear enormous wooden bells of teak or mahogany, measuring a yard wide sometimes. These have wooden tongues that sound with a hollow clapp-clapp as the animals plod through the water. One feature of the island's annual New Year's festival is a race among the finest of the water buffalo. For this occasion they are bedecked with fanciful headdresses and bells more enormous than usual.

On the neighboring island of Java the yellow color of brass is popular for all metalwork, and here the water buffalo wear brass bells of a peculiar helmet shape. The everyday bells are rather rough and plain, but for special festivals the Javanese bring out helmet-shaped bells of gleaming, golden brass and these are intricately engraved with symbolic figures.

Since in India bulls, rather than cows, are actually the sacred animals, they wear the finest collars. Masterful pieces of metalwork worthy of Nandi himself, they consist of metal plaques hinged together and hung with ornate crotals on both sides. The standing figure of a bull ornaments the clasp. Being associated with Krishna and thus venerated, though not truly sacred, the cows in India also wear fancy collars. Often they are made up of blue and white beads laced through one or more bells. The collars reserved for the "bell" cow, or leader in each herd, are very special and not readily available in a collector's market. When an old one is acquired, it is certain to have been used according to tradition. When the leader of a herd dies, her collar is removed and passed to her eldest daughter, but not before it has been reconsecrated by a Brahman priest in a three-day ceremony.

CAMEL CHIMES

When looking for either a camel or an elephant bell, collectors have a wider selection than is sometimes realized. The most commonly pictured types—and both are favorites with collectors—are the dangling cupped chimes for the camels of Iran (Persia) and the spherical bells with tiger-claw closings for the elephants of India. Yet they are not the only kinds associated with these beasts of burden.

Early depictions of camels and elephants at work give a good indication of the assorted types of bells they have worn at various times and places. The first known drawings of camels wearing bells were found on the walls of Persepolis, capital of ancient Persia, and here the bells are small crotals on chains. An eighteenth-century print shows a Syrian camel equipped with more distinguished-looking bells, row upon row of them hanging on a high board fastened to his back. Early illustrations for Caesar's *Commentaries* picture his triumphal procession of elephants festooned with large bells hanging at their sides and strings of crotals resembling sleigh bells on their chest bands. Colorful prints show the early maharajas of India seated in howdahs on their elephants and parading through the streets of Benares. The lavish trappings include bells of various sizes on the elephants' ankles and even around the howdahs.

The elephant bell with tiger-claw closings is seen in some collections as an old specimen of fine, heavy brass without decoration. More commonly seen are the colorfully enameled ones produced in large numbers for India's tourist and export trade. The work on these is very intricate, and the workers who do the enameling are said to use brushes made of only a single hair in order to follow such fine traceries. These more modern types come in graduated sizes, from miniatures as small as a walnut to large ones as big as a grapefruit. The largest ring with a deep and resonant tone befitting an elephant's stately tread. When worn in pairs, their measured chiming is unforgettable.

258. *From an old print showing a Syrian wedding party. Lead camel is well bedecked with bells. Note tiers of them swinging on a board fastened to his back.*

259. *The old and the new in elephant bells from India, where the name for them is* jang. *The old one (at left) is nearly double the weight of the new.* PRIVATE COLLECTION

260. *Curious old bell from Thailand, in a primitive but sturdy wooden cradle. Very ably designed. By collective consideration of experts, this has been adjudged an elephant bell.* MOSLEY COLLECTION

Although the significance of the tiger-claw closings on this particular elephant bell may have been forgotten, they originally served a protective purpose. On the theory that like repels like, this feature of the bell supposedly scared off the elephant's chief enemy—the tiger.

A very rare type of bell from Thailand has, by collective consideration, been termed an elephant bell. The Thais have a genius for welding artistic elements from disparate cultures into something essentially their own, which may account for the unique construction of this peculiar bell. Large and flat, it hangs in a crude wooden frame of obvious age. Sometimes the frame is set on rockers so that the bell sounds as it rocks back and forth. Not all of them are made with clappers, however; some are struck from the outside with padded sticks. The unanswered question in the minds of collectors is just how this bell could have been used on an elephant, unless perhaps an attendant was assigned to carry it.

Occasionally this same type of bell has been offered for sale as a temple bell. Apparently the one displayed at the Chicago World's Fair of 1893 was on exhibit as such, complete with a gong stick wound in red wool. It was labeled the gift of the city of Bangkok.

Probably the largest of the long Persian camel chimes yet seen in a private collection boasts eight bells cupped together and weighs forty

261. *Extremely heavy old animal bell, undoubtedly from Cambodia, of the same type portrayed on large stone figures guarding ancient Cambodian temples. Its archaic beauty suggests ceremonial rather than normal work use. Unusually fine casting, with each smaller section of the mouth depicting a horrible monster and the two larger ones representing huge tongues between sharp tusks.* HALPERIN COLLECTION

pounds. Except for their blue-beaded tassels, many of the chimes are undecorated. When they do display emblematic designs they are doubly desirable, of course. The blue beads found on the tassels are turquoise from Persia and are regarded as talismans to prevent bodily harm. Such beads also decorate another typical Persian camel chime, the old neck chains laced with tassels and assorted bells.

Because of the size of the early camel caravans and the value of the cargo they carried, every precaution was taken to ensure their safety. Major caravans running from Mecca to Damascus in the Byzantine Empire generally required three thousand camels, and with their merchandise were valued near one million dollars. Like the blue-beaded talisman, bells had their role in helping along the treasure-laden camels and keeping them together in the track-

263. *Detail of Persia's (Iran's) national emblem as it appears on camel chime.*

that opened an "antique attic" had a room literally fitted with camel chimes of every description hanging from the rafters. Such collecting bonanzas are not likely to be repeated today, although isolated examples of odd camel bells continue to filter through from such countries as Turkey, Egypt, Arabia, and Pakistan.

264. *Turkish camel bells of brass, with typically Mohammedan decorations in flat relief. Background is blue and red baked enamel.*

262. *From Persia, an old camel chime with traditional blue beads. On the largest bell, in low relief, is the Persian national emblem. For a time this went undetected under layers of grime.*
PRIVATE COLLECTION

less desert. Once considered pure myth, there is now thought to be some merit in the idea that the music of bells can prove both comforting and exhilarating to the animals wearing them. And if the music of bells could do that for the dour and balky camels, small wonder their drivers used bells aplenty on them.

The day of the long camel caravan has faded, however; and for those who have not yet added an old Persian camel chime to their collection, it is none too soon to start searching. A decade or two ago, a collector seeking such a bell was not surprised when a dealer pulled out a boxful to choose from. One prominent Chicago store

265. *Persian camel chain and a single camel bell from Arabia.*
PRIVATE COLLECTION

266. *Wooden camel bell from Ethiopia. Note the outline of a reclining camel incised on the front.* ESTHER OAKES COLLECTION

Among the oddities are the anklet bells used on performing camels—larger bells hanging from the neck would be bothersome while the camel is dancing or racing. The anklets are hollow brass circlets with pellets rolling inside. They are tied on either just above the knee or above the foot.

An altogether different camel bell and one difficult to categorize is known to collectors as the U.S. Cavalry bell, supposedly used on camels imported by Secretary of War Jefferson Davis for transporting supplies among army posts in the arid Southwest. The project was experimental and doomed to failure. Neither the camels nor the army personnel could adapt to the situation. By 1861 the last remnants of the camel corps were corralled near army headquarters in Los Angeles and eventually auctioned off.

That bells were used on the several dozen army camels is an established fact, but whether the so-called U.S. Cavalry bell was the official one is another question. Several area museums own documented examples of old bells once used on these animals, but only one is of this type. Too, there are written historical records alluding to bells on the army's camels; yet these leave the reader feeling that the bells described were some brought by the native drivers who accompanied the animals. One such written record describes the chief driver, Hi Jolly, arraying himself in his native costumes and hanging "strings of bells around his camels' necks, with great strings of bells hanging down to their forelegs."

Nevertheless, in the minds of collectors the idea persists that the U.S. Cavalry bells were designed for use on Jefferson Davis's ill-fated camel corps. Opinion here relies in part on two 1951 letters from the old Starr Brothers Bell Company, stating emphatically that before they were destroyed by floods, the company had the original government commission papers ordering them to design and cast such bells, the mold for which they still possessed. Subsequent investigation at the National Archives in Wash-

267. *Anklets for animal wear. Each is of bell metal and has pellets jangling within. Circular style (Greek) and crescent (Arabian) are modern. Center anklet, circa 1800, has heavy patina and is decorated with grotesque animal heads. From Lahore, where dancing camels wear anklet bells to encourage a rhythmic performance.* PRIVATE COLLECTION

ington, though, failed to uncover any such directives.

Collectors also point to the work of Mrs. A. S. C. Forbes, whose replicas were always of authentic bells from America's past. She must have considered that this U.S. Cavalry bell had been purposely designed for the camel corps, for she made hundreds of replicas from the only two surviving originals she ever found. With each she issued a brief history of the originals, pointing out the intended purpose of the bells and the elements of their design: a spread eagle with arrows; stars and sunburst; also a five-pointed star radiating over the entire top surface of the bell.

Each owner of a U.S. Cavalry bell must draw his own conclusions on the conflicting backgrounds of its origins. All find agreement on one point, however—that by the law of averages very few collectors own an original. Starr Brothers were still manufacturing and advertising the U.S. Cavalry bell as late as 1925; and Mrs. A. S. C. Forbes was still making replicas when she retired and sold her foundry many years later. Inevitably the majority of collectors own a replica rather than an original once belonging to Jefferson Davis's camel corps—if indeed such originals ever really existed.

THEY ALSO WEAR BELLS

Collectors who specialize in animal bells are convinced there is no other category offering greater variety of size, shape, material, tone, and historical lore. This may well be true. Almost every kind of creature that has been at all domesticated by man has been belled at one time or another while serving him. The ponderous yak, the speedy reindeer, the tall and ungainly llama, even the little barkless dogs of the Congo and the coconut-picking monkeys in Malaysia— all are frequently pictured wearing bells. (See Color Plate, V.)

From the animals' standpoint these are "the little bells that cheer their task," as Robert Browning expressed it. From their masters' standpoint the bells serve to locate the whereabouts of the animals. And for isolated frontiersmen and shepherds the bells on their sheep, goats, and pigs can serve in place of a gun to protect the wearer from predatory animals.

Almost any one of these animal bells presents an interesting study in craftsmanship and use. Of them all, the sheep bell is especially rich in historical lore. Though the music of sheep bells is vanishing today, in olden times there was lively competition among certain Old World shepherds who made a hobby of gathering bells that "rang together prettily." On wandering into country fairs and markets, they spent hours going over the piles of bells on sale there, holding them up to the ear to try their tone and selecting those that fitted the scale of rings they were assembling. The simplest way of fixing a bell to the animal's neck was by a strap; but this was not the way of the good shepherd interested

268. *Old shepherd's bell, from Peru. The elongated shape is typical of bells some shepherds carried, the better to help lost sheep find their way. Note the fine representation of Inca sun god.* PRIVATE COLLECTION

269. *The somewhat controversial U.S. Cavalry bell.* WALTERS COLLECTION

in the comfort of his flock. He went to infinite trouble to shape and carve yokes of boxwood, holly, or yew, and he gave many hours to painting them in bright colors.

Like their larger counterparts, the cattle bells, those for use on sheep were made in a variety of styles and sizes. The earlier ones were handmade from sheet iron coated with bronze or brass. The ones shaped like a small tankard and known as canisters were riveted at the top and down one side. Others were wedge-shaped and went under the unlikely name of cluckets. The largest in either style were about the size of a pint measure and were usually reserved for the old bellwethers.

Among American blacksmiths who established themselves as experts in crafting sheep bells was one J. A. Robey of Utah. His idea was to design sheep bells to please immigrant herders of all nationalities, and he built a profitable business doing just that. He became known as *Yierro Kouthounas,* meaning "Old Man Bellmaker." Robey's own favorite type of sheep bell was patterned after a Greek chime of one bell cupped inside another.

Such historic lore relating to bells used on small working animals is seemingly endless; inevitably it also invites excursions into neighboring areas—for example, into the sportsman's use of bells on dogs and falcons. Falconry is an age-old sport demanding some tiny but very special bells as part of the falconer's gear. Unbelievable as it may seem, there are individuals who specialize in collecting even these midget bells, some of them centuries old, others made right here in America today for the mascot falcons at the United States Air Force Academy.

7

The Figural Bell

As WITH DOLL COLLECTING, the more one finds out about costumed figurine bells the more there is to know; and in tracing their history, many odd bits of information come to light at the same time. Consider, for instance, the matter of the little booted or slippered feet that swing as clappers in some of these statuettes. Collectors are agreed that those with well-turned feet for their clappers are genuinely old, if not antique. But perhaps not all are aware of a fine historical precedent for the "footed" figurine bell.

An ancient bell-shaped Grecian figure has two legs attached with copper wires in much the same manner that later bell-shaped figures have legs swinging as clappers. This early example probably served as a devotional idol sometime around 700 B.C. A hole through its head indicates that it may have hung in a tomb, with its dangling legs showing to advantage. Interesting as such tiny feet are in a bell, they do not show when the statuette simply stands in a collection. It must be remembered, though, that most of the earlier bells were—like the Grecian example—made to be used as well as admired; and when they were lifted to ring, the feet were pleasingly noticeable.

The matter of daintily shod feet is only one of several factors helping to determine the relative age of statuette bells. True, collectors can appreciate these costumed figures without knowing the exact period of their manufacture; but

in view of the great number that have been reproduced, copied from old bells, it is wise to be guided by a few cautionary considerations in examining a bell of this type for purchase. Probably no one of the considerations is infallible, and not all of them need apply to each bell. But used where applicable, they can help to distinguish the truly old from the more modern figures.

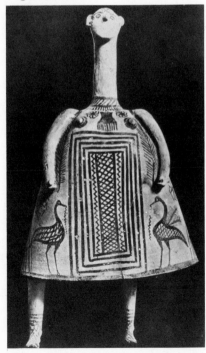

270. *Ancient Greek bell. The legs of the figure act as clappers. Used as a devotional idol. Circa 700* B.C.

271. *Two figurine bells of glass.* Left: *Frosted, possibly Heisey glass.* Right: *Camphor-satin glass of Dutch make.* PRIVATE COLLECTION

272. *Detail of the figure shown in Color Plate II of Meissen bells. Lady is admiring a lavaliere from the open jewel box she holds. Meissen mark in border of skirt. Circa 1780.* PRIVATE COLLECTION

Patina, dents, and other imperfections of age can all be cleverly faked; but thus far fakers have not created an artificial groove around the inside of the skirt, where the clapper has worn the metal while striking it repeatedly in the same place over the years. The presence of this sign of wear is almost proof positive that the bell is of some age. Its absence, however, does not necessarily mean the piece is of recent manufacture. A genuinely old bell that went unused for a long period may very naturally exhibit an interior as flawless as the day it was made.

Evaluating the quality of the brass and the sharpness of the artistic details, both in the dress and in the physical features, will prove helpful in many instances. Old fine-grained brass that is satin to the touch has yet to be duplicated. Nor can the finely chiseled features of a really well-cast portrait bell be duplicated in a reproduction made from a worn mold that has been used and reused. Granted, an old bell may show signs of wear; but if it was well executed to start with, some remaining evidence of sharply detailed workmanship is sure to be apparent at some point on the figure. Workmanship on the figure's hair and hands is especially revealing. Is the hair merely represented, or are striations evident? Are the hands merely blunted representations, or are the fingers defined? These are typical of the questions collectors learn to ask themselves if they wish to be selective in acquiring portrait bells of bronze or brass.

Evaluating those made of either porcelain or glass is another matter. So very few figure bells are of glass that there is little opportunity here to be selective. A few European examples are seen from time to time, and in this country there are occasional recent examples, like the little camphor-satin bridal figure in Heisey glass and the opaque milk-white colonial lady in Westmoreland glass.

Except for certain Japanese productions, old figure bells of porcelaneous materials have not been reproduced to any extent; and if they bear a potter's mark, this can usually be accepted as authentic. The ceramic figures from Japan are relatively easy to distinguish from the older and infinitely more desirable figure bells of European make, such as those of English Staffordshire, German bisque, French faience, and other comparable wares. Taken as a whole, these more fragile figure bells really do not present the collecting problems found in the brass ones. Certainly the larger ceramic figures do not—those lovely but rare porcelain and majolica portait bells eight and ten inches tall.

It is one thing to search for and acquire character bells and quite another to group them in some kind of order. The more decorative and

273. *Large figural bell featuring a plantation child. Colorful majolica ware.* MOSLEY COLLECTION

274. *A barmaid, her money pouch hanging at her side, serves mugs of foaming ale. A highly prized bell among the larger ceramic figures. Majolica.* ROSEMARY KELSO COLLECTION

275. *Looked upon as artistic masterpieces, the nun and the monk are favorites among collectors. Depth of color varies, but nun's habit is always gray and monk's robes brown. He carries a light blue tankard. Skin color and the modeling of features are always strikingly well done. Majolica.* PRIVATE COLLECTION

fragile ones stand out well, scattered individually among other glass and porcelain bells. But because of their greater numbers and more evident historical associations, the metal character bells seem to call for a few groupings.

There are several possible groupings and also some instances of bells that make a natural pair, side by side. Many depict actual personages—royalty and people of accomplishment—and a few represent recognized fictional characters. Others depict genre folk—milkmaids, cooks,

276. *Bisque figurine bell representing Lucrezia Borgia. Head and clapper are attached, and head moves from side to side. Circa 1770.* WINSTON JONES COLLECTION

277. *Nodding figures. Above: Mama dog and mama cat have their young snuggled close. Both of French manufacture. The pomade seller, a bearded Scotsman, straddles tub as he hawks his product. Below: Mother-and-daughter pair of Oriental ladies, made in Vienna. Center figure is a Chinese male dancer.* PRIVATE COLLECTION

chimney sweeps, and others of menial rank. In between these two extremes are quite a few middle-class figures. Finally, there are some that seem to belong together because of similarities in occupational, geographical, or historical backgrounds.

Then there is that special type of figurine bell designed with a head that nods. However they fit these into their groupings, collectors need no urging to feature their nodders as prominently as possible. Invariably nodders depict persons of particular interest, for one reason or another. Old Mother Hubbard and Lucrezia Borgia are typical of the assorted persons portrayed on bells having a nodding head. It is just as well to note at this point, however, that collectors are at variance as to whether all nodders qualify as bells. More will be said of this in the final chapter.

Whatever the informal groupings, the overall effect is one of femininity. Bells of this type are of necessity limited to figures whose manner of dress affords a skirt to serve as the bell and accommodate its clapper. Thus the roll call of male personages who can qualify is definitely limited to people like Napoleon wrapped in his military cloak, and friars or other religious figures whose habits are suited to the bell form.

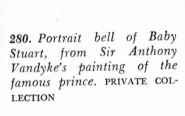

279. *Napoleon's cloaked figure accommodates the bell form very well.* PRIVATE COLLECTION

280. *Portrait bell of Baby Stuart, from Sir Anthony Vandyke's painting of the famous prince.* PRIVATE COLLECTION

278. *Heavy Sheffield figure representing Mother Hubbard and her dog, as portrayed in Walter Crane's interpretation of her for his Mother Goose illustration. Crane's conception of the dog was taken from a peculiar type of poodle popular in Rome while he lived there. Satin silver finish. Marked "Elkington Plate."* PRIVATE COLLECTION

Though male portrait bells are rare, those of children are rarer still. Aside from some little Dutch children there are scarcely any, and this is surprising because children have long been a favorite subject with artists.

This lack, however, is more than compensated for by one extraordinarily beautiful bell in the likeness of a well-known child figure. This is the full-length portrait of Baby Stuart, later James II of England, after the painting by Sir Anthony Vandyke. Although creating brass figurine bells may be classed among the minor arts, surely the artisan who created Baby Stuart must have aspired to be more than a mere

craftsman. He has captured so well the Vandyke-type modeling of the little prince's chubby features, and spared no detail of the rich lace trim on his costume. The figure is a perfect likeness in every way.

There is yet another overall impression in any grouping of figure bells. Doll collectors point out that for some inexplicable reason most dolls are made to look straight ahead; a few look to the right, but only an occasional one glances to the left or up or down. This same observation, curiously enough, applies to portrait bells. They are usually made to assume a posed and straightforward stance. It is the exceptional one that appears to be walking, or working in a seated position.

It is rather a national American trait to insist on specific answers to all questions of identification, and that trait can be carried to extremes if collectors try to identify by name every por-

281. *Lorna Doone's identity reveals itself only after she turns her back.* PRIVATE COLLECTION

282. *Miss Edith Cavell's name is engraved along the front border of her skirt. As a prisoner of war, her hands are manacled.* MC KINNEY COLLECTION

trait bell. Not all of them were intended to portray one certain person; and even some that were so intended are quite likely of persons unknown today. More probably, like all portraitists, the artists creating these bells sometimes wished only to show a villager typical of the times or a costume typical of the region. Any local acquaintance may have served as model.

Admittedly, it is sometimes difficult to perceive the original intention of the bellmaker. Happily a few of these portraits in brass have the name of the subject cast right on the costume. This gives unalterable identity to a figure that might otherwise go unrecognized by the collector. Lorna Doone, with her name incised on her skirt, is of interest as a fictional character; without the name, she might pass as any young girl.

Even with many figurine bells standing forever nameless, the list of those instantly recognizable is sufficiently long. It includes the great and the near great, those who have had a determining influence on history. Among royal figures, Elizabeth I appears in several poses ranging from those a few inches tall to one more rare figure nearly a foot in height and said to be taken from a Hilliard portrait on canvas. Her beautiful but tragic rival, Mary Queen of Scots, stands stiffly whaleboned into a bodice and farthingale embroidered with a panel of

Scottish thistles. Marie Antoinette, the most ill-fated among the queens of France, is identified in two different figurine bells, one of which could well be identified also as a likeness of Madame Pompadour, another royal lady of the French court and favorite mistress of Louis XV.

It is entirely possible, as collectors realize, to have two or more figures showing quite different representations of one and the same person. Fashions have never been static, and in the span of a lifetime quite a number of dress styles and hairstyles are adopted. Thus, Jenny Lind is seen in two and possibly three different figurine bells. Most common is the one of her wearing the ruffled skirt she liked to affect and a bonnet to match, her head tipped back as if she were ready to burst into song. This is the same figure popular in all kinds of Jenny Lind objects, from doorstops to tea cozies.

A far rarer bell is the large figure of her dressed much as she appears in a fresco by Niels Stevns. Here she is singing "at home" before

283. *Famous queens in familiar poses.* Left: *Queen Mary (consort of King George V), Mary Queen of Scots, and Princess Eugénie.* Right: *Queen Anne (of the same period as Elizabeth I but more stiffly garbed), Marie Antoinette or perhaps Madame Pompadour, and Marie Antoinette carrying a butterfly net.* PRIVATE COLLECTION

Hans Christian Andersen and is her more natural self. The style of dress and the hairdo are entirely different from those in the ruffle-skirted figure, yet in each instance the artist has been true to the Swedish Nightingale as she really lived and dressed. Her natural hair was blonde and worn in corkscrew curls, a style pop-ular in the 1840s and 1850s. But while on tour with P. T. Barnum, Jenny Lind felt that dark hair would give her a more striking image on stage. She wore a black wig with the hair parted in the middle and drawn back. The effect of this hair change is lost in the small brass por-trait bells of her ruffle-skirted figure, but in the

284. *A Russian princess in gold (wash) and black, originally the property of a lady fleeing the Russian Revolution. Detailing extends even to her fingernails. Hand holding envelope is movable. Her story: the princess holds a love note and ponders her reply.* VOSBURGH COLLECTION

285. *A masterpiece in bronze, this twelve-inch figure leaves nothing to be desired in its faithful depiction of Jenny Lind as her natural off-stage self.* RINGLAND COLLECTION

286. *The impressive and much discussed Saint Christopher bell.* RINGLAND COLLECTION

287. *Fictional characters, perhaps. Only little Becky Sharp, heroine of Thackeray's* Vanity Fair, *is positively identified. Based on illustrations, these identities have been suggested for the others: Lucy Locket; the witch plotting her evil in* Hansel and Gretel; *and the kindly but palsied old hag in* The Eve of St. Agnes. *She carries the bowl of delicacies for the young lovers.* PRIVATE COLLECTION

beautiful and colorful counterparts by Crown Staffordshire her hair showing under the bonnet is jet black. (*See* Color Plate VI.)

A somewhat controversial figure in bell form is the large representation of Saint Christopher carrying a likeness of the Christ on his shoulder —or so the figures have been identified. Concentrated study at forums, however, has raised some doubts from time to time as to whether the bell is, after all, a representation of Saint Christopher. It is the identity of the seemingly adult figure he carries that is disturbing, even to some who nevertheless still believe the piece does represent the legend of Saint Christopher and the Christ Child. Depictions of these same figures in other mediums tend to show the saint carrying a child, not an adult.

However, the heart of this whole legend revolves around Saint Christopher's picking up the Child on the banks of the river to carry him across, then finding his burden growing heavier and heavier until, upon reaching shore, he discovers he has been carrying the fully grown Christ. In the opinion of Dr. Adalbert Kretzmann, a widely regarded authority on religious art, this is undoubtedly the facet of the legend the bell is attempting to present.

Dr. Kretzmann's expertise in the world of church art enables him also to resolve the other disturbing aspect of this figure Saint Christopher carries—that is, the unlikely appearance so in contrast to the more customary and slightly ethereal representations of the Christ seen in much of the church's art. Dr. Kretzmann points out that such an appearance has historical precedent, however, and is a fitting one considering the bell is of Eastern Europe provenance:

It is quite evident that the present picture of St. Christopher which you have is one of the early Volga Valley representations. The churchmen there were always under the ambivalence of the Eastern and Western views of Christ. The Eastern view insisted on the Isaiah 53 description of Christ as the only authentic description in the Scriptures. "There was no beauty that we should desire Him." The Western Church began to build its concepts around Psalm 45, "He is the fairest of the children of men, grace is poured into His lips."

Viewed against expert opinion and recognized artistic canons, this impressive bell stands

288. *The Iron Maiden of Nuremburg in miniature bell form.* PRIVATE COLLECTION

289. *Bells in pairs.* Left: *These two figures are now known to be part of a series, with others of like dress and posture carrying everything from human heads to tankards.* Center: *Two ladies of eclectic costuming, cast as single bell. Identifies with no single period or region.* Right: *Florence Nightingale and Clara Barton in their respective nurses' outfits.* PRIVATE COLLECTION

after all as a convincing portrayal of the Saint Christopher legend. Fully understood, it takes on new historical interest for the collector and even a certain aesthetic merit all its own, quite apart from the artistic standards looked for in the metal arts of Western Europe.

In addition to bells that characterize renowned individuals, either real or fictional, there are those that are personifications—as it were—like the Iron Maiden of Nuremberg. The original maiden was not an actual person, but an eight-foot-high medieval torture device that in 1965 Sotheby's auctioned to Adrian Conan Doyle for more than six thousand dollars. It now stands in a Swiss castle maintained as a memorial to Mr. Doyle's father, Sir Arthur Conan Doyle. The statue, shaped like a young girl, once opened on hinges to an interior of spikes that impaled many a victim. The miniature bells copied from this statue do not open as do some other replicas, but the hinges on the cloak are clearly visible.

Pairing portrait bells seems the natural thing to do with such figures as Clara Barton and Florence Nightingale. Both are dressed for their nursing duties, Clara Barton as she appeared in the Franco-Prussian War while entering the city

of Strasbourg with the German soldiers, and Florence Nightingale as she served in the Crimean War. Among the ceramic portrait bells that constitute a natural pair are the miniatures of Uncle Toby and his fair wife Agnes. With

290. *Miniature pair portraying Uncle Toby and his fair wife Agnes.* PRIVATE COLLECTION

291. *Genre figures portray an irate Irish cook "speaking up" to a demure little milkmaid and a girl clutching a duck.* PRIVATE COLLECTION

292. *Old lacemaker at work. Bronze.* Circa 1820. *companion shows that air of distress common to g figures of aged folk.* PRIVATE COLLECTION

her rotund figure, she makes a fitting mate for the traditionally hearty Toby. Like their counterparts in pitchers, the Toby bells are very colorful. Each little two-by-three figure is decorated in five colors.

A certain few figurine bells need not be paired, for they already appear as twins cast or molded in a single statuette. One of these castings portrays two fashionable sisters who defy identification, and for very good reasons. The figures are pure fantasy, their costumes illustrating so well the artistic license sometimes taken in designing figurines. The result is a wholly eclectic outfit of hats that are Mexican in feeling, collars and cuffs like those seen in seventeenth-century Germany, and full skirts of the nineteenth century.

Many a figure that cannot be positively identified by name can nevertheless be satisfactorily identified as a type of character. The genre characters are almost always recognizable as types; and they constitute an interesting category from an artistic point of view, each one faithfully reflecting the humble tasks of the time. Though they portray unknowns, they convey an emotional reality that is linked to a particular person under particular circumstances —the weary sadness of an old lacemaker bent over her spindles; the smug content of a Dutch

lass clutching a flighty duck; or the belligerent look of an irate Irish cook after a scapegoat to blame for mischief in the kitchen.

Furthermore, although the average portrait bells are cast in quantities from a mold, a few of the genre figures appear to be individually sculptured—they have the homespun quality of an Eberle bronze. Such bells display a vibrant charm and naturalness lacking in most bells coming from a common mold.

Somewhere between the extremes of genre folk and those of more aristocratic mien there are many figures of middle-class types. Here, however, it is difficult at times to decide whether a certain figure belongs to the middle class or to the aristocracy. There is no rule of thumb to abide by, for example, in the case of a well-dressed person from the seventeenth or eighteenth century. With the rise of a wealthier middle class, sporting fine clothes was no longer the privilege of the aristocrats. In an attempt to preserve social distinctions, laws were passed prescribing what could and could not be worn by various classes. Queen Elizabeth forbade commoners the ruff and the farthingale; in France, brocades were reserved for royalty. But few of the laws were upheld, and the royal class could do nothing except complain that one could no longer tell the potboy apart from the

293. *Figure with all the attributes of a soothsayer, with letter* M *on his skirt to suggest he is Merlin.* PRIVATE COLLECTION

294. *Modish ladies, probably representative of upper middle class. Both royalty and commoners wore the butterfly headdress, like center figure.* PRIVATE COLLECTION

lord or the serving wench from the lady she waited upon. The middle-class trend toward fashionable dress could not be halted.

Closely related to the middle-class figures are those in a small special group depicting court entertainers and soothsayers, some of the latter having a large M embroidered on the skirt—presumably indicating they represent Merlin. The court entertainers include the little jester, that tragicomic figure who adopted bells on his costume out of self-pride. According to Arthurian legend, the jester was filled with envy because knights of the court rode off to battle carrying with them bell-trimmed shields to announce their coming. Left behind, an insignificant figure, the jester sought to make himself more important by attaching bells to his costume, thus drawing more attention to his antics.

Even without any personal identifications of the figures involved, those dressed in regional or period costumes offer an engaging study in

terms of fashion history. French faience figurine bells display the varied native costumes of the old provinces, each with its distinctive headdress. Studying the customs that prompted each manner of dress provides an excursion into French provincialism. The headpiece on a figurine is often a convenient index to the period represented. A butterfly headdress on a woman betokens a Flemish style of the late Gothic era in the fifteenth century. The tall conical hennin marked the ultra in head fashions during

295. *Touring troupes of masked and costumed actors in the eighteenth century provided attractive subjects for European factories making decorative figurines. This lady holding a mask is representative of such actors. Modern copy of an old figure.*

296. *French faience figure in provincial dress.* LA ROSE COLLECTION

295

296

medieval days, and several variations of it appear on various brass portrait bells

Small costume accessories are a further clue to the period portrayed. One appealing portrait bell that can be placed in its proper historical niche by such a clue depicts a lady carrying a muff. From the cozy interior of the muff a small dog peers out. The muff is small and the dog even more diminutive, so that the significance of the two could well be overlooked. Together, however, they definitely place the costume in the French Renaissance, when tiny muff-dogs were a new caprice of the period. They were indispensable to the correct appearance of the fashionable lady. A directory dated 1692 lists the approved Parisian shops making muffs for these pampered little dogs.

FOLK ART FIGURES

Folk art has been defined and redefined, and it embraces objects of every description. In the world of dolls—which have a kinship of sorts with character bells—the term simply denotes those dolls of primitive construction where individual traits are secondary, where the primary interest is in traits common to a certain type of individual. This distinction can be carried one step further in the case of character bells.

There are a considerable number of bells of this type that have little or no modeling of the features. Instead, the face is painted or incised on a flat surface. Arms and hands, too, may be merely represented, not defined. Accepting this decidedly arbitrary and very limiting cri-

297. *Folk art in bells.* Top row: *Two bells from Portugal* (left) *and a peasant woman of Brittany* (right). *Portuguese angel is of Secla ware, a famous folk pottery in Portugal.* Bottom row: *Two end bells from Hungary and straw figures from Ecuador. Polychrome glaze on priest is unusually attractive, the signed work of award-winning Margit Kovacs. Prim lady in straw and her pet both have bells enclosed.* PRIVATE COLLECTION

terion, these can be considered the folk art figures among bells; and they share another distinction that sets them apart, for they are likely to be made from somewhat perishable materials —straw, clay, wood, or at best, a quality faience. Whether a craftsman is skilled or unskilled, if he engages in native art he usually employs whatever material is conveniently at hand. This means that most folk art figures are of some material other than brass.

Crudeness is not a detriment to collectibility in seeking examples of folk art. It is in fact one of the attributes of native art from some areas. This is not to say that all folk art figure bells appear crude in their workmanship. Some, except for that lack of definition in the features, are finished with nicety and even a degree of artistry. As the work of the common people and not the cultured classes, however, they tend toward the primitive. It is this very quality that accounts for the difference, say, between a religious figure from the hills of Portugal and one from the Royal Dux-Bohemia Manufactory.

Occasionally there are little humorous touches, which may or may not be intentional. Frequently the humor seems to spring more from the mind of the viewer than from the hand of the craftsman. The straw ladies from Ecuador, with bells woven inside the figures, are not intended as particularly humorous. It is easy to visualize the craftsman earnestly weaving in and out with contrasting colors to create a face of straw, and it is quite unlikely that he is striving for any certain "look." Yet to see a finished group of these straw ladies is to smile at their expressive faces—some haughty, some flirtatious, some bored. All accidental expressions, but amusing to the viewer and typical of the rewards in collecting what might be termed offbeat bells.

Surprisingly enough, since these are expressions of the common people, the types of characters in folk art bells are by no means limited to the genre class, although many are peasant types or servants. But church dignitaries, madonnas, well-bred ladies—all these and other

298. *Wooden monk with nodding head, once a monastery prayer bell to alert the monks when prayers ended. Features are more sharply defined in this piece, yet it qualifies as folk art, the work of an individual wood-carver. Very old and richly hued brown wood. Circa 1750.* RENICK COLLECTION

comparable characters can be seen in the group, cutting across widely separated social strata and revealing this in their bearing and their manner of dress. Regardless of the figure's rank, however, there is always a lack of sophistication in the pose. This naturalness is part of the charm of folk art figures. It gives them a more varied appeal than can be found in their somewhat stiff and sedate counterparts of brass.

And just where may folk art figure bells be found? They come from Wales, Finland, Portugal, France; almost every country has its native artists who prefer experimenting with primitive mediums. Some like Margit Kovacs of Hungary or John Ffrench of Ireland have made a name for themselves because of their figure portrayals. Others are unskilled marketplace artisans who have no thought of artistic standards.

Mexico is of course home to many such craftsmen. An entire collection could be built around folk art figurine bells found here. Some would be of the traditional black volcanic ash, but there would also be the unglazed terra-cottas, some having embroidered skirts, and still others quite colorfully glazed. The range of original native figures crafted in Mexico is unmatched in any other country, and customarily many of them are made in bell form.

ANIMALS AS SUBJECTS

Among European and American sculptors there have always been those with a penchant for animals as their models. Animals as subjects have attributes that enable the artist to achieve a strong decorative design along with a pronounced naturalism, two highly desirable qualities in any art object.

It is inevitable that animal likenesses, even more than the human form, lend themselves to decorating bells. Proof lies in the mental profiles that come to mind in a partial roster of the creatures artists have called upon to inspire their designs for bells—among birds: the parrot, crane, owl, eagle, goose, stork, and rooster; and among other creatures: the horse, bear, llama, dog, cat, fox, chimpanzee, rat, and tortoise. As for the naturalism inherent in animal figures, the more skilled artists have managed to preserve that even while striving for anatomical accuracy.

Collector interest runs high in finding a bell that displays truly artistic sculpturing of an animal figure, but bells of this description are far from common. Although affection for birds and

300. *Here the viewer can anticipate each action as it is about to happen.* PAUL FISHER COLLECTION

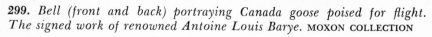

299. *Bell (front and back) portraying Canada goose poised for flight. The signed work of renowned Antoine Louis Barye.* MOXON COLLECTION

animals as models is demonstrated in the work of many internationally famous sculptors, few of these have thought to involve their lively models in designs for anything as small as bells.

The French sculptor Antoine Louis Barye (1795–1875) did, however. In his bell portraying a Canada goose poised for flight he has subscribed to the belief that a work of art, if it is to have life and movement, should mirror a moment just before something is about to happen. The viewer then has the satisfaction of completing the action in his mind. This belief Barye shares with a good many other sculptors, but beyond that he far exceeds them. Others have tried to imitate his pieces and failed. Starting as an apprentice to a goldsmith, he became interested in self-studies at the zoological gardens in Paris to perfect his anatomical knowledge. He established his own bronze foundry, where he specialized in figural bronzes of animals and carried on extensive experiments to perfect his patinas. Eventually he founded the famous Animaliers, a school dedicated to the study of animal sculpture.

Although animals and birds are not commonly cast as parties of the first part enfolding the entire bell, as it were, they are nevertheless the focal point of interest when they are well articulated with the bell itself. A chimpanzee balancing a bell, or a bear standing to play a bell in the shape of a base viol—these are well articulated. Another fine example portrays a

301. *Anatomical accuracy has not been sacrificed to create this convincing portrayal of a chimpanzee balancing a bell. Bronze on mahogany base. Total height: 15 inches. Nineteenth century.* PAUL FISHER COLLECTION

302. *The wolf from* Little Red Riding-Hood. *In his interpretation of this story-book character, the designer has employed not only a degree of originality but considerable artistry. Viewed from any angle, the figure has appeal. Nineteenth century.* PRIVATE COLLECTION

303. *It is easy to relate to the poignant story depicted in this uniquely contrived bell. Note the use of textured metal to create the appearance of fur on the bears. Nineteenth century.* VOSBURGH COLLECTION

HANDLE INTEREST

Figures of animals and birds are a convenient inspiration for handles on bells. Some of course lack definition and are quite static, displaying little life or movement; others, especially of birds, are so highly stylized that they bear little resemblance to their prototypes in nature; but some few are worked into convincing portrayals, and usually the bell attached to a handle of superior workmanship is also a thing of beauty and not just another bell.

The old Russian craftsmen seldom did things by halves. They knew well how to articulate the various parts of an ornate bell. There is no better example than in an exquisitely beautiful old one of finest brass, with Russia's symbolic two-headed eagle as its handle. Composing the bell are three heads in high relief, each wearing a crown. These represent Czar Michael and his two wives. The ancient origin of the double-

304. *Two old turtles of German manufacture head the procession. Only the first has a back of genuine shell. The last two are modern examples of damascene work from Toledo, Spain, and brasswork from Korea. Head and tail ring these mechanicals.* PRIVATE COLLECTION

papa bear attempting to break the bars on a cage imprisoning mama bear, the cage resting atop a low table bell. For one so small, the papa bear shows magnificent vitality. He seems literally alive and breathing hard as he exerts pressure on those bars until they bend before him.

305. *Russian masterpiece featuring the two-headed eagle symbolic of the czars. Nineteenth century.* RINGLAND COLLECTION

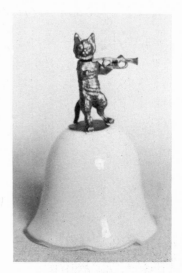

306. *Nipper, the little dog who became the model for Victor's famous trademark* His Master's Voice. *Portrayed in silver and signed by the French artist Pellier.* PRIVATE COLLECTION

307. *Heavily ornate bell with likeness of horse and foal composing the unusual handle. Under garlands of roses on the dome, jockeys race. Clapper in form of coiled snake. Nineteenth century.* MC KINNEY COLLECTION

308. *Vienna bronze miniature on opaque white glass bell. Instrumental cat nods his head as he plays.* PRIVATE COLLECTION

headed bird has many overtones of meaning, its identity and symbolism varying with the country in which it is found. In Russia it is the eagle, symbol of the Czars during the Romanov dynasty (1613–1917). The artist has given this symbolic bird the realistic appearance of an eagle so that the handle is instantly recognizable and identifies well with the portraiture on the bell.

Although a figural handle of superior workmanship can typify a certain creature and even exhibit a degree of individuality, this individuality is seldom directed toward a particular animal known by name. An exception to this generalization stands in the likeness of that famous little English dog, Nipper, whose figure became the Victor trademark. His trademark pose has been captured in the handle of a silver bell signed by a French artist, Pellier. Whether Monsieur Pellier copied Nipper's likeness from the living model or from a painting made of him, is unknown. Nipper belonged to the Barraud family of Liverpool. Whenever the family's gramo-

309. *Masterly modeling on a small owl adds the crowning delight to an already beautiful Italian Renaissance bell.* VOSBURGH COLLECTION

ing full-length figure, sometimes seated, or perhaps merely as a bust. So far as their identity is concerned, these figural handles fall into the same categories as do the figurine bells. The majority of recognizable individuals are admir-

phone was playing, he sat peering wistfully into the great horn-shaped speaker. His pose took the fancy of an artist, who painted the little dog's portrait without any thought of its becoming famous.

The human figure as a handle on bells is seen in much the same way that it appears in major pieces of sculpture: sometimes as a stand-

313. *Carved ivory handle portrays William Tell and son. The father carries a sheaf of arrows over his shoulder. Nineteenth century.* MC-KINNEY COLLECTION

314. *A bell ordinarily seen with only a loop handle here has a handle of baffling interest. Standing figure is that of Perseus with his Gorgon's shield, which appears to be an original attachment for this bell. Yet its association with the scenes on the dome is obscure. Those show Assyrians bringing in heads and prisoners to be recorded. The captives are Israelites, and to emphasize their humiliation they are portrayed barefoot.* PRIVATE COLLECTION

able persons of historical or literary note; but now and then there are likenesses of scamps and rascals, even morally abhorrent individuals like Satan himself.

Probably no single person of note has topped more bells than Napoleon Bonaparte. In different characteristic stances he appears on assorted bells. Of the two more ornate ones popular with collectors, one shows in relief the eagle emblem especially designed for Napoleon to represent imperial power as once traditionally attributed to the Romans. The eagle grasps the thunderbolt, a symbol for Jupiter's power to destroy his enemies. The other bell shows in bold relief scenes from the Battle of Waterloo and is appropriately inscribed around the lip:

L'EMPEREUR BATAILLE DE WATERLOO

NAPOLEON A WAGRAM

Joan of Arc is another popular subject, appearing sometimes as a figural handle and some-times as a full figurine (see Ill. 315). Her likeness standing as a handle on a plain bell is adapted from a sketch made by Jean Dominique Ingres (1780–1867) for a painting he was to make later. His aim was to present the Maid of Orleans as a classical figure, heroic and perfectly proportioned. She is dressed in her suit of armor, wearing a cross on her breastplate and holding a standard in one hand. Charles VII gave the Maid a valuable suit of armor before she rode off to Orléans. It was made to her measurements; and buckled into it, Joan looked like a smaller version of the typical fifteenth-century knight. This is also an apt description of her appearance on the handle of the bell.

Her armor, approximately fifty pounds in weight, consisted of helmet, cuirass, various leg pieces, and six separate parts for each arm. Her steel cap was properly called a salade; but unlike those usually worn, hers was not fitted with a visor. Though in some battles she may have worn a type of helmet with a hinged visor, she

186

315. *Three interpretations of Joan of Arc. As a handle, her figure is taken from a sketch by Ingres to show her fully clad in armor. At left she appears in partial armor. At right, as the simple peasant figure.* PRIVATE COLLECTION

316. *A cherub as handle serves to focus attention on the significance of this Holy Grape Harvest Festival Bell. He carries an armload of fruit, and around the dome are children gathering fruit. The bell was secured in the aftermath of World War II. A fleeing monk had rescued it from Monte Cassino monastery just before the bombing. Nineteenth century.* MOXON COLLECTION

317. *Joy impels this comic figure wearing the Fool's costume. He is a part of an eight-man morris dancers' team; it is his job to amuse the crowds with his antics.* VOSBURGH COLLECTION

wanted her face to show clearly. Her purpose was not to fight but to lead by being seen and heard. On the bell where her armed figure stands as the handle, her face is clearly visible under her helmet.

Almost every category of bells seems to have some that can be collected in a series, so to speak. The figure-handled type are no exception. There are, for instance, the little English bells with characters from Dickens's novels as their handles. More importantly, there is one

318. *Handsome and early bell of silver. The bust of Saint Anthony. Spanish, possibly from Lisbon, where Anthony is a favorite saint.* Circa 1700. SPEAR COLLECTION, PETER WHITE MEMORIAL LIBRARY, MARQUETTE, MICHIGAN

320. *Six figural handles on bells of similar base, part of a series of undetermined number. Only identifications are Napoleon (above, left) and Shakespeare (below, right). The little draped* putto *seems out of place with more historical-looking persons.* Above: MYRL HUENE COLLECTION *and a private collection.* Below: MC KINNEY COLLECTION

319. *Silver stirrup bell from Peru. Head forms the bell. Imitative of the terra-cotta portrait stirrup vessels of the Mochica culture,* A.D. *400–600. The stirrup on those was used as a pouring spout as well as a handle.* PRIVATE COLLECTION

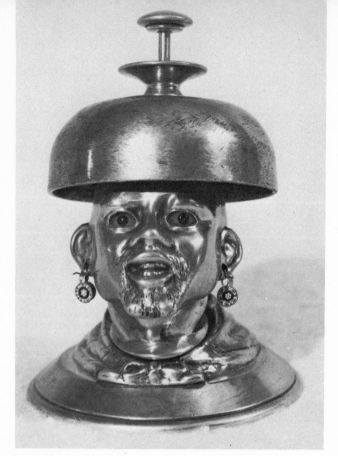

321. *Call bell from Austria shows Chinese influence. Earrings are cloisonné Circa 1800.* WINSTON JONES COLLECTION

322. *Bell from Freiburg, Germany, represents drunken angel grasping the bell rope and spilling a stein of beer. Circa 1855.* WINSTON JONES COLLECTION

323. *Oriental figure with nodding head holds a twirler bell, umbrella style. He represents a Chinese schoolmaster pointing the "finger of wisdom." Circa 1870.* PRIVATE COLLECTION

324. *A Japanese lady stands under a parasol hung with three lacquered bells. Of the two figures posed with her, the lady is the signed work of Hori-E-Yoshi-Zumi, a noted Japanese sculptor.* PRIVATE COLLECTION

special brass bell familiar to many collectors and seen with any of half a dozen or more male figures as handles. Some of the individuals portrayed are identifiable, but others like the *putti* figures are merely types. The bases for these bells vary only slightly and are always of the same geometric pattern. The entire series is considered to be of English make, even though one or two of the handles are figures wearing Eastern rather than European garb.

Handles are not the only means of accommodating figures to bells. Clever artisans with a flair for originality of design have found innumerable ways to exhibit figural interest, sometimes having the figure support a bell, sometimes articulating the two in a manner even more novel. Among human figures artfully accommodated to bells is one known as the Indian Princess. She is expertly and fittingly involved in the design. She sits Indian fashion on a cupshaped bell, holding a beater in each hand. The arms pivot in unison so that flipping the upraised beater releases the lower one against the bell. The two tiers of bronze ormolu mounts under the bell enrich the piece. Here reptiles intermingle with deeply chiseled and luxuriant foliage appropriate to the setting of the story behind the bell.

This is an objet d'art of French origin—and typical of the French artisan's preoccupation with American Indian figures in the late eighteenth and early nineteenth centuries. Starting with the story of Pocahontas and Captain John Smith, there are many tales of an American Indian princess who pleaded for the life of a captive being held by her people. One such story—and the one represented by this bell—especially intrigued the French writer Chateaubriand while he was traveling in North America. He wrote the romantic tale as told to him and published it in *Le Mercure de France* in 1801. Shortly thereafter, many illustrations of the figures involved in the romance appeared on French art objects.

The tale concerns Atala, daughter of a North American Indian chief, who fell in love with

325. *The Indian princess bell. Said to portray Atala, daughter of an American Indian chief. Circa 1830.* PRIVATE COLLECTION

Chactas, the chief of another tribe, who was her father's prisoner. She delivered him from death and fled with him. The legend goes on to relate that Atala later took her life after recalling that her mother had exacted a promise from her, never to marry. Supposedly Atala is the figure on the bell. A mate to this piece is said to show the figure of her beloved Chactas, positioned in rather similar fashion on a bell of like French design.

8

Bells as Toys

In the words of antiques columnist Dorothy Hammond, searching for children's playthings of an earlier era has become a mania with present-day collectors. Bell buffs are no exception, for they have their own very definite groups of toys to seek. These range from ancient and primitive clay rattles to the fashionable gold and silver baby bells of colonial days, and from simple rolling bell toys of India to the complex animated bell ringers popular in America a century ago. Not all the baby rattles constitute toys in the strict meaning of the term; but for practical purposes all are included here, inasmuch as most bell collectors welcome appropriate examples from all areas of children's playthings.

The age-old belief that wearing necklacelike rattles would protect children from harm was undoubtedly the basis for the earliest tiny bells and rattlelike toys given them as playthings. Our knowledge of bell toys from this earliest period is fragmentary, at best, and based largely on specimens discovered during excavations. Tiny crotals have been found buried with children in the catacombs at Rome, and the use of bells on the Roman child's *crepundia* has already been noted. In Pompeii excavations yielded a metal circlet hung with bells, the circlet being fastened to an ivory handle, or gum stick, used for teething.

An Egyptian pottery rattle in the form of a hollow cow containing pebbles may be seen in the Metropolitan Museum of Art. Other early rattles in the same museum include the terracotta forms of an owl and a pig, both from Cyprus. Pig rattles of baked clay are common to a number of early civilizations, perhaps because pigs were often sacrificed for the special preservation of young children.

CORAL-AND-BELLS

There are few records of bell toys during the Middle Ages. William Horman's mention of a baby rattle is one of the few references. In his *Vulgaria* published in 1519 he remarks, "I wyll bye a rattell to styll my baby for cryenge." Beginning in the sixteenth and continuing through the eighteenth century, however, there developed what was literally the golden age of baby bells. Numerous examples in gold and silver were executed by metal craftsmen of the day both in Europe and in America.

Choicest of all from this era, in the estimation of many, are the coral-and-bells. Customarily these were more or less of a single style, fashioned on a cylindrical stem having a whistle at one end and at the other a gum stick of ivory, coral, or some similar hard substance. Between the ends the slim shank expanded into a bulbous body holding tiers of gold or silver bells.

Coral-and-bells made appropriate christening gifts for the babies of wealthier families. They were considered ideal presents for the occasion, not only because they amused the infant and provided teething comfort but because they protected him against all witchcraft. According to superstitious belief, the coral itself as well as the sound of bells had the power to charm against bodily harm. Appropriate gifts they may have been, but perhaps not always appreciated by the babies. The great English essayist Joseph Addison once related: "I threw away my rattle before I was two months old and would not

326. Coral-and-bells, England. Silver and coral. By Richard May and Jane Dorrell, London. Circa 1775. COLONIAL WILLIAMSBURG, WILLIAMSBURG, VIRGINIA

327. Silver filigree rattle belonging to George IV. CROWN COPYRIGHT RESERVED. BY GRACIOUS PERMISSION OF HER MAJESTY THE QUEEN

328. Coral-and-bells, England. By Joseph Taylor, Birmingham. Circa 1791. LOS ANGELES COUNTY MUSEUM

make use of my coral until they had taken the bells away from it."

Many seventeenth-century portraits of Flemish and English children show them grasping a coral-and-bells, or whistle-bells, as they were sometimes called—especially when the teething stick was made of a substance other than coral. One of the earliest of such portraits (*see* Ill. 334) dates from 1622 and hangs in the home of an English lord at Stapleford Park, Leicestershire. It is a study of Lady Abigail Sherard with

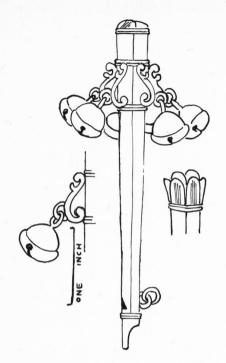

329. *Coral-and-bells, France. Gold and pink coral. Circa 1660–1690. Brought to Newport, Rhode Island, in 1696 by Gabriel Bernon, a Huguenot refugee. Now the property of the Rhode Island Historical Society.*

330. *Rattle, American. Gold and coral. By Daniel Christian Fueter. Circa 1760.* GIFT OF MRS. FRANCES P. GARVAN, JAMES GRAHAM, WALTER M. JEFFORDS, AND MRS. PAUL MOORE. YALE UNIVERSITY ART GALLERY

her son, later Lord Leitrim. The little boy's whistle-bells hangs from a wide velvet band passing over both shoulders.

Children of well-to-do parents in America also appear in portraits either wearing or holding elaborate gold or silver baby bells. The portrait of a New York Dutch baby, Jacques de Peyster, shows him holding the same gold whistle-bells with a rock crystal stick that is on ex-

hibit in the Metropolitan Museum of Art. John Hancock had a "wissel and bells," as did infants in the John Quincy Adams family. Martha Washington ordered one from Philadelphia in the 1790s, presumably for her first great-grandchild.

Martha's gift may well have been selected from an advertisement in a colonial gazette. As early as the 1760s whistle-bells were being widely advertised by colonial silversmiths, mostly as London imports. In his charming booklet *American Baby Bells,* Harry B. Weiss quotes a number of such notices. Though usually sparing of words, a few give more exact details—as in

331. *Silver rattle with mother-of-pearl handle. Circa 1850.* MUSEUM OF THE CITY OF NEW YORK

332. *Silver whistle-bells, Spain. Circa 1870.* PRIVATE COLLECTION

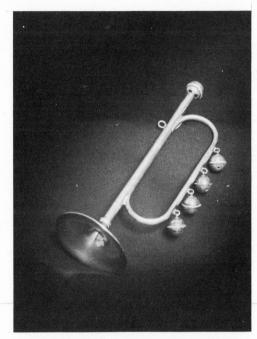

333. The whistle-bells idea adapted to a child's horn-with-bells. Horn still plays. Silver. England. Circa 1800. PRIVATE COL-LECTION

duplicated very closely the European examples they knew. For this reason, unless they are marked such pieces cannot easily be attributed to specific silversmiths. Because of stringent laws requiring hallmarks of English silversmiths, their whistle-bells are more likely to reveal a mark. The most sought after is the H.B. of London's famous lady silversmith, Hester Bateman.

The collector seriously intent on acquiring a colonial whistle-bells needs to realize that English silversmiths continued making these fancy

334. Detail from portrait of Lady Abigail Sherard and her son, later Lord Leitrim, wearing his whistle-bells. In one hand he holds a single tiny bell. England, 1622.

the *Pennsylvania Gazette* for December 15, 1763, where Edmund Milne of Philadelphia of-fers:

> silver whistles and bells,
> with corals chaised and plain,
> just imported

During the latter part of the eighteenth century, a number of famous American gold- and silversmiths are known to have started making exquisite specimens of coral-and-bells for children of the "carriage trade." Boston, New York, and Philadelphia were the earliest centers for the art of silversmithing, and most surviving examples were made in these centers by such men as Daniel Christian Fueter, Jacob Ten Eyck, and Phillip Syng. The latter was offering in 1763 ". . . a neat gilt silver whistle and coral with eight bells." Paul Revere, too, made silver rattles and "wisles."

Many of the colonial silversmiths were primarily of Dutch or French Huguenot or English extraction; and the baby bells they fashioned

playthings until 1850, and from 1880 to 1915 two New York firms made replicas. All the later ones somewhat resemble the colonial in form but they are smaller and less expensively made;

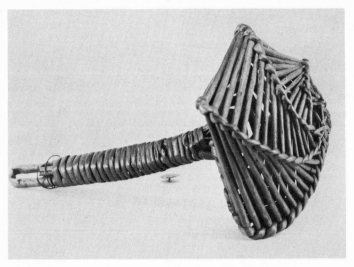

335. *Willow rattle. Circa 1835.* MUSEUM OF THE CITY OF NEW YORK

and the coral or the rock crystal teethers are replaced by cheaper ones of bone or mother-of-pearl.

Silversmiths from colonial times on have always fashioned many smaller types of baby rattles also. As silver came to be used more commonly for trinkets, and as a greater proportion of the population was able to afford their purchase, the demand for such little playthings increased and they were produced in quantity.

336. *Victorian baby bells. An acorn-shaped bell and a miniature double-chiming bell, both on turned rosewood handles, from Gong Bell Manufacturing Company. Circa 1890. Fragile rattle woven of reeds has bells inside. Stitching in three colors. Alaska. Circa 1900.* PRIVATE COLLECTION

Today they make attractive collectibles, offering varied appeal in their designs and having the added advantage of being easily displayed.

The earlier ones date from the eighteenth century, probably made by English or European silversmiths. These are little hollow effigies of birds, animals, ships, et cetera, with silver bells suspended from them. The later effigy types of the nineteenth and early twentieth centuries are also of hollow sterling but with pellets encased in the figures, which in turn hang and rattle from a bone teething ring or a pearl stub. The figures are recognized childhood favorites: a clown, Humpty Dumpty, or an elephant. Many of these "jester" or "stub" types, as they were called in the trade, were made by firms like Unger Brothers of Newark, New Jersey, and sold at Tiffany's, Peacock's, or other leading jewelers.

Babies in less well-to-do families also played with a variety of rattles made of wood, wire, tin, even straw, wicker, and cloth. But these conformed to no special pattern until about 1850 when the "umbrella" type of wood and wire rattles came into vogue, along with a few cast brass types produced by the early makers of sleigh bells.

The umbrella-shaped rattle is held aloft on a turned wooden handle with a whistle in one end. From the central stem above the bell, four blue beads are suspended to act as outside clappers. There are variations, some more elaborate than others, but all with blue beads as clappers. These supposedly protected the infant from harm. Even today, in certain countries necklaces of blue beads and bells are placed on babies to ensure their safety.

Other oddly assorted baby rattles of pioneer days were oftentimes homemade and typical of only a limited geographical area. In the South, for instance, it was customary for babies to wear little rattles made from tin snuffboxes containing pebbles and jacketed with colored yarns; in Sitka, Alaska, babies of the Tlingit Indians wore tiny rattles made from the crop of a goose, the outside woven of grasses.

The great majority of these more primitively styled baby rattles were fashioned by unknown artisans who never advertised but merely enjoyed making toys in addition to their regular work. Among the handcraftsmen who kept right on working alongside America's growing factory system were potters and various weavers, who also included bells and rattles among their wares. Frances Lichten's *Folk Art of Rural Pennsylvania* tells how the local potter was often the source of children's bell toys:

> Besides all manner of dolls' dishes and whistles shaped like birds, the potter made dolls' heads and infants' rattles—clumsy hollow cats or deer with clay bells inside, planned to be shaken by adults for infant entertainment.

The wide range of possible "finds" in this area makes the search for rattles fascinating but sometimes frustrating. Made of perishable mate-

337. *Umbrellalike rattles with amulet-type blue beads as clappers. Bells stained in bright colors. Late Victorian.* PRIVATE COLLECTION

rials, few of the cruder ones survived beyond the youngster's babyhood, and today they are rela-

338. *Baby's rolling rattle in brass wire work. India. Miniature tambourine with bells. Netherlands.* PRIVATE COLLECTION

339. *Mechanical Heubach doll holding bells. These sound when arms move.*
NORMA JEAN'S DOLLS

tively scarce—more so than the cherished and more expensive silver types.

All these fragile rattles were soon supplanted by more sturdy types, once the sleigh bell manufacturers were established and branching out into the making of toys. The musical sound of real bells on playthings appealed to both parent and child. As the population flourished and the demand for bell toys increased, other manufacturers also took over producing them on a large scale.

340. *Chinese infant entertains himself with tiny bells.*

ANIMATED BELL RINGERS

For the East Hampton foundries, it was but a short step to start making toys involving bells from their stock in trade. Of these companies, the N. N. Hill Brass Company manufactured the greatest variety of rattles: single and double chimes, dumbbells, and teething-ring rattles of every description. They also made many styles of little boys' driving reins for playing horse— of cloth with two bells, at five cents each, and of leather with twenty-eight bells, at one dollar. As late as 1918 their catalogue still pictured more than sixty styles of rattles and reins.

Their closest competitor, the Gong Bell Manufacturing Company, offered a similar line but of course with a few specially patented toys of their own design. One was a little baby's bell consisting of an acorn-shaped bell fitted to a neatly turned rosewood handle.

Older children, too, were offered new and amusing toys after manufacturers realized the possibilities in combining bells with the always fascinating action of wheels. Appropriately called bell ringers, these new toys were introduced in the late nineteenth century and were an immediate sensation. At varying periods during the heyday of their manufacture (1880–1920) wheeled bell toys were made of tin, iron, heavy stamped metal, or a combination, but always with one unchanging principle—when pulled or pushed along the floor, one or more bells would ring at intervals, either by internal motion or by the action of animated figures.

The first experimental ones were merely a pair of fancy wheels with a bell on the axle between them. Then horses, riders, and drivers were added, and from here it was a natural move to designing the more elaborate animated bell-ringer toys, the most popular type of all. To properly classify as an animated bell ringer, the toy must have some movement of a figure involved with the ringing of the bell.

That authoritative volume *Toys in America* gives an excellent overall idea of the varied figures and subjects incorporated into the de-

341. *Child's chiming toy called "Trinity Chimes" operates from small keyboard. Colorful lithographs decorate front panels. From the Schoenhut toymakers. 1903.* PRIVATE COLLECTION

signs of the bell ringers. Some were inspired by Mother Goose characters, as for example "Ding Dong Bell, Pussy's Not in the Well." This elaborate toy of 1888 involved a clown, a boy, a cat, and a well in its action. Others capitalized on characters or events with timely historical appeal. When the World's Columbian Exposition was staged in Chicago in '93, there was the Christopher Columbus toy, very ornate, with Columbus standing in front of his ship, surrounded by sailors. For the Spanish-American War there was "Teddy Roosevelt and the Rough Riders," and to commemorate the discovery of the North Pole in 1909, "Admiral Peary and a Polar Bear."

The descriptive catalogue names assigned these intriguing toys were in themselves often indicative of the action involved, as in "Hee Haw" or "Boy Pulling Cat's Tail" or "Jonah and the Whale." This last, produced by the N. N. Hill Brass Company, shows the whale swimming in a very blue ocean. With each revolution of the wheels a bell rings and the whale swallows Jonah, only to have him pop out, ready to be swallowed again.

342. *Animated bell ringers, illustrated from Gong Bell Manufacturing Company catalogue.*

N. N. Hill and the Gong Bell Manufacturing Company were the most competitive producers of animated bell ringers, although other firms made them during their period of greatest sale. Of particular interest are those from makers of mechanical banks like the J & E. Stevens Company, a top manufacturer in this field.

One of the satisfactions in collecting old bell ringers lies in the fact that they can usually be documented, either by studying early company catalogues or some of the numerous books on antique toys, or by visiting an outstanding collection. One of the most rewarding and delightful exhibits is maintained by the Perelman Antique Toy Museum of Philadelphia. Some sixty

bell ringers are included, all handsomely displayed and carefully documented.

Another satisfaction in this collecting area is the realization that advertisements for such toys can be relied upon, for no reproductions have been made. Though far less common now, for-sale notices like this with its nostalgic pricing were still fairly common in the 1950s:

Four iron early, rare bell toys; not the nickel plated type, but rare painted iron. First: monkey on log, 6½" long, pounding coconut on bell, $25. Second: iron chariot, 4 wheels, large iron goose rings bell; 6" long "WADDLER," $15. Third: iron chassis, Indian rings two bells when wheels move, 6" long, $12. Fourth: large iron clown on chassis, rings two bells when wheels move, $12.

343. *Typical bell ringers made by the N. N. Hill Brass Company. All except horse-drawn bell qualify as animated type. To ring bell, elephant's tusks move up and down; bear and clown, from side to side.* PRIVATE COLLECTION

9

Dual-Purpose Bells

EVERY EPOCH OF BELLMAKING has had a few special phenomena that distinguished the period or the place and were not repeated elsewhere. One of the more interesting instances arose in the Victorian era when silver-plated table appointments of all kinds were status symbols in the middle- and upper-class American home. The American tradition of improvisation came to the fore here, and as a result bells were incorporated into the designs of silver spooners, silver napkin holders, silver toast racks, et cetera, et cetera. These were what might be called dual-purpose bells, since they not only served to call the household maid but also served as an in-

tegral part of the object's ornamental design.

Pieces of this description were popular because they satisfied the Victorian fondness for both the practical and the ornate. It is fitting that they be looked upon mainly as pieces of Americana, for silver plating reached its peak of development in the United States. This is not to say that many comparable articles of silver plate were not also produced in England; but during the years just prior to and following the Civil War, there were approximately two hundred silver-plating establishments in the United States alone. Most of them were scattered along the Eastern Seaboard, with a heavy con-

344. A Victorian spoonholder could accommodate its owner's collection of sterling spoons. Left: *Bell housed in base is rung by pressing side lever. Applied silver leaves around holder.* Center: *Tap bell of the type seen also on castors.* Right: *Bell housed in base is rung by pushing the plunger in the center stem. Decorative figural feet.* BAXTER COLLECTION

345. *Silver napkin holders. Base forms housing for bell that is rung by depressing the center rod. Marked "Wilcox Silver Plate Co." Circa 1867.* PRIVATE COLLECTION

346. *Silver sugar and creamer in stand fitted with bell. Marked "Simpson Hall Miller Co."* MOSLEY COLLECTION

centration in the Connecticut River Valley.

Obviously, then, unless a particular article is in some way marked or is illustrated in a given catalogue, or unless its patent dates can be traced, it is not easily attributable; and even catalogues are not always helpful, for it was common practice among early silver manufacturers to exchange among themselves parts of articles they made. This was done on a regular contract basis, so it is possible in old catalogues to see pieces of like design shown by several companies.

The majority of silver manufacturers purchased plain metal bells from firms like Reed & Barton or Meriden Silver Plate Company, then decorated them to suit, and fitted them as they wished to silver-plated vases, revolving castors,

and the like. There was almost no limit to the number of conceits to which those ingenious individuals attached bells. Rogers Brothers, noted Connecticut silversmiths, in 1878 came out with an eleven-inch piece having a toothpick holder on top, a vase to one side, and a spoon holder on the other side. Under all this was the tap bell.

The revolving table castor, with its full complement of bottles for spices and oils, was probably the most popular of all such items, and it appeared quite frequently with a bell either on or under its handle. Catalogues featuring this item often stated that a bell handle could be furnished with any castor when desired. One such catalogue advertisement showed

16-inch castors with bell @ 6.25
18-inch castors with bell @ 8.50
separate bell handles   @ 1.50

In the total number produced, probably waste bowls ranked second to the castors. In less polite terms, these were the "slop" bowls used for emptying the dregs of cups at the table. They appeared most frequently in catalogues issued between 1870 and 1900, wherever silver-plated

347. *Silver table article of unspecified purpose. Large initial* S *is engraved on holder, for Belle Skinner of the family famous as makers of Skinner silks and satins, Holyoke, Massachusetts.* MELHORN COLLECTION

tea sets were advertised. Those having a bell are footed and of rather squat proportions, the better to accommodate a large cup-shaped tap bell underneath.

In general the popularity of castors and other large table articles in silver plate dates from the early nineteenth century. They were produced in the greatest quantity, however, between 1850 and 1900. Some of the most elaborate pieces, like the so-called cathedral castor, appeared just prior to and during the 1880s. These later designs represented the epitome of elegance. They also represented more or less of a grand finale to the era of silver-plated table appointments, for by 1900 the vogue for them had run its course.

Even though individual articles are not always attributable, it is sometimes possible to date a silver-plated table piece tentatively after studying its style of decoration. For example, a waste bowl with a frosted finish and brightly polished cuttings more than likely belongs to the 1890s. "Satin bright cut" was a new decorating style just introduced in the preceding decade. On the other hand, an article of plain, gleaming silver decorated only with a beaded

348. *Silver vase with tap bell. Foliate engravings. Overall design shows* art nouveau *influence. Marked "Reed & Barton."* HAMLIN COLLECTION

edge may date much earlier. The beaded edge was a type of decorative treatment applied to early (before 1860) silver objects of otherwise plain design.

The entire silver electroplating process employed on these objects owed its origin to the Birmingham, England, firm of G. R. & H. Elkington, which in 1840 was the first company ever to be issued a patent for silver electroplating—a process using a metal base of nickel alloy that was shaped and assembled down to the last detail before being coated with only a very thin deposit of silver. Often there was a mark incorporating the letters *EPNS* (electroplated nickel silver).

349. *English plated-silver toast rack with free-swinging bell. Marked for Roberts & Belk, Furnival Works, Sheffield. Crest not identified. Circa 1880.* PRIVATE COLLECTION

In 1846 this process was introduced to America by Rogers Brothers, and it became the common property of all American manufacturers of silverware. Even so, the finishes on the completed pieces differed from one firm to another because not all silver coatings were of a uniform thickness. Since the only guarantee on the amount of silver was the maker's reputation, brand names and the phrase *Quadruple Plate* were looked upon as indications of a heavy deposit of silver.

UNDERSTANDING HALLMARKS

Although most dual-purpose table bells are found on articles of silver plate, a few are seen on similar articles of sterling. This is particularly true of those from Britain. The British sterling pieces bring the collector face to face with the need to understand hallmarks. The laws requiring and regulating such markings have never extended to silversmiths in America, but England has long required that sterling be stamped according to rule, thus testifying to the quality of the metal.

In simplest terms, a full set of hallmarks must always consist of four distinct stamps confirming the maker, his town, the sterling quality of the piece, and the date it was made. The maker is customarily identified by his initials; the town mark for pieces made in London is a leopard's head and for pieces made in Birmingham, an anchor; the standard mark for sterling content is a lion passant gardant; the date mark is a letter, which is changed every year.

From Britain there is also the matter of table articles in Sheffield plate. Sheffield plate developed when it was discovered that a layer of silver could be fused over copper ingots. The resulting plate could be shaped and decorated so that it looked like silver. At first the makers of Sheffield plate were prohibited from marking their work, but later it became legal for firms within one hundred miles of Sheffield to put their name and an emblem on their work. Since these makers were silversmiths, most of whom maintained high standards, they reserved their

350. *Illustrating modern London hallmarks. Maker's initials at left. Sterling silver standard lion mark at left center. London's leopard (he lost his crown in 1821) town mark at right center. Date letter for 1964 at right.* COURTESY OF THE WORSHIPFUL COMPANY OF GOLDSMITHS

marks for their most valuable pieces. A crown was the most common Sheffield emblem used as an assurance of good quality, but in 1896 this mark was prohibited by the assay office. As might be expected, a few makers of Sheffield plate saw fit to act less scrupulously and these stamped their work with rows of tiny puncheons deceptively like hallmarks for sterling.

MORE BELLS IN DUAL ROLE

Bells in a dual role combined with table articles are by no means limited to silver. In pressed glass of the late nineteenth century there were butter dishes with a lacy edge supporting a cover in the shape of a bell, complete with clapper. These are most commonly found in the Currier and Ives pattern, in either clear, amber, blue, or apple green. Combination pieces in blown glass are not unknown either, but are extremely rare. One example is seen in the Dutch beaker with silver bells ornamenting its handle, as shown earlier among illustrations of old European glass bells.

For centuries there have been wine cups made with tinkling bells as a base. History tells of Humbert II, Dauphin of Viennois, in 1338 drawing up a document of privileges granted to a certain glassmaker—privileges allowing use of a certain forest area "on condition that the latter supply annually for his [the Dauphin's] house one hundred dozen glasses in the form of bells . . ."

Bells have been combined, too, with various objects for the dressing table, objects such as ring holders, stands for watches, and all sorts of cases and porcelain pieces meant to hold jewelry. Many of the porcelain holders are made in two sections, with the top that lifts off being the bell; quite often the top, or even the whole piece, will be made in the likeness of some dainty or else amusing figure.

With the start of the Victorian era, both British and American inventors began to bombard their government patent offices with all manner of specifications for objects incorporating bells

351. Butter dishes with bells serving as covers; colorless pressed glass. Left: Currier and Ives pattern. Threaded handle. Right: Standard pressed pattern with frosted leaf design. PRIVATE COLLECTION

in one way or another. Despite the unrelenting prejudice against Victoriana on the part of many, it must be admitted that designers of that period produced ideas for some unique articles such as no one had thought of before.

352. Paperweight bell. Heavy faceted weight is surmounted by arborlike arrangement supporting tap bell. Camphor-satin gnome sits drinking from keg. Brass mounts. PRIVATE COLLECTION

353. Match holder with striking surface, bell, and an ashtray combined. Iron weighted base. All other parts, brass. From an old English pub. MC LEAN COLLECTION

The various ways in which bells were worked into some of the designs is nothing short of amazing. One of the most unusual British patents in this category called for a bell to be built into a vessel for ice water. Specifications

for the design included also a receptacle for matches and a flower vase, with the bell push being fitted into a little pump for delivering the ice water. Many combination articles for smokers included a bell and some or all the other necessary parts: cigar cutter, matchbox, ash tray, and snuffbox.

A British writer of the day told of staying at a seaside hotel where both guests and staff were driven to the point of annoyance by so many bells sounding at the least excuse. Some were hidden in plant stands or they stood in plain sight on top of paperweights. Others were incorporated in toothpick receptacles or in holders for outgoing letters at the hotel desk.

It is true that most of these intricately contrived combinations keep roughly to the chronological limits of Victoria's reign from 1837 to 1901, but a number of new ideas for designs cropped up well into the Edwardian age that followed. A British patent was issued in 1902 for "an electrically operated cigar lighter, cigar cutter, ash tray, and bell; advertisements or pictures could be put in a frame at the side, and the top could be used for a money-box."

There are three dual-purpose bells of American origin which, although more conservative in conception, are of considerable interest. All three are of the late Victorian or the early twentieth century era. One is a bronze doorknob

354. Bronze doorknob showing bell push. Mechanism is housed in plain knob at other end of axle. No patent date. PRIVATE COLLECTION

355. Circular three-footed brass trivet combined with a bell. Tapper flips up directly over one foot. Extremely heavy. PRIVATE COLLECTION

with the bell push imbedded in the ornate outside knob and the bell itself encased in the plain inside knob. Some of these show a patent date for the year 1897. Another combination couples a very melodious brass bell with a heavy round brass trivet. A stylized tulip motif is cut into the trivet and is quite appropriate to its circular shape. Round trivets in themselves are more rare than those of horseshoe shape, for instance, and are said to have been a specialty of the Victorian era. Coupled with a bell, one of these is of course doubly rare.

A third combination piece of unusual interest, and one that is uniquely American, is a lamp and an ashtray combined with a bell. Only three of these are known to exist, all

357. *Wayside bell cote accommodating a thermometer is bronze with gilt ormolu trim. Bell and cross are of brass. Marble base. From Vienna.* PRIVATE COLLECTION

three being either the off-duty or else the experimental work of craftsmen at the N. N. Hill Brass Company (*see* Ill. 356). The lamp is in the form of a tree trunk with a large frog resting at one side of the base. The bell is concealed within the frog. An adjustable leaf-shaped ashtray—presumably it is that—rises from the base on the other side.

Although they were greatly preoccupied with designing them, American and British inventors held no monopoly on these combination pieces. The French had a fondness for combining dainty porcelain objects with metal bells. In Austria at least three different arrangements were designed involving thermometers and bells mounted together on a fancy base.

356. *Lamp, ashtray, and bell combined in a single table object, with the bell concealed in frog. Painted throughout in natural colors. One of only three known to exist. N. N. Hill Brass Company.* PRIVATE COLLECTION

INKSTAND COMBINATIONS

The basic idea of bells in dual role was not wholly original with the Victorians, though they capitalized on it to an extreme. Earlier employment of bells in conjunction with other articles was far more restrained, though, than in the Victorian period. Evidence of this is seen in the use of bells on early inkstands, or standishes, as they were originally called.

To acquire a completely equipped inkstand with its original bell is a major delight in anyone's collecting experience, for there is a considerable body of literature on early inkstands that makes research on them rewarding. They enjoyed a long period of development, apparently being known for many years before they were used to any extent. Henry VIII owned probably the earliest silver specimen still in existence. It is a small tray hallmarked for the

359. *Georgian inkwell with original well of dark blue glass and original quill pen. Cover with cupid finial is also the bell. Rococo silver. Marks unidentified.* PRIVATE COLLECTION

358. *Ink standish is made up of six pieces: candle holder, bell, penholder, and three vessels. One is for ink, one for either sealing wax or pounce, and one for sand to sprinkle over wet ink to dry it. Spain. Circa 1700.* BECKY MAYER COLLECTION

year 1630; but after that date nearly a century elapses before there is much attention focused on the standish.

Until the Restoration, writing furniture in England and America consisted largely of the portable desk. Convenient and comfortably designed desks evolved with the William and Mary period (ca. 1685–1720). It was then that inkstands of silver were wrought for the first time as standard articles of sale. They created a richly elaborate accessory for the newly fashionable desks.

Actually, the silver standish is looked upon as a development of the eighteenth century. In Georgian England the highly ornate standish was a favorite gift of appreciation among members of the royal family, suitably engraved with crest and monogram. In this age of impeccable taste and gracious grandeur, the sterling silver standish reflected Georgian satisfaction in beautifully matching appointments. There was of course a gracefully shaped tray with an elaborate rim and knurled feet. On it were vessels for ink, pounce, and wafers—each unmistakably matching and hallmarked. A popular variation was to omit the wafer box and place a bell between the ink and the pounce pots, this to ensure the prompt appearance of the servant who was to dispatch the letter. After about 1745 the bell was sometimes fitted to the wafer box as a cover.

Much of the pleasure in an antique inkstand lies in its equipment. Each piece will be in correct proportion and will have a definite purpose if it is an original and undeniable part of that particular standish. Some inkstands held more than three articles, for there was the matter of cleaning the pen and some accommodation was needed for pens and knife when not in use. Preparation of the feathered quill pen required a razor-sharp pocketknife to point and slit the quill.

Anyone acquiring a standish as much for its bell as for its other fitments should be cautioned to make certain the bell properly belongs. As one writer on the subject of Georgian inkstands points out, a Georgian sterling bell with its spreading rim and baluster handle is in itself of great value, and there is a temptation on the part of some to remove the bell from the tray and sell it separately. To quote, in precise terms, from one expert: "A George I bell ten years ago [1957] sold for about $700 and fetches at least $4,200 today [1967], and later examples are correspondingly high in price."

There were, of course, inkstands priced to fit all degrees of wealth. Some very handsome ones in Sheffield plate and in porcelain were designed with bells as a part of the fittings. And within one hundred years of the Georgian period the inkstand was being copied in finely finished brass.

Only a few standishes by early American silversmiths have survived, but more of the nineteenth-century brass ones can be seen in collections. For the most part, these reflect the changing designs seen in their English counterparts. Some of the early brass ones show a traditional oblong tray, perhaps with a heavy

360. *Early wrought-iron floor stand with candle-cup, bell, and bell ringer incorporated into its design.* SHELBURNE MUSEUM, INC.

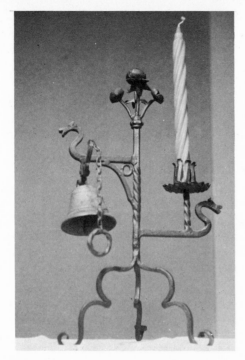

361. *Early wrought-iron table stand involving candle holder and bell.* BROWN'S ANTIQUES

gadrooned rim; later ones created under the influence of art nouveau exhibit curving trays with fanciful ornamentations. Both the Barton Bell Company of East Hampton, Connecticut,

362. *Pair of English brass candlestick bells. Bells operate with wheel and chain. Circa 1840.* PRIVATE COLLECTION

and the Gould-Mersereau Company of New York manufactured inkstands with bells among the fitments. Those from Gould-Mersereau were being advertised in 1899.

OLD CANDLESTICK BELLS

Probably the most universal and also the oldest articles involving bells in their design are candlesticks. The combination of sound and light is somehow a natural one, and one that was employed centuries ago to exorcise darkness and the evil spirits associated with darkness. The combination of bells and candleholders is also natural from an artistic standpoint, for there is a close relationship between the proportions of an ordinary handbell and those of an early brass candlestick with its trumpet-mouth base.

Natural as the combination seems in retrospect, collectors can nevertheless only surmise how the idea first flourished. Was it inspired by the use of candlesticks in the early church? Monks of the tenth century were already molding candleholders of bell metal. While presiding at the altar a priest may have struck a candleholder unexpectedly as he held it aloft, thus causing it to emit a bell tone. Upon hearing that accidental tone, any enterprising artisan could easily progress to the next natural step and incorporate a clappered bell in the base of a holder. In any event, ecclesiastical sticks involving bells are favorites with collectors; and because of the religious symbolism attached to candles in the church, these ecclesiastical sticks are usually works of great artistic beauty.

Their use as altar appointments, however, is only one of several applications for lighting devices of this kind. Persian households used a richly chased brass holder with a clapperless bell inserted on the stem midway between the candle-cup and the saucerlike base. In old English taverns a combination brass candlestick and bell was kept conveniently at hand for lighting guests to their rooms. When not being used for that purpose, the piece served as a call bell. Under the candle-cup was a swinging bell com-

363. *Candlestick bells of varying composition and design.* Left to right: *Modern Spanish wrought-iron, with bell doubling as snuffer. Old Peruvian silver. Old Dutch iron, with bells hung in imitation of Holland's circular carillons. Old Persian brass. Early American wrought-iron, with opaque pink glass bell, tapper, and snuffer.* PRIVATE COLLECTION

plete with a miniature wheel and chain for activating it. Spanish gardens were sometimes lighted with a wrought-iron candleholder having a small brass bell suspended from a chain. The little bell could double as a snuffer, if necessary. American craftsmen of the nineteenth century also used wrought iron to fashion rather intricate parlor pieces combining candlelight and the sound of a bell. Some were floor stands, and on these the elaborate mounting for the bell might be copied from a European counterpart involving the figure of a bell ringer.

And of course for centuries there have been Far Eastern combinations of this description, as already noted in surveying Oriental bells. The artistic possibilities in combining light and sound have long been appreciated in the East. More often than not, the combination hinges upon some animal form—in China, perhaps a dragon; and in India, a cobra. Their sinuous bodies are readily adaptable to supporting both a candle-cup and a bell in some graceful manner.

So the roll call of candlestick bells can be continued from one land to another. Candlesticks are of versatile design to begin with. Consequently they can accommodate bells in unexpected and varied ways, each combination naturally being fashioned in the art idioms of its own day. For the collector all this spells a potential collecting area of unusual interest.

10

On Starting a Collection

TASTES IN COLLECTING BELLS, like tastes in reading, travel, music, or fashion, can be international or national, timeless or archaic, exploratory or purposeful—in a word, eclectic. Therein lies the joy in this hobby of collecting something that can be found in so many shapes, materials, ages, and origins.

Pleasurable as such varied prospects may appear to the beginner, they also impose on him a certain responsibility in the matter of choosing wisely. Discrimination in buying comes gradually, however. As a past president of the American Bell Association, Helen Baxter discussed in *Hobbies Magazine* the building of a bell collection. From her own experience and that of others she wisely pointed out that inevitably the beginner tends to be a gatherer. Then almost automatically he finds himself becoming a collector in the true sense of the word, wanting to be selective in order to acquire bells having some relevant significance.

The experienced collector has usually evolved his own set of criteria for judging what, in his estimation, makes a bell a worthwhile acquisition. Personal preference and purpose carry considerable weight here, though, and it is presumptuous to think that what is worthwhile for one collector is equally so for another. Someone wanting a showcase collection will select bells displaying the greatest visual beauty. Someone else of more historical bent will come to feel that form and appearance in a bell are of minor importance, that for him age and rarity are better criteria of value. Each beginning collector must experience a certain amount of indecision, of trial-and-error buying, before finding his own avenue of interest and ultimately arriving at his own ideas of worth when purchasing a bell.

LEARNING BY VIEWING

On the other hand, the novice wants to become knowledgeable before too long and thus avoid prolonged trial-and-error buying, for that can prove costly. There are no shortcuts to becoming better informed but there are many pleasant ways of doing so; and all of them involve viewing bells whenever and wherever possible, either at first hand where they can be touched and examined or in photographs with explanatory text.

Membership in the American Bell Association (the headquarters are at Tarentum, Pennsylvania) offers countless opportunities to view and study bells belonging to collectors scattered throughout the United States and several foreign countries. Members receive an illustrated monthly publication and are eligible to join regional chapters in their area. At the regional meetings and also at the annual national convention there are always ample opportunities to view the collections of others.

Visiting antiques shows and shops also helps the novice to widen his knowledge of bells, especially as it concerns their worth in dollars and cents. This is a phase of collecting to be discussed with diffidence, for there are sometimes wide discrepancies in the prices asked for identical bells. Such differences are inescapable because so many factors enter into a dealer's price—what he has paid for the bell, what he knows about it, what competition dictates or, equally important, does not dictate in the case of rarities. A collector needs to weigh these considerations before judging dealers' price differentials.

It is all the more difficult to say anything helpful to a beginning collector about the prices he can expect to pay for bells because many factors also enter into his personal attitude on the matter—whether he has unlimited bank accounts, whether he is willing to pay any amount for bells he very much wants, or whether he believes in judging the cash value of a bell by its intrinsic worth. This last approach is the more prevalent and sensible one, but one that requires a good deal of homework on the part of the collector.

The abbreviated price guide at the conclusion of the book reflects current trends in the values being placed on antique bells. Beginners who do not have unlimited funds for collecting may wish to study this. In so doing, perhaps they will find themselves in a better position to choose those types of bells that will bring them the greatest satisfaction for their money.

Subscribing to a magazine in the antiques field is a wise investment. Following the advertisements of reputable dealers helps in keeping abreast of current offerings and values, since most dealers today are quite well informed about bells, now that they have become more than a minor collectible. Although it is entirely possible for anyone of modest means to acquire a quality collection of bells, at the same time few fine collections are being established today at bargain-basement prices. The sophistication, affluence, and avidity of collectors have conspired to keep prices relatively high on really good bells. And though the amateur may not be so aware of this until too late, he may regret passing up a truly desirable bell simply because it seems *slightly* overpriced. Far better to acquire it, unless the asking price is out of all reason. As Miss Baxter pointed out in her *Hobbies Magazine* discussion, the opportunity to acquire one particular bell may never come again.

There are few articles and books dealing exclusively with bells. Still, a collector need not always limit his reading to that subject alone. Articles and handbooks on related subjects—porcelains, glass, metal arts, for example—offer useful information so that the amateur can more easily recognize bells of a certain ware when they appear.

Museum publications and the museums themselves are excellent sources for study. Though there are no major American museums devoted entirely to bells, many have numerous examples on permanent display. Attention has already been focused on the fine art glass bells (*see* Ill. 201) at the Butler Institute of American Art in Youngstown, Ohio. Then, too, almost all museums include outstanding specimens in their special exhibits from time to time.

The best viewing is frequently in museums limited to certain areas of interest. Here the viewer has the delight of coming upon bells unexpectedly, bells the museum considers merely incidental to its area of interest but which loom as major attractions for the enthusiastic bell buff. For those fascinated by the musical aspects of old bells, there is no finer viewing than among the musical instruments at the Smithsonian. Anyone studying bells from primitive cultures can find invaluable information from browsing around the dioramas and artifacts belonging to the American Museum of Natural History. The Woolaros Museum on the Osage Reservation in Oklahoma includes a fine showing of authentic bells and rattles here and there among its American Indian exhibits. Still more Indian ceremonial and horse regalia with bells attached are on view at the Yakima Frontier Museum in the state of Washington. Western team bells are also to be seen at close range here. With a small amount of effort, anyone who travels can locate additional museums offering viewing satisfac-

364. *Bell cote at entrance to Granite Glen Museum, Evergreen, Colorado. Bell is from Ebenezer in the Pines, a Danish Lutheran church once in Evergreen. The Crown Prince of Denmark rang the bell at the dedication of the church.* WINSTON JONES COLLECTION

365. *Dinner gong on view in Teddy Roosevelt's home, Saga more Hill, Oyster Bay, New York. Made by a London firm and mounted on four-foot elephant tusks from an elephant Roosevelt shot in Kenya, 1910.* THEODORE ROOSEVELT AS SOCIATION

tion for almost every collector regardless of his concentration—whether he pursues bells of a single period or bells of a single type.

The finest and most comprehensive private collection open to the public on a regular schedule is housed at Granite Glenn Museum, Evergreen, Colorado (*see* Ill. 364). The bells represent the lifetime collecting efforts of the museum's owner and curator, Winston H. Jones. The building proper holds the smaller collectibles, and the surrounding grounds make a picturesque setting for large bells, some weighing a ton, and all in handsome mountings appropriate to their type—the church bell in its cote, a large Japanese one in its torii arch.

A smaller but highly selective collection is on display in the Peter White Memorial Library of Marquette, Michigan, the collection being from the bequest of Mrs. Franklin Spear, a prominent Marquette resident and a charter member of the American Bell Association.

There is a great deal of satisfaction, too, in viewing bells as an integral part of the furnishings in restorations. Seeing Abraham Lincoln's doorbell suspended in the entrance hall of his Springfield home enlightens the collector as to how those odd spiral-hung bells once appeared in actual use. Observing a pair of nineteenth-century English brass candlestick bells in Washington Irving's dining room at Tarrytown, New York, helps to visualize the way such pieces were used to ornament and light a room of the period.

COMPOSITES, FAKES, AND REPRODUCTIONS

A certain amount of buying is apt to be done sight unseen or at auctions where the items have not been examined beforehand. The unwary amateur may be somewhat disillusioned on acquiring for the first time a bell that afterward proves to be a composite one, particularly if it is poorly assembled. All bells are of course assembled in being manufactured, unless they are cast as a single object. The assembling here is done according to a prearranged design, however; but bells that are made up of parts not originally intended for each other are looked upon as composites.

Kept in proper perspective, one or two of these are not necessarily objectionable in a collection. They may in fact demonstrate how telltale clues reveal such bells for just what they are—assembled, or "married," pieces, as they are known in the antiques trade. The great majority are brass animal bells or sturdy handbells to which someone has fitted a figural handle. The urge to assemble bells quite frequently originates when a craftsman is tempted to "create" handles from appealing figures; and sometimes these are not only skillfully attached but are of a brass that matches the bell surprisingly well without any refinishing. The practiced eye of an expert, however, detects the artificial attachment. The clapper is almost always a further clue to a composite. All too often the heavy rusted tongue typical of an animal bell, or even an old handbell, is allowed to remain. If another clapper has been substituted, the heavy and rusted suspensory ring still remains as evidence.

Composites are by no means limited to metal bells. There are examples in glass, assembled in all sorts of ways, many of them in a sense fakes because no one of the parts really belonged to a bell in the first place. A light shade with a handle inserted in the top, a bell-like bottle with the bottom ground out and a handle added—these and similar contrivances, no matter how artfully assembled, are fakes when they are offered for sale as authentic bells. Fortunately, most reliable dealers will not knowingly handle assembled pieces.

Then there are fakes of another kind that are far harder to detect. These may be pre-Columbian pottery bells made only yesterday, as it were, or they may be priceless porcelain bells with faked potters' marks, or modern cut glass

366. Four composite bells of brass. Handles significant and well attached. **Left** to right: *Stork, representing the Low Countries where they nest; Scandinavian troll smashing bell he traditionally despises; a Laplander's handiwork; the red star of Russia, as seen on spire at University of Moscow.* **PRIVATE COLLECTION**

367. *A string holder in Thousand Eye pattern glass converted to a bell rests on underplate of related pattern.* PRIVATE COLLECTION

bells "worked" over to appear brilliant and sharp. Even museum experts are at times helpless to distinguish between the genuine and the fake, as are the very people who make the genuine articles. On one famous occasion in London, officials from Ireland's Belleek manufactory were asked to distinguish their cups and saucers costing 23s. from certain fakes costing 5s.9d. They were unable to tell them apart! In view of such inability on the part of experts, dealers and collectors cannot hope to escape an occasional error in judgment.

Reproductions, like composites, need to be kept in proper perspective. Most collectors have no quarrel with quality reproductions of antique bells per se. Priced right and sold for what they are, they can be either accepted or ignored by the individual collector. The quarrel arises only when reproductions are sold as originals and at prices only originals should command. For many beginners these "new bells with old charm" serve to acquaint them with figures and patterns they may never have seen before and may never acquire in the original. Even so simple a pressed-glass pattern as Hobnail, for example, is difficult

368. *Clear-toned crystal bell with luminous air twist shaft. Contemporary.* COURTESY OF STEUBEN GLASS

to find in an original bell; yet the collector who lectures before clubs delights in telling of the once-upon-a-time popularity of this pattern and of its four-hundred-year-old German ancestry. Showing a reproduction in Hobnail glass is certainly not out of place in this instance. The very fact that it is being reproduced is evidence of the pattern's repeated popularity.

There is also the question of contemporary bells, originals coming from today's craftsmen.

A growing number of bell collectors, unless they are dedicated to collecting within a single period, tend to take an interest in the modern artist's creative designs. By collecting and exhibiting a certain amount of contemporary craftsmanship they feel they are preserving examples for the future, examples that all too soon will no longer be contemporary but may suddenly become collectors' items. As one director of a major museum aptly expressed it, when challenged about acquiring too much contemporary art: "But if you don't collect it, even against your taste buds, you've made a great mistake, because you'll only have to go round and collect it later."

Of course, there are contemporary bells and contemporary bells, and some have little to recommend their being preserved for posterity. At the other extreme are the sparkling Steuben glass bells of contemporary design. These illustrate so well the fact that age and rarity are not necessarily the sole criteria of meaningful value. Bells of Steuben glass are available to anyone wanting them, and the name under which they are sold is a familiar one. But here the familiar name is an advantage, representing the highest quality in crystal and enhancing any collection. In the final analysis, as countless collectors agree, it is the intrinsic worth of a bell that counts, age and rarity notwithstanding.

Royal Copenhagen is another familiar name now famous for several distinctive designs in contemporary bells. To own one as an example of the work done under the firm's innovative Tenera program is to acknowledge appreciation for modern young designers' ideas. The bells are but one article among many resulting from the experimental studio set up at the Royal Copenhagen Porcelain Manufactory. Here six young Scandinavian women artists blended their ideas with the experienced craftsmanship of the firm's leading ceramist. Even to the untrained eye, it is apparent that the designs justify the name given the products from this experimental studio—Tenera, meaning "The Young–the Budding–the Spirited."

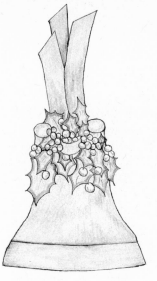

369. *Colorful faience bell made by an Oregon ceramist. Pink body, red and green holly, gold handle. Contemporary.* PRIVATE COLLECTION

370. *Winged Pegasus stands as a meaningful handle on contemporary metal bell. Design inspired by classic mythology. Japan.* WALTERS COLLECTION

371. *Bells and birds from Royal Copenhagen's experimental Tenera program.* ROYAL COPENHAGEN PORCELAIN MANUFACTORY, LTD.

372. *Contemporary bell of colorless spun glass. Bird finial and rim both stained in turquoise.* PRIVATE COLLECTION

Some of the things being done by contemporary workers in spun glass are also inviting to many collectors. Bells of this lacy glass, contemporary though they may be in concept, represent an art that first flourished centuries ago. As early as 1696 there were English allusions to the showmanship and skill of men and women "who lately wrought and spun glass publick."

DOCUMENTING THE COLLECTION

Documentation of a collection takes on added importance with passing time, but unfortunately it is also a task easily laid aside until the collection has grown to such proportions that the mere thought of cataloguing it is onerous. The time to start a written record, as any seasoned collector will testify, is while the collection is being initiated—or very soon afterward. There are valid reasons for this advice. It is far less burdensome to set down descriptive details, one bell at a time, while purchasing data remains clearly in mind. Later findings can always be inserted in the catalogue; but despite good intentions, unrecorded facts from the time of purchase are likely to be forgotten.

It may be an exaggeration to claim that the pleasure of piecing together their background equals the pleasure of searching for the bells themselves. Nevertheless, there is a certain satisfaction in making a habit of cataloguing each bell as it is found. In entering the specifics of origin, composition, and age, the collector must examine his bell closely and bring into play all that he has learned.

The matter of estimating the age of a bell presents a challenge that even scholars with all their expertise cannot always meet with any degree of precision. The use of the term *circa* permits a little leeway, since in the antiques trade it indicates a period of ten years either way from the date given. But that flexible span is of minor consideration when experience indicates that collectors customarily err in assigning antique bells too early a date, often with a probable error of two or three centuries.

In dating bells of more recent make, collectors are guided—and sometimes misguided—by the United States import law that took effect in 1891 and required that the country of origin be marked on all imports. It is commonly believed that every bell having its country of origin clearly marked was made after 1891. There is much evidence, though, that many firms were so proud of their fine workmanship that they had been marking country of origin on their pieces before the law required it. Moreover, the lack of such marking does not prove that a certain bell was made before 1891 either. After all, the law pertained only to imports; bells purchased by individuals traveling abroad might or might not be so marked.

Determining the place of origin is sometimes a challenge when the "country of origin" mark is lacking. Some bells are stamped with the native term meaning "registered," and this gives an immediate clue. In France the term is *dépose;* in Sweden, *deponert.* Lacking any such clues and lacking any pertinent inscription, the collector is left largely to his own devices in determining what he can on this point. There is no magic formula, but comparative studies with documented bells can prove helpful.

Working in close proximity with bells while cataloguing them frequently reveals imperfections that had previously gone unnoticed. These should be meticulously noted in the description. At this point, the novice may question whether he would (or should) have purchased this piece had he known of its imperfection. Collectors in general are of two minds in their viewpoints here. As a rule they avoid bells that are chipped, cracked, or drilled, if only for one reason—the impairment of tone. Perfectionists go even further and advise never buying anything not in flawless condition, thus ruling out bells with missing clappers, dents, and the like. However, not all collectors are perfectionists. In the case of a rare bell with a *minor* blemish, a bell that would add immeasurably to a certain grouping, who is to say that it isn't wise to acquire it—irrespective of the flaw if that is truly a minor one? Those who argue in this vein point out that many objects like bells have often seen long usage outdoors or they have suffered damage from fire or flood. This very usage that may have resulted in minor flaws is the same that gives the bell historic worth.

A minor flaw in a bell naturally raises the question of repair and restoration. If a collector is something less than a perfectionist, and if he is willing under certain circumstances to accept a bell with some slight imperfection, it does not follow that he believes in restoring it to erase all trace of the flaw. Some prefer that the minor imperfection remain as evidence of the bell's active past. Others prefer seeing a bell restored to its original condition. With these divisive viewpoints, beginning collectors will not find any ready answer to their question as to whether restoration affects a bell's value. It is worth noting, however, that curators condone restoration when it becomes necessary and when it is professionally supervised. When the director of one of the country's leading art museums was being interviewed on this very subject, he frankly declared that if the public saw the actual state of some acquisitions before restoration, retouching, and so forth, they might be very much surprised, even shocked.

Another question that amateurs want answered is related not so much to documentation as to the care of bells—cleaning and polishing them. Should they or shouldn't they be cleaned?

373. *Only careful cleaning brought out the symbolic beauty of this handsome bell. When found, it was unrecognizable under layers of rust and grime. The mark* DEPONIRT *indicates it is not a piece of Americana, as might be supposed, but was registered as Swiss made. Symbolism includes the Statue of Liberty, an eagle, and a shield of thirteen stripes marked* COLUMBIA. CONARD COLLECTION

Here again there is no consensus. Bell collectors appear to be about evenly divided in their preferences. Some prefer keeping their bells in the condition in which they were found. Others like to see the metal clean and glowing, serving to recall how the bells looked originally. One objective argument that may well be taken into consideration favors cleaning because sometimes, under a layer of grime, significant markings will be found. Buffing, though, is recommended only in certain instances; it is likely to obliterate the very markings that cleaning is intended to reveal. Even more important, archaeological bells and early Oriental bells should *never* have their patina removed.

These are but some of the many aspects of starting a bell collection. An inquiring mind, time, and experience will help to acquaint the beginner with others.

11

Related Realia

BELLS AS A MOTIF in the world of design appear in so many mediums that scarcely any collector can resist a few related objects. They range from mere trivia to articles that are collectible in their own right, costing as much as, or more than, actual bells. Where space is no problem, bell buffs sometimes extend their collecting interests to old chiming clocks with conspicuous bell mechanisms; music boxes relating to bells either in appearance or in the melodies they play; or various figurines in the likeness of bell ringers. Two of the most charming pieces in this last category are the Royal Bayreuth figural creamer of a colorful colonial bell-ringer and the Royal Doulton figure of a town crier (*see* Ill. 376), also colorful. Some years ago Sotheby's auctioned a curious trio of bell ringers, three Bavarian uniformed bandsmen made of silver with nautilus shell torsos. Each carried a bell and a music portfolio.

Where space is at a premium, papery realia and objects that can be displayed flat hold more appeal. Stamps, coins, and buttons employing a bell motif are all top favorites in the way of related collectibles, as are old sheet music covers and art prints (*see* Ills. 377–381). Although prints may involve the use of considerable artistic license in picturing bells, many interpret the roles of quaint old bells realistically. These can lead down interesting bypaths of knowledge.

Old horse brasses require little space and add a decorative note to walls where horse bells hang. These brasses have the added advantage of having been very closely associated with horse bells and used with them on harness trappings. Moreover, though some were simply cast in the pattern of a bell, some were cut out to accommodate small bells and these of course are extremely rare. They lost their bells years ago, most of them.

Like the bells with which they were used, horse brasses have enjoyed a long history. Their origin goes back to Roman times, or even earlier, when they were looked upon as amulets to protect the horse from what was believed to be the evil eye. Gypsies liked them for their magical properties, liked to see the sun glinting on each polished surface—supposedly to direct away unwanted evil.

These brasses became most popular in England with the accession of Queen Victoria, and there were hundreds of designs to choose from, either geometrical or figural or heraldic. Comparatively few of the geometrical were ever patterned after a bell, probably not more than a dozen, and so a great deal of searching is required to acquire any assortment with this motif.

There are two kinds of brasses to collect: old ones cast prior to 1900, and modern ones that are machine-stamped copies. The copies are faithful but much lighter in weight and much more crude than the cast brasses, which could weigh six or eight ounces apiece. The cast ones can readily be identified by the evidence of stubs at either side on the back. With these stubs

374. *Gilbert Curfew Clock. Bell strikes the hour. Gilbert Clock Company, Winsted, Connecticut. Circa 1910.* SPEAR COLLECTION, PETER WHITE MEMORIAL LIBRARY, MARQUETTE, MICHIGAN

375. *Music boxes that play bell-like melodies. From Austria, Switzerland, Germany, and Russia.* PRIVATE COLLECTION

376. *Town crier with bell in hand, as portrayed in a Doulton fine china figurine.* ROYAL DOULTON FINE CHINA, LTD.

the polisher could hold the disk firmly in a vise, then later file them down. Hopefully the collector looks for the older brasses, especially those that are mounted on harness trappings the way they were originally used—either individually on face pieces that hung down the center of the horse's forehead, or in groups of three to eleven on the martingale that reached from the collar to the horse's girth between the forelegs.

PLATES AND TILES

Certain editions of the well-known Danish Christmas plates and Easter plaques commend themselves to bell collectors for their colorful accents and for their scenic depictions of historic bells. The first Christmas plate was made at the Bing & Grondahl porcelain works in 1895, more

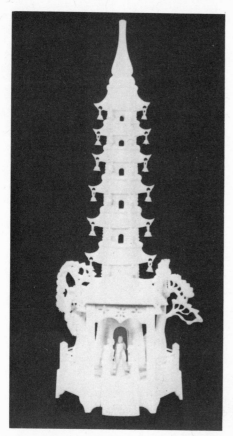

378. Bell founder's advertising token. Obverse: F. A. JENSCH : BELL FOUNDER : 1035 S WELLS ST. : CHICAGO. Reverse: MADE TO ORDER FROM 1 LB. TO 50,000 LBS. : ESTABL. 1857. PRIVATE COLLECTION

377. Chinese carved ivory pagoda, which relates well to Oriental bells. CONARD COLLECTION

379. Detail of large brass button known to collectors as Owl in the Belfry. Two-dimensional pierced work on belfry. PRIVATE COLLECTION

or less as a concession to the Old World custom of royalty giving to each of their servants a Christmas platter heaped with fruit and candies and other goodies. Later the plate was kept as a wall decoration. The Bing & Grondahl introductions proved popular, and in 1908 the Royal Copenhagen Porcelain Manufactory issued its first comparable Christmas plate. The Christmas plates from both firms have been produced annually ever since, but always in limited editions. At the end of each seasonal run the molds are destroyed and the plates immediately become collectors' items.

With few exceptions the plates are of a uniform seven-inch size. The most noticeable exception is the larger anniversary plate issued each fifth year by Bing & Grondahl. The colors are always in shades of blue and white and the scenes are appropriate to winter and the Christmas season. The designs are the subject of much thought and dedication on the part of Denmark's leading artists, who are steeped in old Scandinavian traditions.

The documentation for each Christmas plate depicting a bell is as follows:

1900 Bing & Grondahl, CHURCH BELLS CHIMING IN CHRISTMAS, shows one huge bell in the tower of the Syv Church in Roskilde, west of Copenhagen. The bell was cast in 1515 by Johannes Fastenove of the Netherlands. Artist: Dahl Jensen.

1920 Bing & Grondahl, re-issue of the above in a larger size, as a jubilee plate.

380. *Old sheet music cover depicts Russian-type troika bells. Four-color litho.*
PRIVATE COLLECTION

381. *English print published by Will Miller, Albemarle Street, London, 1895, portrays street entertainers performing with bells.*
PRIVATE COLLECTION

1934 Bing & Grondahl, CHURCH BELL IN TOWER, shows bell ringer pulling rope ringing single large bell in tower of church on Christmas Eve. Artist: Immanuel Tjerne.

1913 Royal Copenhagen, SPIRE OF FREDERIK'S CHURCH, shows bells in the spire of this beautiful circular marble church in Copenhagen. Artist: Arthur Boesen.

1942 Royal Copenhagen, BELL TOWER OF OLD CHURCH IN JUTLAND, shows a single bell in the tower of a typical Danish church, most of which were built in the twelfth and thirteenth centuries. Artist: Nils Thorsson.

Less well known but equally interesting and decorative are two bell motifs found on other series from these firms, series that have long since been discontinued. From 1904 through 1925, small six-inch Christmas plates bearing a somewhat stylized design were produced by Royal Copenhagen. The last issue is the only one with a bell motif, in rich cobalt blue against yellow and white blossoms. The inscriptions used on this series are much like those on the regular series of Christmas plates from Royal Copenhagen.

From 1910 through 1935, Bing & Grondahl made a series of Easter plaques suitable to cover the flue openings when the heating stoves were taken down in the spring. The 1927 plaque shows the bell ringer pulling a rope to sound the bell in its cote atop a hill. In the background a beautiful Easter sunrise emblazons the sky. The plaque is inscribed PAASKEN—1927. (*See* Color Plate VIII.)

Since bells have never been produced by Holland's Royal Delftware Manufactory, De Porceleyne Fles, their Christmas plates designed around a bell theme become all the more desirable as examples of their much admired workmanship. De Porceleyne Fles is the sole surviving firm of the thirty original Dutch potteries established in 1650.

To serve as a guide in seeking a Royal Delft Christmas plate, the following are the issues depicting bells—though the list could be extended to include a number of other scenes featuring church spires and bell towers. In searching, it is well to know the exact title of the design because plates of several different subjects are issued annually.

382. *Large American horse brass. Silver and brass. Heavy casting. Inscribed* AWARDED TO PRIZE WINNER OF THE PENNSYLVANIA WORK HORSES PARADE ASSOCIATION :: OCT. 16, 1907. PRIVATE COLLECTION

383. *Old horse brasses carrying original bells.* MUNICIPAL MUSEUM, HULL, ENGLAND

Year	Artist	Subject
1915	L. Senf	(Glory to God) Christmas Bells
1918	L. Senf	Christmas Bell
1929	P. Senf	Christmas Bell (Christmas 1929)
1937	P. Senf	Bell (Christmas 1937)

Unlike their smaller Danish prototypes, the designs for which are chosen on a competitive basis, these Dutch Christmas plates are the work of staff artists. In the case of the ones with a bell scene, the artists were a father and son whose combined years at the Royal Delft firm spanned nearly a century. Starting in 1878, Leon Senf —and later his son—experimented with many unique mediums in an effort to originate distinctive designs for the plates and also for the tiles that have made this manufactory a leading name in delftware.

No Royal Delft plates were produced during the Second World War and for some years afterward. So that the tradition would not die, however, Christmas cloisonné tiles were produced from 1946 through 1954. The 1947 edition depicts a bell tower and a winter's scene viewed from within.

Some interesting English tiles with a bell motif were made at the Minton works, a prominent name among the great porcelain firms at Stoke. An offshoot of their work in Victorian times was the making of encaustic tiles. Among the patrons for their venture was the architect Augustus Pugin, who used Minton tiles in decorating the new Houses of Parliament.

Minton's tile business prospered and glazed tiles became high fashion for fireplaces, also for reredos and other aspects of church architec-

384. *A border characterizes the designs on Royal Copenhagen Christmas plates.*
ROYAL COPENHAGEN PORCELAIN MANUFACTORY, LTD.

ture. At the Philadelphia Exhibition of 1876 a complete chimneypiece of brilliant Minton tiles aroused great enthusiasm. But the most curious of their tiles depicting bells does not happen to be colorful. Rather, it is a somber graveyard scene in black and white and is thought to have been designed for a scheme of church decoration. Since Minton tiles were produced chiefly for architectural purposes, finding single ones is a relatively rare experience. Any that are found appear never to have been used and are therefore assumed to be a designer's samples.

385. *Minton tile in black and white, probably designed as a church decoration about 1880. Stamped:* MINTON CHINA WORKS : STOKE UPON TRENT. HALPERIN COLLECTION

386. *Popular inanimates: Huntley & Palmer bell-shaped biscuit tin is flanked by paperweights decorated in Norwegian rosemaling.* PRIVATE COLLECTION

387. *Incense bell, a unique inanimate designed to hold incense over a lamp. Gold-green laced glass applied to ruby base cased with green glass. Loop for hanging. Signed: A Jeam. Circa 1890.* RENICK COLLECTION

388. *Bread tray in John Hancock Liberty Bell pattern glass. Milk white. A choice Centennial Exhibition piece by Gillinder & Sons.* MOODY'S MUSEUM, MCGREGOR, IOWA

INANIMATES

Inanimates exercise a fascination for many bell collectors and fit in quite well with their major collection. Inanimates are best described as quiet objects having the shape and appearance of a bell but not functioning as one—that is, not ringing. Paperweights, banks, inkwells, biscuit tins—all these and dozens of other utilitarian articles can be found as inanimate bells. Frequently these are copies of specific bells, even to their inscriptions. During the latter half of the nineteenth century the vogue for tins was at its peak. In common with most other biscuit manufacturers of that period, Huntley & Palmer of Reading, England, packed theirs in a wide range of different tins shaped like soldiers, steamers, bells, and so on. The one shaped like a bell is prized by collectors, for it spares no detail in copying an old village church bell quaintly inscribed WHEN YE DOE RINGE I SWEETLY SING.

Liberty Bell glassware is in itself highly collectible and is assuming added importance now that our 1976 bicentennial looms near. Much

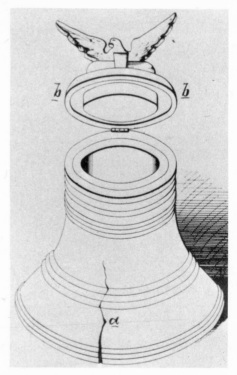

389. *Glass vessel typical of the many being patterned after the Liberty Bell around 1876 and later. Patentee: Edward Finney of Philadelphia.*

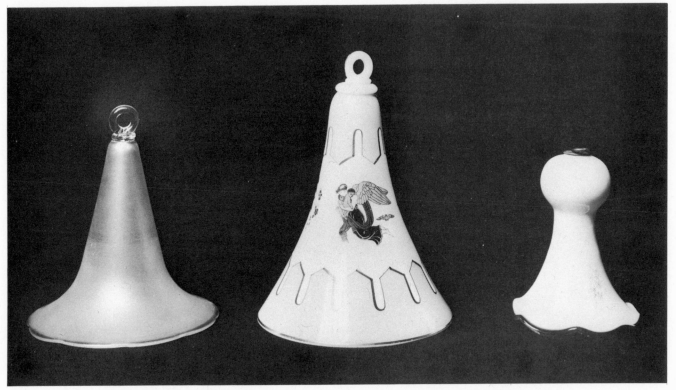

390. *Three Victorian smoke bells of unusual beauty.* Left to right: *Camphor glass; cased glass in soft brick rose and brown, with figures representing night and day; milk white glass with fluted rim of cobalt blue.* PHOTO, COURTESY OF BERENICE DU BOIS

of it is in pattern glass, but included in this ware are several patents for articles shaped to a likeness of the Liberty Bell. These were made from the mid-1870s through 1914 and even later. Most favored of such pieces are those made and sold by Gillinder & Sons in 1876, right on the grounds of the Philadelphia Centennial Exposition. According to Ruth Webb Lee, one bell shape so made and sold was the little glass candy container with a metal arrangement on top by which it could be hung. Each was inscribed PROCLAIM LIBERTY THROUGHOUT THE LAND and 1776–1876 CENTENNIAL EXPOSITION. Other inanimates patterned after the Liberty Bell but not made specifically for the Centennial were flowerholders, lamps, and a combination jelly glass and money box. This last was manufactured by Robinson & Loeble of Philadelphia as ". . . a glass vessel for holding jelly, &c, that when the

contents are removed the vessel or receptacle may be used as a toy savings bank. . . ." Both the candy and the jelly holders, like most similar Liberty Bell articles, were produced not only in clear glass but in blue, green, and amber.

Smoke bells were originally a part of Victorian hanging lamps, to keep the smoke from soiling the ceiling. These and the rare forcing bells used to propagate plants are interesting abstract adaptations of the bell form and are popular with collectors who are connoisseurs of old glass. There are scattered literary references to both these forms, as well as a few special studies of them—all of which helps to extend the collector's knowledge in areas relating to bells.

Smoke bells make an especially interesting study because they can be found in metal or porcelain or glass. The last-named are either pressed or blown glass, usually in color, and of such

391. Blown glass forcing bell, one of sixteen originally blown for a rose fancier to use in propagating plants. Clapper artificially attached for decorative effect. Height: 16 inches; diameter: 16 inches. VOSBURGH COLLECTION

varied types as clambroth, camphor-satin, and marble. Regardless of composition, smoke bells display a variety of shapes from flat saucerlike to tall conical. Rims may be smooth, scalloped, or fluted, and on some blown-glass ones the rims are stained. Though the majority of these bell shapes are undecorated, a few show quaint old-fashioned scenes painted in color. All in all, there is a considerable collecting range here.

When the old hanging lamps went into discard, the smoke bells that had hung over the glass chimneys were rescued and put to some other use; or they were kept simply for ornamental purposes. In literature on the subject are several charming vignettes as to how Victorian ladies used their smoke bells. One English-woman took hers to cover her wineglasses, thus creating bell-like covers. Another story comes from Paris, where in a French movie a conical smoke bell appeared as a slow but well-timed and efficient way of snuffing out a candle. The heroine was seen to place a smoke bell over her bedside candle flame, giving herself just enough

392. Traditional jungfrauenbecher *with swivel cup. Glass is patterned in green, blue, and lilac. Outlined in gold.* CONARD COLLECTION

393. *Silver marriage cup. Circa 1870.* S. DORMONT COLLECTION

394. *Glass jungfrauenbecher without swivel cup. Enameled inscription in German reads: "all happiness to him who drinks."* PRIVATE COLLECTION

395. *Molenbeker (mill-beaker). Latticinio glass, with a silver mill. The Netherlands. Circa 1650.* RIJKSMUSEUM, AMSTERDAM

time to get into bed before the light extinguished itself from a gradual lack of air.

It seems appropriate to conclude a roundup of related realia by looking at two types of figural articles that in recent years have been enthusiastically adopted by bell collectors. One is the *jungfrauenbecher,* or marriage cup. Most of these are either of sterling or of glass, in the likeness of a woman wearing a bell-shaped skirt that forms the larger cup and holding a smaller cup that swivels, between hands held overhead. Traditionally the groom drank from the larger cup at the same time the bride drank from the smaller; beyond that, stories of the *jungfrauen-*

becher differ. One story claims that each drop of wine spilled foretold a year of sadness.

Numerous variations were made, especially in Germany, where many in enameled glass were designed without the cup that swivels. Here a figure was just a decorative handle on the

396. *Elephant nodder combined with a candleholder. Gray and white ceramic with brilliant blue and gold trim.* CONARD COLLECTION

beaker. These variations were not used in the same way as the kind with the swivel cup. Instead, the idea was that the beaker had to be drained before it could be set down. Using this principle, the Dutch made a special wager cup in the shape of a windmill. The arms of the windmill were set spinning, and the bettor had to empty the glass before the spinning stopped.

All these variations of the *jungfrauenbecher* bear some resemblance to bells; but a more valid reason for associating the two lies in recalling that in the sixteenth century, and even earlier, bells had been harnessed to wineglasses in one way or another—either as a base for the glass or as its handle.

397. *Bell-like figures with heads that nod as weighted clappers swing. Couple in masquerade dress are blue-and-white Staffordshire trimmed in gold. All others are softly tinted bisque.* PRIVATE COLLECTION

NODDERS

Another type of figural that has been adopted into bell collections in recent years is the nodding figure in various ceramic mediums. Here the factors associating such figures with bells are a bit more nebulous and confused by two opposite points of view. In the antiques trade, ceramic nodders are not considered bells; most collectors are guided by this viewpoint. They consider such figures as related realia only, inasmuch as what passes for a clapper is usually a weight for the purpose of activating the nodding head or the hands or other movable parts.

Nevertheless, there are those who make no distinction between ceramic nodders and metal nodders. The latter have always been accepted as bells, so why not the same acceptance for ceramic nodders, since they have as much tone as, say, earthenware bells? Such acceptance seems reasonable considering that some doll collectors matter-of-factly include these figures among their dolls, even though they were originally made more as ornaments for parlor whatnots and mantels. Bell collectors would seem equally justified, then, in numbering these same figures among their bells, if they so desire.

However they are regarded, ceramic nodders have an appeal all their own. The figures are expressive. Many display the lighthearted sophistication characteristic of porcelain figurines; others have a rustic charm; and some are raffish, even comic. Not all are images of human beings. Nodding figures of animals were just as popular with the Victorians who were so fond of these ornaments.

There is no evidence that such ornaments ever were made in America. They are, for the most part, of Staffordshire or other glazed porcelain, French bisque, or Mexican pottery; and some are of Oriental origin, although many of the Oriental figures are European in make. One of the few specific references to the designing and production of these nodders goes back to the days of Louis XV. Madame Pompadour maintained a factory for fine bisque ornaments, and figures with nodding heads are known to have been made there.

It is the animation in nodders that gives them special appeal. Those with only a head that moves are by far the most common, but a few display as many as three movable parts. Head, hands, tongue, and eyes could all be weighted to move independently. Properly weighted and balanced, a head might nod for as long as thirty minutes. In a world largely unanimated a century ago, little decorative objects such as these must have seemed unique. There are anecdotes of children and invalids who amused themselves for hours, watching the movements of a nodder. It is this animation, of course, that partly explains the more than casual relationship between these quaint ornaments and bells—at least in the minds of a good many collectors.

Price Guide to Antique Bells

THIS GUIDE is in no way intended as a device to "set" prices for either collector or dealer. Rather, it is a reflection of those prices at which bells are already being sold. With very few exceptions, descriptions and values are based on actual recent advertisements or other listings from bona fide dealers, and are for bells in good condition unless otherwise noted.

As observed earlier, this brief listing is included primarily to give the beginner an over-all idea of prices in various categories. The seasoned collector is already aware of the price ranges for many of the bells described. It is a foregone conclusion that some collectors will find they have paid more for a particular bell than the highest price quoted here, whereas others are known to have paid even less than the lowest price. This merely substantiates what has already been said about price differentials.

Prices on some types are seemingly fantastic, as on American souvenir glass bells; yet the rarity of these bells, which were once fairly common and inexpensive, becomes clear upon hearing of the experience of a dealer who recently purchased several hundred souvenir items in glass and china and found not a single bell.

Luristan bell w. stylized horse figure top, 2″ size	$20.00 to $25.00
Aztec copper bell, 3″ teardrop, conventional design	20.00 to 30.00
Indian gourd rattle, beaded handle w. tiny bells	18.00 to 30.00
Mayan clay rattle, ancient figure in native garb	95.00 to 200.00
Oriental gong, 16″ exquisitely carved teak frame	135.00 to 160.00
Chinese mandarin hat-button bell, medium size	22.50 to 35.00
Oriental enameled bell w. small figure as handle	15.00 to 35.00
Ogre's head rattle on long handle, crude	40.00 to 50.00
Chinese coolie carries two gongs on pole across shoulders, 16″ o/a	45.00 to 60.00
Tibetan dorje bell, bronze, approx. 8″, much worn	40.00 to 50.00
Late Satsuma bell, lavish gold trim	18.00 to 25.00
Japanese bowl gong, 18″ dia., red lacquer stand	50.00 to 70.00
Flat gilt gong, or Japanese *kei,* phoenix bird dec.	40.00 to 60.00
Hindu temple bell, deity handle, nicely detailed	20.00 to 45.00
7″ Evolution bell, handle a two-sided figure	18.00 to 25.00
Masseur's bell, figural handle, punch work base	18.00 to 24.00
Pair heavy old anklets hung w. temple dancer's bells	50.00 to 70.00
10″ African bell, brass, shape of skeletal figure	30.00 to 40.00
Large iron double bell used by Nigerian chief	30.00 to 40.00
Meissen table bell, applied flowers & fruits	37.50 to 50.00
German Delft table bell, crossed hayforks, 3½″ size	20.00 to 25.00
Old Bohemian glass bell, enamel on white over color cut to clear	35.00 to 45.00

9" Nailsea bell, white loopings, steeple handle .... 80.00 to 95.00

6" Glossy Burmese bell, rich coloring, clear handle .... 200.00 to 250.00

Royal Bayreuth tapestry bell, scenic, blue mk. .... 35.00 to 65.00

Royal Bayreuth bell, Sunbonnet Babies, unmkd. .... 65.00 to 150.00

Evangelist bell, religious figure as handle .... 30.00 to 40.00

Apostle bell, 6" size, heavy, sharp detail .... 50.00 to 65.00

Old brass monastery bell on bracket, Latin inscriptions .... 50.00 to 60.00

Hemony bell, middle size .... 60.00 to 95.00

Hemony bell, largest size .... 125.00 to 150.00

A. R. P. bell, signed G & J, 1939, black from use .... 27.50 to 37.50

Spanish priest's, or Saint Anthony's, bell, sterling, heavy chain .... 22.00 to 30.00

M O P tap bell, French, on soapstone base .... 45.00 to 60.00

Rare Russian enamel bell by Carl Fabergé .... 850.00 to 1500.00

Iron tortoise bell w. genuine shell, press head/tail to ring .... 90.00 to 100.00

Iron frog on lily pad holds gong as umbrella. Mkd. Germany .... 25.00 to 40.00

Colorful 5" French faience bell .... 12.00 to 15.00

Brass bell shape of windmill, 3½" size .... 12.00 to 15.00

Charm, metal from Old Chicago Ct. House bell. Certificate .... 15.00 to 20.00

Glass commemorative bell, Columbian Expo., frosted handle .... 18.00 to 25.00

Signed Heisey crystal bell .... 20.00 to 25.00

7" cut glass bell, brilliant and deep cut .... 37.50 to 45.00

Amberina bell, pressed glass .... 32.50 to 45.00

Custard glass bell, pressed pattern .... 40.00 to 50.00

Brass-mounted Wavecrest tap bell, pastel colors .... 100.00 to 195.00

Small art nouveau bell, silver .... 8.00 to 15.00

Tiffany tea bell, heavy silver, signed .... 30.00 to 42.50

Quaint twirler held by little girl, nickel finish .... 15.00 to 20.00

Unusual twirler, shape of high-seated bicycle, EPNS .... 65.00 to 80.00

Souvenir advertising bell, ruby glass, gold lettering .... 35.00 to 85.00

Brass, trolley-car conductor's overhead bell w. bracket .... 25.00 to 40.00

Large Sanctus chime, tuned bells under brass shell .... 40.00 to 60.00

Rod of bells from early parlor organ, attached hammers for playing ...... 100.00 to 125.00

U.S.N. ship's bell, complete with yoke, small 9" size .... 50.00 to 65.00

Large ship's bell, English, dec. design .... 185.00 to 225.00

700-lb. bronze church bell, all parts for mounting .... 225.00 to 500.00

Old farm dinner bell, steel alloy .... 35.00 to 70.00

30 cast brass bells, 1¼", on original 6-ft. leather strap .... 40.00 to 75.00

25 graduated bells, largest 2½", on 7-ft. strap, original leather .... 75.00 to 100.00

Conestoga wagon bell, 5 bells in iron band 25" across .... 35.00 to 50.00

Fancy old sleigh bell, initialed NS .... 3.00 to 5.00

From Thailand, primitive metal animal bell in wooden rocker, 15" o/a .... 150.00 to 190.00

Heavy Persian camel chime, nest of 4 bells, 16" o/a .... 125.00 to 150.00

Old Kentucky cowbell, original paper label .... 3.00 to 8.00

Heavy figure bell, Saint Christopher carrying Christ .... 50.00 to 65.00

Brass Napoleon bell, bust of Emperor, scenes & wording .... 18.00 to 25.00

Porcelain bell, lady in 18th century dress. Mkd. Germany .... 15.00 to 20.00

5" brass lady bell, medieval dress, feet for clappers .... 35.00 to 40.00

Small brass bell, Jenny Lind in ruffles & poke bonnet .... 16.00 to 22.50

Brass nodding head bell, old lady carrying dog .... 50.00 to 60.00

Sterling baby bells, 5 on M O P ring & whistle. Dated 1859 .... 50.00 to 67.50

Coral-and-bells, 4½" hallmkd, 2 bells missing .... 125.00 to 150.00

Child's sterling whistle, 4 bells, 6" o/a .... 22.50 to 25.00

Animated bell ringer, Indian rides galloping horse, 7½" long .... 35.00 to 45.00

Floor chime, 9½" long, tin trotting horse, iron wheels .... 25.00 to 40.00

Floor chime, 4½" long, tin horse, break in one wheel .... 25.00 to 65.00

Gilbert curfew clock, 4" brass bell in arch .... 75.00 to 100.00

5-bottle castor set w. bell in handle .... 65.00 to 125.00

Matched pair tavern candlestick bells, English brass .... 135.00 to 150.00

Selected Readings

Bailey, Henry Turner. *Symbolism for Artists, Creative and Appreciative.* Davis Press, Worcester, Massachusetts, 1925.

The Bells and Crosses of the Glenwood Mission Inn. Riverside, California, 1938.

Coleman, Satis N. *Bells.* Rand McNally & Company, Chicago, 1928.

Collections of Objects of Religious Ceremonial in the United States National Museum. United States National Museum, Bulletin 148, 1929.

Dictionary of Folklore, Mythology and Legend. 2 vols. Funk and Wagnalls, New York, 1950.

Edgerly, Beatrice. *From the Hunter's Bow: The History and Romance of Musical Instruments.* G. P. Putnam's Sons, New York, 1942.

Freeman, Dr. Larry. *Early American Plated Silver.* Century House, Inc., Watkins Glen, New York, n. d.

Hearn, Lafcadio. *Glimpses of Unfamiliar Japan.* 2 vols. 1894.

Howe, Jane. *Your Guide to the Spanish Mission Bells in New Mexico.* Battenburg Press, Norman, Oklahoma, 1956.

Lascelles, B. A. *Unpublished Letters.* Privately owned. 1950.

Lavine, Sigmund A. *Handmade in America: The Heritage of Colonial Craftsmen.* Dodd, Mead & Company, New York, 1966.

Lockwood, Isabel. *Oriental Brasses.* Arthur H. Clark Company, Glendale, California, 1915.

McClintock, Marshall. *Toys in America.* Public Affairs Press, Washington, D.C., 1961.

Markham, Major C. A. *Chaffers' Handbook to Hall Marks on Gold and Silver Plate.* Reeves and Turner, London, 1924.

Morris, Ernest. *Tintinnabula.* Robert Hale, Limited, London, 1959.

Omwake, John. *The Conestoga Six-Horse Bell Teams of Eastern Pennsylvania.* The Ebbert and Richardson Company, Cincinnati, 1930.

Richards, H. S. *All About Horse Brasses: A Collector's Complete Guide.* Printed in England, n. d.

Sage, Elizabeth. *A Study of Costume.* Charles Scribner's Sons, New York, 1920.

Salley, Virginia Sutton. *Royal Bayreuth China.* Portland, Maine, 1969.

Savage, George. *Porcelain Through the Ages.* Penguin Books, 1963.

Sullivan, Michael. *A Short History of Chinese Art.* University of California Press, 1967.

Thorn, C. Jordan. *Handbook of Old Pottery and Porcelain Marks.* Tudor Publishing Company, New York, 1947.

Weiss, Harry H. *American Baby Rattles.* Privately Printed, 1941.

Welch, Holmes. *The Practice of Chinese Buddhism: 1900–1950.* Harvard University Press, 1967.

Whitlow, Harry H. *Art, Colored and Cameo Glass.* Riverview, Michigan, 1966.

Index